Grief Labyrinth

Grief Labyrinth

✦

A Mother's Journey After the Death of her Daughter

Carole Lindroos

9/2010
Lesley,
May your healing journey
with grief be filled
with blessings.
With love,
Carole Lindroos

iUniverse, Inc.

New York Lincoln Shanghai

Grief Labyrinth
A Mother's Journey After the Death of her Daughter

Copyright © 2008 by Carole Lindroos

iUniverse books may be ordered through booksellers or by contacting:

iUniverse
2021 Pine Lake Road, Suite 100
Lincoln, NE 68512
www.iuniverse.com
1-800-Authors (1-800-288-4677)

Because of the dynamic nature of the Internet, any Web addresses or links contained in this book may have changed since publication and may no longer be valid.

The views expressed in this work are solely those of the author and do not necessarily reflect the views of the publisher, and the publisher hereby disclaims any responsibility for them.

"Odes of Solomon" from *THE ENLIGHTENED HEART: AN ANTHOLOGY OF SACRED POETRY,* Edited by Stephen Mitchell, 1989, HarperCollins Publishers. Used by Permission.

ISBN: 978-0-595-47712-8 (pbk)
ISBN: 978-0-595-91974-1 (ebk)

Printed in the United States of America

In Loving Memory
My Daughter

Inga Van Nynatten
July 27, 1970 – September 2, 2000

Contents

Acknowledgements

Many people have supported me in writing this book. My daughters Erika Carlson and Jill Elkin consistently followed my progress and encouraged me, especially after reading my first draft. Many thanks to Laura Scott, who first introduced me to the labyrinth and Naomi Sullivan, who mentored me at QuaLife. I am deeply appreciative of Tama Kieves, who helped me to claim that I was a writer. Cynthia Morris and my Friday book-coaching group were of tremendous support. I owe many thanks to my Thursday morning writing group: Sharon, Linda, Laura and others. Our connection, collective energies, tears and laughter were a constant source of spurring my creative writing. Many thanks to Kirsten Wilson who awakened me to the stories held in my body. I want to thank my friends Vera Berv, Linda Bennie, Myrna Bottone, Liza Carlson, Dvora Kanegis, Kim Mooney, Darci Myers, Priscilla Press, Sue Thompson and Karen van Vuuren for their unique ways of caring for me through my writing process. I want to thank all my Argentine tango dance partners and friends, who were a source of healing for my heart and revitalization for my spirit. Thanks to Jeanne Dussault and Gail Opsahl who made contributions to the resource pages in the appendix. Thank you Vera for taking my photograph for the cover. I am grateful for my meditation instructor Janet Solyntjes. Her warmth, compassion and genuine presence have consistently guided me. Without my editor, Liz Netzel this book would not have come into being. She always believed in me and her open heartedness not only supported my writing, but my grief journey.

My deepest appreciation to you all.

Introduction

Grief Labyrinth is about Inga, my daughter who died from breast cancer at the age of thirty on September 2, 2000, and my subsequent grief journey. This has been a pilgrimage to the depth of my soul. The book opens with an automobile accident that shatters my windshield. At that moment, I ask myself, "What is going to happen that will completely change how I see the world?" Inga dies eleven weeks later. I learn to embrace death, be my own best friend, find gratitude and learn to trust myself again. Over the course of a seven-year journey, my broken heart transforms into an open heart.

This book is for my family, for those who came before me and those who will follow me. It is for all mothers, daughters and granddaughters affected by cancer. It is for everyone who is grieving. My hope is that health care professionals will read it to see into one mother's experience so they might better understand and serve others in their communities.

Since I began this book, my heart has opened to the world. Inga's death broke my heart, broke my spirit and crushed my being. I did not think I would survive the tragedy. I fell into the darkest pit of despair where nothing seemed to matter except being with her one last time. When my brother died in 1969, I briefly visited despair and then once again, when I was diagnosed with breast cancer. However, Inga's death left a hole in my chest from which I felt I was bleeding to death. I wanted to die, for then I could see her again. Shattered by the reality of death, grieving both privately and openly in the world, I discovered my heart reformed, regenerated. The empty cavity in my body where my heart once lived became a pool of mystical waters where I saw my own reflection, my true self for the first time. My heart was broken open to receive love and a soul-filled connection with those I encountered everywhere I went. Here is how I would describe the change: Now when I hand the homeless man or woman a dollar on the street corner, I feel their pain; there is no separation between us and my pain is their pain. I discovered my open heart.

I have discovered my body's wisdom and learned that conversations with parts of my body inform me of my deeper self. My toe with its deep understanding of the nature of my stubbornness reminds me to walk gently. My neck-wringing judgments have loosened their grip on my throat. My gut instincts are the most accurate and I trust their advice. My tightened jaw reminds me to relax and let go of my old need to control the world in order to feel safe. My body is a receptacle of so much sensual pleasure as well as aging reminders. I love walking naked after my bath and feeling the silken texture of the sheets as I slip into bed. My body seems to thrive on rice and vegetables for breakfast. I have learned to really listen more to its preferences and reach less for the sweet instant gratification of my old comfort food friends, cookies and chocolate.

No one knows what a mother experiences when her child dies. No one who has not lived through it can really understand, only sympathize with how one imagines it to be. By telling my story, I found my own healing. By circling through the grief labyrinth repeatedly, I began to understand my own grief and befriend myself. I wanted to read other grieving mothers' stories, but found there were not many books available. I wrote because I felt I had to write and learned the value of writing in my healing. I wrote the same stories repeatedly until they melted into each other. I went from not knowing what I needed to finding exactly what I needed. As a grief counselor, I learned from the inside what it really means to be listened to. I needed others to be quiet and listen. I needed to be in silence and listen to myself. Deep listening is not something to be taken lightly. It is profound. I heard the depth and breadth of my own pain.

When I began writing, my book was to be solely a memoir. I aspired to create a tapestry of remembrances about my daughter Inga, her life of thirty years, her death and her advice—her constant advice of "trust me." Embarking on this journey without her physical presence, my hope was to rediscover trust in myself along the way and heal my immense grief at her death.

In her memory, ***Trust Me*** is etched on a rock at the trailhead in Prospect Park near Austin, Texas where Inga lived. "Trust me," Inga would say. "You can build a legacy that will go far beyond you and will be remembered with much gratitude by thousands and thousands of people." Inga was a trail planner with the National Park Service and she loved to hike high in the mountains of Colorado as well as the areas surrounding her home in Austin, Texas. In this, we are different; while I too enjoy mountain byways, my journeys tend to be those of inner life, as a seeker of healing.

Professionally, at the time of Inga's death, I was the program director at QuaLife Wellness Community, a small nonprofit in Denver, Colorado, that educates and supports individuals and families affected by cancer. I made a career change in 1985, studying psychology and then getting my master's degree in contemplative psychotherapy from Naropa University. As a licensed psychotherapist, I had been working with cancer patients, their family members and those grieving for more than a decade. My specialty in the psychosocial cancer field came about because of my own personal family history. My aunt died of breast cancer when I was four years old, my mother was diagnosed with breast cancer when I was eight years old, my brother died of cancer when I was twenty-five years old and I was diagnosed with breast cancer when I was thirty-six years old.

I wanted to create a road map for my grieving self and now my hope is that my map may be helpful to others. Although every person's journey is very different, what is common to all is the power of choice. It may be a simple choice such as what to do when you wake up and you feel lousy. If you are feeling only heartache and you have nothing scheduled, you still have choice. You can curl back up under the covers or you can do something else. Sometimes it may be best to just stay in bed and pull the blanket up over your head and sometimes not. My hope is that what I have written gives you hope. You will need to decide what is helpful for you. Make your choices for yourself. If you choose to stay under the covers one day, then so be it; rest well.

Time has been my healing salve in my grieving, but I have used many resources as well. I have walked and talked with friends and family members; I have been in grief art therapy for a year and counseling for another year; I have worked with my dreams, prayed, meditated, and journaled; participated in a grief group; attended Compassionate Friends meetings; soaked in bubble baths, hot tubs and hot springs; had many massages and cuddled with my cat Perry. I have studied Buddha dharma, watched tear-jerking movies and danced Argentine tango. Burning tears, anger, guilt, disbelief and numbness have been my companions, along with insights, compassion, and laughter.

The Labyrinth: A Sacred Tool

A most valuable support has been the process of walking the labyrinth, an ancient spiritual tool. The labyrinth has been used by many cultures and religions for over 4,000 years. There are many varieties of labyrinths which have been found in churches and cathedrals, as well as in landscapes. They were designed primarily for being walked as a meditative experience, originating during the Crusades when pilgrimages to Jerusalem were no longer safe to embark on. A labyrinth has a single, winding purposeful path from the mouth or entrance to the center and back out again. Unlike a maze, it has no dead ends or wrong turns.

The labyrinth experience is a profound metaphor for the grief process. There is only one way to walk, which is forward. So it is with grief. The only way through is forward, with many twisting turns and going back and forth over what seems like the same territory. After we journey to the center of our grief, to the center of ourselves and the center of the labyrinth, we can then slowly return to re-enter the world anew. The circuitous labyrinth path offers hope and healing to all who enter. Each walk is unique, as we are each individuals with unique journeys as time passes. The labyrinth offers a safe refuge to navigate the emotional world of grieving. There is a beginning, middle and an end to the labyrinth walk, which helps us to contain the often-overwhelming nature of grief.

"The labyrinth is an archetypal image of wholeness that helps us rediscover the depths of ourselves." So says Dr. Lauren Artress, Canon Grace Cathedral, San Francisco.

The Chartres labyrinth pattern has eleven circuits. The path is narrow enough that you need to focus to stay on the path yet not wide enough to let another pass without stepping aside. There is no one way to walk a labyrinth, just as there is not one way to be in grief. Each of us walks the labyrinth at his or her own pace. The journey is never direct or straight. It takes unexpected, unplanned and authentic turns. By the simple act of putting one foot in front of the other, we arrive where we are supposed to be. What happens inside the labyrinth can be a metaphor for life as well as grief.

For some people, walking a labyrinth is a time for peaceful reflection, a stroll in the woods. For others, the experience is profound and comes with transformative insights. You can use labyrinths to find hope and inspiration during your grief. It can be used as prayer, ritual, remembrance and time alone with your loved one. The experience can calm, energize, clear, or give meaning or understanding. It can facilitate letting go, change, transition and reconciliation.

A ritual recognizes life changes and offers the opportunity to fit things together again. Reflecting on where you are can turn the simple experience of walking the labyrinth into a mind/body/spirit connection with the potential for wholeness. Thomas Moore in *The Education of the Heart* tells us that rituals are "… any action that speaks to the soul and to the deep imagination whether or not it all has practical effects … Even the smallest of rites of everyday existence are important to the soul." A ritual is a structured experience designed to celebrate life. It creates a container in which we can learn more about ourselves and our relationships with others. A ritual deepens our connection to our psychological and spiritual center. With the labyrinth, many rituals are possible. There are many ways of "fitting" the changing events of life together to make things whole.

You can create a labyrinth walk with the intention of healing your grief. This can be done alone or with a group, with any type of labyrinth. I am appreciative of the teachers who have brought labyrinths alive for me on my grief journey.

To use the grief labyrinth you need first to locate one. This may be an outdoor walking labyrinth or you might start by using a finger labyrinth.

The finger labyrinth is a small version of the walking labyrinth and can be made of various materials. Usually it is three-dimensional in order to allow your finger to follow the path without having to look at it. There is a copy of my personal finger labyrinth included in the back of this book. Many finger labyrinths are portable so you can use it anytime without having to travel to a full sized one. Have a notebook or some plain paper available too in order to jot down your thoughts and insights.

First, reflect on your grief process and remember your loved one who died. Looking at old photographs can stir memories. You might ask the question, "Will using this labyrinth be helpful for me?" Then start your walk and release any thoughts or feelings as they come up. Walk as slowly as you would like, stopping as you feel inclined. When you arrive at the center, just notice what happens. Is there an answer for you, any guidance or any inspiration to continue grief labyrinth healing work? When you feel ready then walk back out, returning to the place where you began. Write in your journal what just happened. What did you discover? What did you feel as you made your way? Maybe nothing. Maybe you feel differently now. Maybe you think you may want to explore the grief labyrinth model more.

Your healing journey is unique; you can take pieces of the resources I used, add resources of your own, and create a plan, which is always your choice to change along the way. I encourage you to write three things you can take action on this week that might help support you in your grief journey. One idea could be to walk the labyrinth three times this week.

Whether you choose to walk the labyrinth or not, the four themes of labyrinth walking can be very helpful as a reference point in healing your grief. Bear in mind that this is not a linear process, but rather a multidimensional route. Healing your grief requires time for reflection, remembering and reviewing your loved one's life and your life with him or her. The structure for this book follows the four R's of labyrinth walking. There is a section on each of the following: Review, Release, Receive and Return. *Reviewing* allows for reflection, remembering and gratitude. *Releasing* is a time of letting go, clearing out, resolving the past and creating space in your life. *Receiving* is the opportunity to open up to other possibilities, a sense of freedom, some relaxation and time to embrace peace and acceptance. Most likely, you will cycle through *reviewing* and *releasing* many times. Then there is time for *returning* to your present life and circumstances, reconnecting with your values and the experiences and beliefs that have given your life meaning. Note that your beliefs may change over the course of your healing time or be magnified.

Grief work is hard work. The labyrinth offers a safe sanctuary where you can both grow through your grief and renew yourself. It becomes a container for grieving, which you can step into and also step out of.

I have walked the Chartres labyrinth in France, Grace Cathedral labyrinth in San Francisco, and many local labyrinths near my home in Boulder, Colorado. I found the finger labyrinth to be of special importance, because I could always have it with me. As a spiritual counselor with a local hospice in 2006, I also used it to assist others in their dying and grieving process. I have also walked the labyrinth to help inform my writing focus, as I continue my healing.

The labyrinth is a sacred path where the mystical meets the ordinary, the divine touches the mundane, and the physical body supports the spiritual body. It is a path of deep silence. In the labyrinth, the mind chatter of daily life can quiet itself. There is space for deep listening.

How to Use the Labyrinth

I mainly walk my simple finger labyrinth. It is 8" by 10" on a piece of Styrofoam board on which is glued a purple satin rounded ribbon marking the path. At the center are three very small colored beads. I walk it using my index finger with my eyes closed. I usually use my right hand, but at times choose to use my left hand.

Before entering the labyrinth, I sit quietly with the labyrinth on my lap and take time to review or reflect on where I am in my grief and life journey now. Often I set an intention for the walk. I may be reviewing the past, remembering what Inga might have said in circumstances in which I now find myself in my present life. I often look at photos of Inga and contemplate those times in her life. I sometimes ask for help and guidance in navigating my emotional life. This may also be in the form of a question I pose such as "What do I need today to support me in my grief?"

After review and reflection, I close my eyes, enter the labyrinth with the index finger of my right hand, and feel the sensation of my contact with the floor of the labyrinth. I notice when thoughts, sensations, emotions arise, release them and return to my finger walking the labyrinth. Usually I move very slowly through the many curves of the winding path. I might stop if strong feelings come up and I give myself all the time I need to move through or with them.

There is not a right or a wrong way to walk the labyrinth, but I notice I do have my own rhythm, which is comforting. As with any contemplative practice, the experiences are greatly varied but I do feel it always seems helpful to calm and contain my often-wild mind. Grief often feels out of control. To walk the labyrinth is a time for containment and centering.

When I reach the center, usually I am a little surprised to feel the three beads, which let me know I have arrived there. Here I rest with an open mind and heart and a readiness to receive. I wait for whatever comes to me. If I have posed a question, I am attentive in particular to my first thoughts. Sometimes a sensation or a simple word may be what stands out. Sometimes nothing really happens. Sometimes I might have a dialogue with Inga there or feel her presence. I have experienced a sense of deep understanding that did not have words, a kind of knowing. Ultimately, I feel my sense of trust has been built anew every time by my arrival at the center. A labyrinth is not a maze; one always arrives at the center. There is also a way to view receiving as not just the time alone in the labyrinth but also from a bigger perspective. Walking the labyrinth repeatedly is not a linear process; the more I walk it the more I find the depth of my wholeness and how sacred life really is.

At some point, I choose to leave the center and return to reconnect to my everyday world with whatever insight or sensation I have received. Usually I feel lighter and my return walk is at a different pace than my walk in. Again, there is no right or wrong way. I do the return walk still noticing the contact my finger makes with the labyrinth. I try not to get into too much evaluation of what has just occurred and to just stay with the experience and sensations. I still keep my eyes closed throughout and often there is a smile, which spontaneously comes as I cross over the entry point opening, marking my finish.

I would like to encourage each of you to walk the labyrinth as you read my story. Take time to delve into your own grief with me. There is a simple Cretan-style finger labyrinth for your use in the appendix or you may choose to walk a full labyrinth if you have one nearby.

May you be blessed on your journey.
Carole Lindroos
July 2007

Review

To begin the walk into the labyrinth one stands at the mouth of the labyrinth, the entry point, poised to review and reflect. Death shocks and numbs us. Remembering brings us to the point of facing the reality of our loss, an important step in the healing process. Photographs have been an important piece in my looking back over my life with Inga. Below is one taken of our family in 1980.

From left to right are Jane Van Nynatten (Fred's mother), Fred Van Nynatten (Inga's father), me, Ann Lindroos (my mother), Gus Van Nynatten (Fred's father), front row, Jill (Inga's seven year old sister), Inga (age ten), and Erika (Inga's six year old sister).

While I kept a daily journal, there are scenes, which only returned to me as I revisited the labyrinth over and over again. Sometimes I would pose a question during this time such as "What do I need in order to heal my grief?" Or I might ask for help from Inga. These questions and requests formed intentions for my labyrinth walk.

In journal format, I documented the last six weeks of Inga's life and then the weeks and months following her death. I have included dreams since they have been important in my journey to discover my unconscious life. Reviewing, rereading and looking back at this time has been painful and healing. To enter the labyrinth of grief is a sacred pilgrimage. It can be life affirming, poignant and joyful at times. I have cried, laughed and gone through many boxes of Kleenex with my finger labyrinth on my lap. Each walk through this life review has melted another layer of sadness into a new kind of freedom for me. The container of the labyrinth offers a way to hold the chaotic nature of the emotions surrounding grief.

My story begins in the summer of 2000.

June 17, 2000

Today I drove to Denver to give a presentation on "Self-Care and Self-Empowerment" at the Leukemia Society's Conference on Cancer Survivorship. While en route to the mid-town hotel on Interstate 25, driving 65 miles an hour, I see some debris in the road. Within seconds, a truck kicks it up and slams it into my windshield. "Wham!" A metal pipe half an inch in diameter plows into me. My windshield shatters. I brake and miraculously I am able to slowly drive over the three lanes to get to the side of the road. I am in shock. I cannot see out of my windshield.

Shaking and in tears, I first think about the experience of being diagnosed with cancer. At one moment, life is just coasting along and out of nowhere, cancer drops in like a bomb.

Minute glass shards cover my dashboard. I hit my emergency blinker lights and ask myself "Do I need help?" Yes, I very much do. I want someone there with me, but no one stops. The traffic continues to race by for 10 minutes or more. Just when I need it, I do not have my cell phone. I start to cry and feel some relief from the tension in my chest, neck and arms. I am angry too. Why me, why now? I ask.

How will I get to the conference? How can I go dancing tonight? The hell with the conference. Am I OK? Touching my face and skin, I brush glass from my lap. No blood at least. Three feet of the windshield are demolished. Around a small central hole, there are cracks across the rest of the windshield. I am able to bend down and partially see out of the left bottom portion. Maybe I can just drive to the next exit and then to the hotel where the conference is being held. Yes, I think I can do that. I breathe deeply. No one notices me. I am angry. So I decide that I do not need anyone right now; I can handle this by myself. (Now isn't this familiar!) The hell with all those speeding cars driving by as if nothing happened here. I pull out into traffic very slowly with my blinkers flashing.

Ten minutes later, I arrive at the conference hotel and park in the garage, relieved that the grey clouds, which threatened rain, did not burst forth. The first person I see up on the conference floor is Nancy, a long time participant at QuaLife where I work as the program director. I tell her what just happened and she asks me "Are you alright? You look so calm." I tell her I need a hug. And I really do. I am so thankful. My life is very different from when I had cancer twenty-one years ago. Is there some deeper meaning here? When something happens to my car, it usually is a metaphor for some part of my life. So I ask myself, "What has kicked up or is about to kick up in my face that shatters everything, that cracks my vision of the world and where I am going?" I do not have the answer, but hold the question. I breathe deeply again.

I am still in an altered state as I give my presentation to the group of 100 people gathered there. I weave the story of my accident into my presentation and feel energized. The group seems responsive and my talk ends with a guided imagery session. This helps to calm me as well as being a tool for those in the audience.

I then go call my insurance agent and find out how to get my windshield repaired. Fortunately, the person who does such repairs has a replacement one for my car and can do the exchange at his house this afternoon. I am hesitant about driving my car, but he is reassuring and gives me directions. He says his place is only twenty minutes from where I am in downtown Denver. While I still do not relish the thought of getting back into my vehicle, I am anxious to get the repair done so head out of town, driving very carefully.

I get lost finding the repairperson's home. When I arrive, Dan awaits me and offers a lawn chair for me to sit in while he sets about his work. He tells me that I am one lucky person, that I must have very good karma. He has never seen a windshield with such damage without more damage to the car and to the driver. He proceeds to tell me about other windshields he has repaired and the people behind them. Some of them did not walk away from their accidents as I have. Dan remembers me from a previous windshield repair to my Volkswagen many years ago. I am still a bit shaky as I step back into my car to drive home with crystal clear vision.

Over the next few hours and days, I tell and retell the story of my accident. That very evening I drove back to Denver to go dance Argentine tango, which is my normal Friday evening outing at the Mercury Cafe. I passed the very spot where the accident occurred and hoped to locate the pole along the side of the road. I did not see it, but hoped to retrieve it both to ensure that it would not harm anyone else and also to keep it as some sort of weird memento.

Everyone I share my story with about the accident responds with awe that I was not killed. People keep telling me how fortunate I am. Then some tell me their stories of those who were killed in auto accidents such as mine. One of my friend's parents was killed when a pole impaled her father, who was driving. I felt horror hearing this image. There was an urgent need for me to repeat my story over and over again.

Several days later, I am standing at a busy intersection, waiting to cross, when I have the thought that I could just step into traffic and either nothing would happen or I would die. That is when I become very aware of the trauma that had occurred for me and how it had affected me. I self diagnose myself with PTSD (Post Traumatic Stress Disorder) and know that I really need help now. I come to a place of "trust me"; I really know the accident has caused damage beyond the physical effect on my car. Now is the time for true healing to begin.

June 21, 2000
Dream Entry
I am riding as a passenger in the back seat of a small airplane. Bill is the pilot and he is going to crash us into the mountain. He states 'It is better to end this lifetime and then I know we'll meet under better circumstances in the next life.'

June 23, 2000
I ask my Dream Guide to help me to understand last night's dream and the circumstances of being given life after my auto accident. I ask, "Who is Bill and is there action I must take to move through my struggle? Why was I given life, saved from death?"

Dream Entry
The man says that he feels he is really getting to know me and like me. He's looking for a special seashell. In addition, I recognize it and tell him where he can find it.

I found the play on the word seashell interesting. "C shell" like "C" for cancer and drop the l's and there is "she". Also Bill is Be—ill. And my friend reminds me that I must have fears about Inga and the possibility of her dying from her illness. No, I don't want to face those thoughts.

Two years ago, Inga, my twenty-nine year-old daughter, was diagnosed with an aggressive form of breast cancer. My fears, hopes and dreams of her have been a roller coaster ride since the day she called to tell me that she had breast cancer.

Depression and heaviness weigh on me, thinking of both the accident and Inga's cancer. A hopelessness and lack of spirit prevail. The more I tell my story, the less relief I feel. Everyone else seems so pleased at my survival and I admit to wishing that I had died in the accident. Later I reach an understanding about how impossible it seems for me to live with Inga's battle with breast cancer. I want to run away from it all.

June 27, 2000

It is the day before my birthday and I have an appointment with a psychotherapist I trust and respect to help me via EMDR (Eye Movement, Desensitization and Reprocessing, a highly effective psychotherapeutic modality to treat trauma). I tell him "I'm at the end of my rope," feeling exhausted and overwhelmed with being alive. As I moved through the processing of the traumatic pieces of my auto accident, I came to the core of what happened. My spirit left my body through that small hole where the pole penetrated my windshield. I was told to return. It was not time for me to leave my body yet. When I asked the reason that I am here, I heard "to listen, to teach, to write." And that is a task for one who trusts. Do I trust myself enough to listen, to teach and to write? What would I write about?

July 18, 2000
Isla Mujeres, Mexico

Yellow fish gather around my feet in the warm, clear turquoise waters. This is a paradise that I have found for Inga's thirtieth birthday celebration. My daughters and I have not been on a trip alone together for twelve years or more without husbands, boyfriends or children. I am so looking forward to their arrivals. Our time together is for the celebration of Inga's birthday and her remission from cancer, fun in the sun, family healing and snorkeling. My middle daughter, Jill, asked us each to prepare for a ritual and the opportunity to tell each other our fondest memories with each other, what we are proud of each other for and what each of us needs from one another on this trip. I was pleasantly surprised when Jill emailed that note to me! All my daughters have always joked about my need for and love of ritual. Now here is Jill initiating a ritual for all of us.

Sunset at the ocean has always been very special for me. It is the time to let go of the day and give thanks for what has been given to me. So I closed with a prayer for the day, and opened to receive with gratitude what would be next. The sun set about 7:45 PM and after my guacamole and margarita, I was off for a shower feeling quite wonderful. Tomorrow they all arrive. I am both looking forward and have some small trepidation stirring within. Will old family issues come up? Will there be conflict without resolution? All will be well; my optimism wins out. I tend to some plans, arranging our swim with the dolphins and make the reservation for our birthday dinner at NaBalam, a wonderful hotel restaurant here on North Beach.

The next day the first to arrive is Jill. We hug and talk, swim and wait for her sisters. Erika and Inga had hooked up in Houston as their planes both had stopovers there from Seattle and Austin, so they would arrive together. I remember the look of sheer glee on Inga's face as she strutted onto the beach and threw her arms up over her head and exclaimed, "This is the best place in the whole world; I want to come to this beach every year forever." We all were so very happy. Later that day Inga asked that we plan to come here together again. Next time perhaps we can come with all the rest of our families. I had pictured all of us on this island together on the many trips I had already taken here. Now it was reality; we were all here. I was incredibly happy in our reunion.

That evening we gather in my room, to do the ritual that Jill had planned before we go out for dinner. Inga says she doesn't want "all that crying stuff," but if it is to happen then better before dinner than after. So we each got out our "notes,"—well those of us who had made some.

July 19, 2000
Inga's Journal Entry
What do I need from each person to make this trip satisfying?
Erika—energy and stillness
Jill—talk more
Mom—fun + listening + helping Jill & Erika & I to relate well

What do I promise to do for each person?
Erika—not make things be my way
Jill—open up to you, listen + get to know the new Jill
Mom—dance!!

Share a memory of joy with each person.
(no entry)

I'm proud of you for ...
Mom—being non-judgmental

having fun
not being a stereotypical Mom
Jill—listening + forgiving
Erika—Being you!
being intense and loud
+ also being a real friend to me

It's Inga who cries throughout this ritual. I feel a bit rushed and unsettled. I am so moved by what each of my daughter's shares. I am so proud of all my daughters for opening up in this way. We each brought photos. I have copies of three photos of the girls as they were growing up. They were adorable children, all with blonde hair and blue eyes. Every Christmas their Dad would take a picture of them with his fencing sword as a marker to show how tall they were. Another picture of them features a pyramid with Inga and Jill on the ground and their little sister Erika balanced on top of them.

As I stare now at Inga's journal, I realize that these were her very last handwritten words. My heart is both full and very sad as I feel the loss of Inga. I am also so sad that she is not here for Erika and Jill. What a loss of their futures together. Erika and Inga had a deep friendship already and it is so painful to me that Erika has lost both her sister and a good friend. For Jill I feel the pain of lost potential, what might have been. Inga needed more time with Jill to move through their unique differences. I wish she had that time. I wish we all had more time with Inga.

The birthday dinner was delicious. I brought a candle from home that played happy birthday and had arranged with the waiter to bring it out on a dessert cake. Inga was radiant, her broad smile beaming. Erika gave Inga a CD "Bust Book and Girls." Jill gave her a book for lazy beach reading and I gave her a disposable underwater camera.

I remember when Inga was fifteen years old and our family was on a vacation on the Cayman Islands. There weren't disposable waterproof cameras at that time, and Inga really wanted to rent an underwater camera. It was pretty expensive as I recall and her father and I didn't want to do it.

She was her insistent self and was determined to have pictures of what she was seeing underwater. So during a siesta time for us, she went off to find where the cameras were available and rented one, using all the spending money that she had. She took the pictures and then told us afterwards what she had done. The photos were not very good quality, but Inga got what she wanted. I reminded her of this story and said that I was sorry that I was so unsupportive of what she wanted back then. The next morning we went for our swim with the dolphins. We were assigned to Roxana and Olympia. I have swum with these dolphins numerous times and each time it has been special. I worried that the swim would be too organized for my daughters or that they might think it was corny. They didn't. The free swim time gave all of us the opportunity to relate with our new dolphin friends. As our grand finale, we each posed kissing a dolphin. These are now treasured memories captured on film and video.

The next days were spent mostly under a beach umbrella and swimming in the ocean. Since the water is very shallow on this section of the beach and also very warm, we waded and sat in the turquoise clear sea for hours on end. We floated together topless and took silly pictures of each other. There was such relaxation and ease.

We all wanted to go snorkeling and there were locals who would pull up their boats and want to sell us snorkeling trips. At first we weren't going to take this route, but eventually we gave in to the convenience and negotiated a price. There were two men aboard, one to captain the boat and the other to snorkel with us as a guide. They took us downstream of the strong current along the main reef and dropped us off with life jackets. Here we were all in the same current, with really no need to swim; we could just be brought along by the natural flow of the water. We saw so many colored fish and we all took pictures with Inga's birthday camera. At the end of the reef, there was a rope to hang on to while we waited together for our boat. The current was so strong that we really needed to hang on to the rope or be swept off. We laughed and joked.

We ate fish tacos and we had guacamole on the beach every day. Of course, there was shopping too. Inga wanted a hammock, which had to be purple, and she wanted a good quality one for the best price. So we looked at every purple hammock on the island. Along the way, she found tie-dyed skimpy outfits for herself and Erika.

The evening before Jill left was an intense emotional time. It seemed as though we were all pressured beyond a point of being able to stay together. What were we trying to do? To connect and love each other more deeply than we had ever done before and we just couldn't do it sanely. There was a blowup and walking off and apologies. Inga stayed out really late that night dancing. It was coming upon us: time to say goodbye. Separation brought many feelings to the surface. And little did we know then how significant it was to be.

First Jill left, then the next day Erika and Inga. When I accompanied Erika and Inga to the ferry, Inga was already starting to feel physical pain. She said her hip was hurting. And I asked if she had medication with her. No, she responded. I asked if she was scared. Yes was all she said. We had played, laughed and cried together and now we were returning home. I felt numb somehow as I said goodbye. I left them and went to the church to light the candle for Inga and all of us. It was the candle I brought for our ritual that began our vacation together.

There was a crowd in the church—some service was going on, and so I left to buy water and returned later. The service was still going on, but I decided to find a seat, which was easy on the left-hand side of the church. I sat close to the front and started to pray. I looked up at some point and to my right was an open casket. I was shocked to realize that this was a funeral. And it was a child, a young girl all dressed in white who had died. My heart just broke right open and all my fears and sorrow about Inga rose to the surface. I was sobbing as the family went forward to kiss their little girl goodbye and they closed the casket and moved into a processional out of the church.

I knew they were walking her to the cemetery on the other side of town. I have previously visited there many times. Mexican cemeteries are so colorful and full of shrines to their loved ones that tell the story of their lives. How could this family survive the loss of their beautiful little girl? I wondered what had happened to her. I cried with them and for them, and I cried for what may be in the future for our family. It took twelve years for all of us women to come together. Would we be able to do it again? Would I die? Or is it possible that Inga could die and we would never see this kind of reunion again together?

Returning to the water, soaking in its sparkling clear essence, I see four yellow fish near me in the protection of my shadow. I think of the four of us, my daughters and me. When will we four be together again? Tears and salt water mixed together both comforted me and brought more fears to the surface.

July 27, 2000
Today is Inga's thirtieth birthday and it is nothing but full of the unpleasant. She calls to tell me it's the worst birthday she's ever had. After the wonderful trip and all, she now has returned home and has a suspicious spot on her spine that is causing her much pain. She will be going for another MRI tomorrow. She is angry at her father, since he did nothing for her birthday—no call, no card, no little something. I too am sad and angry.

July 29, 2000
Dream Entry "Water Leaking in at the Corner"
I look over to the right and it's a corner that is leaking water in the foundation. I yell for help—there's water all over the floor.

I awaken relieved that it's only a dream. What is leaking? I think of emotions. Water as the unconscious, the leak meaning boundaries that are not firm. I am taking in water, taking on that which is not mine. I need help repairing this leak. In the dream, I yelled out. This is a good sign; I am so used to handling everything on my own.

July 31, 2000
Inga is no longer in remission; the cancer is back in her sacrum. She tells Jill fifty seconds worth of information and instructs her to call Erika

and me. It is unusual for her to call Jill first and I thought maybe she had felt closer to her after our trip to Isla Mujeres.

I am feeling numb, wanting to cry and unable. My tears are just under the surface and there's anger too. There is something I know I need to do and that is to contact Fred, Inga's father. The decision to email him seemed best for me. In the past phone conversations don't happen due to him being unavailable or when we are on the phone, I don't get in all I want to say. I am proud of my direct and kind message that follows.

Fred,

I added your name to my email list for Inga's Healing Circle many months ago. I never heard that you received and/or appreciated receiving updates in this way. I also never heard your support of Inga's healing through the prayers, meditation or beliefs that I alluded to could be any means of your choice.

Inga has requested that I remove you from this email list. I understand that she doesn't choose to give you an "easy" way to effortlessly know her circumstances. I did not understand or support this choice at first and have thought this over for several weeks now.

Moreover, I have come to believe that I prefer to honor her wishes. I am removing your name this evening before my next update, the reason being that I value my relationship with Inga. I was distressed to hear that you did not manage to wish her a Happy Birthday on the day she was born. (I also noted that you didn't manage that for Jill either ... being that I was at Jill's house on her birthday, so could gather that information on my own.) I find your behavior really cruel and heartless. And there are no excuses. Are there? It is just if no one reminds you, it doesn't happen. Didn't you tell me that you were going to make changes? Well I don't think abandoning your daughters is a positive change. Especially since Inga is in so much distress. It is your responsibility to BE a father, not expect your daughters as women now to continue to take care of you.

You are inexcusably absent of heart except when there is benefit for yourself.

May you find the strength and courage to do what is right by Inga. She needs to be loved, respected and told the unspoken. She needs to know that you are proud of her. I still remember when your mother finally told you that directly.

I continue to practice forgiveness which helps me a lot. You might do well with it yourself, both for yourself and for others.

Carole

Writing and sending this off clears the air for me. I worry so much about Inga and ask myself if I have done enough for her. I have been having so much trouble sleeping; I pray for a good night's rest to fortify me.

It's now five days after Inga's birthday and talking with her on the phone I ask her if she has heard anything from her Dad. No she hasn't received any contact from him and I am really mad, but not surprised. Inga states, "I am relieved, since it just confirms what I already know." Now I wonder what exactly did she know. Did she feel unloved or just ignored, unimportant to him?

August 8, 2000

Here I am in the Phoenix Airport heading to Austin. I talked to Roy, Inga's friend and realtor who helped with her house purchase. Her college friend Laura, who lives in North Carolina, has been visiting and supporting Inga for the past week along with Roy. They both agreed that Inga cannot be alone. She is in pain all the time and can't seem to eat much or manage driving either with all the pain medication she is on.

I packed my bags and after three hours of sleep headed out to the airport, having purchased a medical emergency ticket with America West. I am so tired and numb, and my back aches. Having just returned from Mexico two weeks ago, I still haven't caught up from that trip. I am in shock too. How could Inga be so sick now when she was swimming, dancing and running on the beach such a short time ago? I very much needed to come here to be with her. A colleague at work helped me make that decision by asking me, "Will you look back on this time five years in the future and regret that you didn't go?" I knew I had to come and I did trust my inner knowing.

I bring two hedgehog doggie toys for Sam and Trixie, Inga's Dalmatians. As expected, it did bring a smile to Inga's face. She was lying on her new couch in her new home looking pale and worn out when I arrived. She didn't want to get up until it was time to leave for the appointment with the doctor. Laura had already left to go home and Roy had picked me up at the airport. It is such a blur, those days of being quiet around Inga, giving her medication and driving her to doctor appointments. Her doctor wanted to put her in the hospital for tests and pain management, but Inga balked at the idea. She wanted to stay in her own house with her dogs and new familiar surroundings. She had just moved into this house on July 1 and had barely unpacked and bought a couch for the living room.

Erika arrives a few days later and what a tremendous help she is. The dream had told me to get help. I feel like I can sleep now and share all that is going on. I am no longer alone.

August 13, 2000

I am not leaving today as originally planned. Yesterday at the hospital, Inga received very difficult news. Another two small tumors were found on T6 and T7 and a suspicious area in her brain. Inga refused a full MRI, due to her claustrophobic tendency in the closed tube scanner. She wound up getting two mg. of Xanex, slept throughout the CAT scan and continued sleeping the rest of the day.

The news overwhelms me, delivered by the nurse whom I had liked a lot previously. There was such a distance as she's telling me what the doctor told her. Her cold neutral voice is both serious and abrupt. We need to make an appointment with Dr. Fain on Monday and establish the next plan. It's all too hazy and I am too worried to leave now. I talked with both Laura and Roy and suggested a meeting with Roy, Erika, Inga and myself tonight to talk honestly.

I did feel better about getting some things out in the open after the meeting about the serious nature of Inga's condition and that she is not able to care for herself alone. There is so much more to talk about. I remind myself to just breathe and take one step at a time.

August 14, 2000

Dr. Fain's office is jammed and we wait almost two hours to get in to see him. When we do he is very direct. The pain needs to get managed and then she can start treatment. She needs the brain MRI which can get scheduled in an open machine. There was such relief for Inga when she could get at least a few small things that she wanted, like a scan in a machine that was not closed since the confinement caused her such terror. Dr. Fain was not overly concerned—or he just never showed it. Need to get an appointment with Dr. Warhoe, the radiation oncologist, to see what she will recommend about the new tumors.

I started a log of all of Inga's pain medications and when she takes them. It's getting really intense as she is taking twice as many medications as when I first arrived 100 mg. Duragesic patch, 1mg. Xanex, Decadron, Hydrocodeine, and Diladuaud for breakthrough pain.

I am worried, yet leaving tomorrow, to take care of some things at home. Erika will do well and we have a plan through the following weekend. It's really hard. Am I doing enough? It's not that I fear that death is near, but I can't really tell where Inga is. She can't tolerate much more pain and is the radiation helping? I can only trust that Dr. Warhoe knows and the radiation will shrink the tumors to alleviate the pressure on her nerves.

Inga wants to create a patio garden. She wants counter space added on in her kitchen. She wants to make copies of the sketch she has in her bathroom of three little kids all on toilets, to give as presents to her sisters. She wants to write her master's thesis. I need to visualize this for her. For me to see myself going to her graduation, her wedding, tubing on the river and hiking in Colorado. Seeing her well, pain-free and taking care of herself and others. I want to see her veins plump and her smile bright like it was just a few weeks ago in Mexico. I am very afraid of what the future holds for her and all of us.

August 16, 2000
Dream Entry
I am eating an end piece of roast beef. The burnt outer edge tastes very sweet and delicious.

It is good to be back at home and taking care of myself. I went to have an acupuncture appointment with Jeffrey Dann. He suggested, as I had already gleaned from my dream, that I should eat some red meat. So I stopped at North Boulder Market and told the butcher about my dream. Only in Boulder would a butcher reply with, "So I think your body is asking you for a nice lean filet mignon. How thick would you like it cut?"

I talked to Erika a lot today. She is doing all right, arranged to go swimming for a while. She is thinking of staying another week. Inga and she are talking and trying to make plans. Tomorrow there will be a test at Dr. Fain's office regarding the brain fluid where the MRI seems to be picking up cancer. Inga's voice is hoarse and she's coughing allot, which causes concern about her lymph glands. It seems like she needs to get back on her chemotherapy regime.

August 17, 2000
I had a very restless night's sleep. I keep tossing and turning and then I hear the words, "It's the beginning of the end." Maybe it was a dream, but I don't recall anything else about it. I know it is the truth.

A phone call from Erika informs me that Dr. Fain told Inga she definitely has brain metastasis and thinks she may only have three months to live. The doctor wants resuscitation orders. Inga will be hospitalized for a catheter and chemotherapy directly run into her spinal fluid. I feel like I am on automatic pilot as I call Jill to tell her the news and ask her to tell her father Fred and his wife Candy. I am hopeful we all will have a window of time for healing. I don't want Inga pushed about being with her father. She said she did not want him to come; she did not want to see him. I feel protective of her. I will get back down to Austin immediately.

Dreamtime doesn't come to comfort me. I toss and turn, cry, and worry about the future. I feel so much agitation, frustration, and just don't know what is best for me. I deserve to recharge, to receive assistance from my dream guides. Please help me, I call out; my daughter is dying. Someone somewhere please help me. I plead that this cannot be true, but I know that it is. My biggest fear is the reality, right now. She is in a lot of pain. I can't bear this.

August 18, 2000

Laura, Inga's good friend from Raleigh, North Carolina has returned and Inga says, "Laura is awesome." Inga ate a turkey dinner the night before and now French toast this morning for breakfast. This is good news and we all need it. Inga's voice is gone and there is the question of lymph node involvement. Inga's friend Roxy visits. Roxy is a long-term Stage IV breast cancer survivor and she's about my age with a grandson, and has been a true friend to Inga since they met early on at a Breast Cancer Support Group that Roxy helps facilitate. I feel relief knowing that Roxy is well and available to support Inga.

Inga always said, "If Roxy can have a miracle then I can too." Roxy was in hospice care 10 years ago and was taken home to die and surprised everyone with a turnaround.

I call to talk to Jill and we get into taking sides regarding her father. It is the same old pattern. I didn't change anything by asking Jill to do what would best be done by me directly. I refuse to rescue him and there's so much pain already. I call to get support for myself from my friend Priscilla, which really helps. From that conversation I realize it would be best to have a non-family member talk with Fred. So I call Laura and ask her advice. She agrees to call Fred and I feel much relief. Sleep now. I really need sleep. Benadryl is about the only thing around that says "drowsiness may occur" so I take it.

August 19, 2000

I awake with the thought that Inga is refusing to sign a Power of Attorney. This really needs to happen. I hope that Laura can talk with Inga this weekend. I am still in shock. My worst fear has always been having something terrible happen to one of my children. The worst thing is happening.

I plead for mercy, I cry out in agony. My daughter can't die. Yet the treatment is not working and she is in horrible pain and state of consciousness that she has ever been in since her diagnosis. It is just a month ago that we were all laughing and playing in the beautiful blue waters of the Caribbean. How can this be happening?

August 19, 2000
Early Morning.
Erika calls me first thing this morning from the hospital. Inga yelled out to her in the middle of the night very agitated and restless. This is so hard on Erika. Dr. Fain did not make rounds and he told me he would talk to Inga honestly about what is going on. Damn!
Same evening.
Inga is at home now, ate a little, and wouldn't talk on the phone with me besides to say, "Hi, I'm sleepy." I send out an email to all the family and friends, which I call Inga's Healing Circle. This list has grown to more than 50 people in the last year and Inga says she feels their support.

Dear Family and Friends,

I need your help and assistance. Inga will be starting Hospice soon. She is currently in the hospital and will go home later today. She has brain metastases and some new tumors on her spine. There is much pain, which is barely manageable. Mostly she is groggy and sleeps a lot. Able now to eat a little, but nausea is still a problem. Inga is a fighter, which now is difficult, because she is unwilling to talk about dying, her wishes and Hospice care.

Erika is with her, along with Inga's good friend Laura. I will be returning to Austin in four days.

It is a very sad and heart-wrenching time. Please pray for her and all of us. I also need to hear from you. Cards sent to her home would be welcome. She appreciates humor, nature, her dogs, family and friends. She says, don't give up on me." It is very hard for her emotionally as well as on all of us. Peace and love, Carole

Sending this email helps me. I don't feel so alone. I decide to go dance tango to find some energy. Even if it doesn't help much maybe, I can sleep at least or have some distraction from this overwhelming volcanic emotion growing inside of me.

August 22, 2000

This is such a heartbreaking time. Inga, please come around. Talk to us about your fears. God, please give us a miraculous healing. No tears came to me until bedtime. What a relief those tears were! It is now clearer to me that going to Australia is not an option. I had been scheduled to travel to Melbourne in early September to give a presentation at an international psycho-oncology conference. I was holding out making a final decision hoping that Inga would get stronger and then I could go. I can still hope for some change for the better and at the same time know that it is too stressful to think about traveling so far away for that conference with Inga being so ill.

August 24, 2000

What a 24-hour period! I am back in Austin and amazed at how Erika has organized, filtered, taken care of, questioned and struggled with important decisions. Inga is only groggy, hardly ever lucid. She is much worse than when I was last here. Her back pain has lessened; she is very anxious and not talking. Her throat is coated with thrush, a side effect of the steroid she is taking to help alleviate her brain swelling and headaches. I started cleaning and washing clothes and constantly checking in on Inga. I brought her cold washcloths for her forehead and started learning Inga's sign language, since she isn't talking. I was on duty for the night shift to allow Erika to get a full night's sleep. It is hot, and I mean hot. Most days it is in upper 90s by 11 AM and stays that way until 9 PM. We have two air conditioners running inside. There is one in the spare bedroom and one in the living room. They are loud but necessary as they are nonstop cranking out ice-cold relief.

This evening a lab technologist came to the house in order to hook Inga up to fluids, since she was so dehydrated. Her vein was very hard to place the line into and Inga's exhaustion so great that we found it quite wonderful for the technician to stop by on his way home from work in order to hook her up. This was someone who Inga felt confidence in and she was very appreciative. Inga is now comfortably settled in for the night.

I went to bed in the study, creating a mattress for myself out of the chair cushions on the floor and a cardboard box for a night table with lamp so I could read. Every 30 minutes I was jumping up hearing Inga's calls for help through the constant blasting sounds of the air conditioner. By 3:30 AM Inga wanted Ativan 1.5 mg. Then I started getting more anxious. Would I hear her call? Was the IV drip OK?

At some point, I notice a slight swelling of the upper left side of my lip. I got up to look in the mirror and sure enough, my lip was double in size. So who is anxious now? I go looking through her supply of meds to find a Benadryl but with all the boxes available, I don't find any. Back to attempt sleep. Sammy girl has now taken over my bed. I love to sleep with Inga's eight-year-old Dalmatian, but in these small quarters I just had no room left for myself, so I kick her out. 5:00 AM, no sleep, 6:00 AM, I get up and look in the mirror to find my entire cheek swollen. I almost want to awake Erika because of what is happening to me, but I refrain.

August 25, 2000

At 8:15 AM I hear Inga rattling around in the kitchen. I get up to check on her and see that the IV has been infiltrated with blood. She had pulled the bag down when she went to the bathroom. I am not a nurse and I just hate this. Erika, help! I yell. I don't know what to do. Calls to the doctor's office finally yield the solution to just pull out the line. Erika is amazing. "I'll do it," she says. And she calmly removes it. Then I am off to walk the dogs. I am grumpy. Why did I bring these damn dogs with me that drag me along? I feel sorry for myself. I am bitching. Erika can't cope with me. She walks the dogs both home and I go off to cry and moan and bitch on my own. It is kind of a relief. Erika had showered while at home and apologizes to me. I wonder now what for. It is so hard and stressful for both of us and she has been here several weeks already.

It is time to get Inga started to take her to her radiation appointment with Dr. Warhoe. Inga asks why she has to go. Erika's answer satisfies her so she gets up with some help, dresses and moves into the living room, flopping down on the couch. Her lethargy, mixed with drugs and pain, makes her seem so fragile and her stubborn nature comes out too. We told her that the radiation was to help with the pain by reducing the pressure on her sciatic nerve. She asks us to cool the car down first before she goes out and asks for a pillow; she is unable to sit up. We help walk her to the car.

Along with buying a new home and furniture in the past month, Inga also bought or rather traded her old convertible in for a green Toyota Rav4, just after she returned home from our trip to Mexico. I remember her phone call back then: "Guess what, Mom, I found a new distraction from all this pain and shit: I bought a new car!" Now just a few weeks later she has only driven it once besides getting it home after the purchase.

At the radiation oncologist's office, Inga lies flat on the floor, having asked for a mat to lie on. She wants the lights out, as they aggravate her headache. Dr. Warhoe tells Inga, "You must get back on the Decadron and then you'll feel better in twelve hours." That's when I just lose it. However I am polite and calmly excuse myself from the room. I start crying uncontrollably and ranting out loud to myself as I pace in the corridor. "Yeah, that's what you say and what if she doesn't? What do Erika and I do at midnight when Inga isn't better?"

Jimmy, the nurse who knows Inga well, comes to talk with me. I ask him "Do you believe there's a cure? Is Inga going to get better? Why isn't anyone talking about what is really going on here?" I tell him what Dr. Warhoe told Inga about the Decadron. Dr. Fain had said Inga could stop the Decadron due to the thrush in her throat and also because it didn't seem to be helping. I tell Jimmy how it is at home caring for Inga with her unmanageable pain. He suggests that we all talk to Dr. Warhoe together without Inga present.

Blame, blame, blame. Damn!!! Dr. Warhoe states that Dr. Fain shouldn't have taken her off the Decadron. She listens intently to my concerns and my question to her about whether the radiation is working. I ask her what they have done to give Inga the facts and a reality check about her condition. Both the nurse and Dr. Warhoe state that Inga does not want to hear the facts, that she has always been in denial. Like that is some sort of disease too. She is only thirty years old; how can they blame her for this? They need a better way to communicate with Inga. The doctors have done this before—Inga hasn't, nor have I.

Dr. Warhoe asks what she can do. I tell her to talk to Inga TODAY about her condition. I also ask for a referral for hospice care. Then she says she's behind one hour in her schedule and has to go to another patient, for some procedure she names that I don't understand. She will come back later. When she returns "all puffed up" she states that she consulted with Dr. Fain and here's what they want to do. Inga must consent to staying at the hospital. Again there is this implication that Inga is a noncompliant patient who checks herself out of the hospital against medical advice. As if somehow Inga is the problem.

We return to the exam room where Inga is sprawled out on the floor and Dr. Warhoe begins the special talk with her. She tells Inga that her condition is a very serious and life-threatening situation. While the tumors on her sacrum have shrunk some, the lack of pain management indicates that there is something going on that may not be reversible. Very kindly she tells her that she may not have long to live and that everyone wants to help her to be pain free.

Inga does not respond at all. She then says, "What's next?" The doctor tells her that she needs to be admitted to the hospital and Inga immediately balks. She doesn't want to go there. She asks will she ever leave the hospital. She fears that she will never leave. This is the first time she implies her own death may be near. There is complete silence.

For several very long moments, no one says anything. Then the doctor tells her she needs to be in the hospital where she will get the best care. We want to get fluids into you, so you will feel better, give you steroids IV, and possibly a stomach plug (in order to give food directly into her stomach). Inga agrees to go to the hospital, but not until she asks again if it could just be for a short time and then she could go home with Mom and Erika to take care of her.

We tell her we want to take care of her, but we are not able to manage her pain and that honestly it is too much for us. We tell Inga we will stay in the hospital with her as much as she wants. Dr. Warhoe asks if there is anything else before she goes off to call in the orders for the direct admission. The doctor leaves and Inga literally pops upright and with two fingers of her right hand, high in the air exclaiming cheerfully, "Tonight we dance."

Oh, Inga, my sweet and funny girl! I thank you for making us laugh in the midst of all this emotional intensity.

At least there are no problems at the hospital to get her moved straight to room 716, a very nice private room on the cancer floor. We call Roy and Roxy to ask them to come over to sit with Inga so Erika and I can take a break. Tomorrow we agree to have a team meeting at noon. What a relief as we go off for a swim and then dinner. Erika returns to the hospital and orders a cot so she can spend the night there beside her sister.

I called Fred tonight. Erika asked me to do it, since she did not want to be in a position of having to convince Inga to see her father. Jotting down a few notes helped me to be clear on what I felt was important to relay to him. I feared being caught in old feelings I have of wanting something from him, which he won't do, and then this results in my feeling rejected and angry. So I was well prepared for the conversation.

I gave him an overview of my thoughts on how the situation with Inga had grown to a critical mass. I wanted no blaming. And stated that I hoped each could repair the core issue that holds their relationship in such a painful way. I told him there are some things I have to offer which are personal, professional and also intuitive knowing. I asked him if he wanted to hear this. "Yes, go ahead," he responded.

The first area is in responsibility. For myself I ask how I created this situation. Therefore, I ask you to look at what you have done and not done to create this crisis situation with Inga. It is not just a matter that Inga does not want to see you due to one small circumstance. You must know in your heart of hearts that you have been responsible for this coming to critical mass, or at least take one-half of the responsibility.

Now there is anger. Here is the area where I know that I have been responsible for modeling unhealthy behavior for all of our daughters. Anger came out of me inappropriately both at them and at you, but it is possible to heal the wrongs of the past. In addition, I would ask you to do that.

Then I asked him, "Would you love Inga even if she never saw you again?" That would be unconditional love. A state I aspire to. I know you mean well, however you haven't demonstrated unconditional love towards her. If she had to ask for things so that you would give them to her, that's conditional love.

I remember the first yoga conference Fred and I went to. The guru was sitting taking questions from the audience. "What is unconditional love?" The guru leaned over close to his assistant and said, "I love you." The assistant said, "I love you." He leaned over again and said, "I love you." The assistant said "I love you too". And once again the guru said, "I do love you." The assistant said nothing. And the guru explained. If every time someone tells you that they love you, and you need to tell them the same back, that is conditional love. When you don't need to tell the person back that you too love them, there is the opportunity for unconditional love.

I then told Fred that if I were in his position, I would choose to take an action that demonstrates my unconditional love. I would write Inga a letter that said all the ways that I did screw up in my responsibility as a father and as an adult starting at her birth through her sixteenth birthday and these past six months. Then I would Fed Ex it to her. I would send flowers and ask her to forgive me. I would come on my knees if need be with humility. There is only the immediate present time. We don't know how long Inga will be with us.

The conversation ended with Fred having said very little but that he'd think about everything I told him. I felt good about being honest, kind and not engaging emotionally with any of my old personal issues with him. I could only let him go and hope for the best.

August 26, 2000

This is another very tough day. Inga's condition is deteriorating. Her agitation and anxiety are extremely high and unmanageable. The nursing care on this floor is top notch and Ativan helps too. Dr. Lucas was making rounds for Dr. Fain and he stated it clearly. Inga is dying. There is no treatment that is helping control the cancer's progression. Her body is starting to shut down. He said it could be a matter of days or a few weeks. Hospice should be involved. Inga has refused over and over again to talk about it. She always says tomorrow, tomorrow we'll talk about it.

I call both Fred and Jill. It is time for them to come. Fred asks if Inga has asked to see him. I tell him no, but relay to him my belief that even if he has to sit in the hallway waiting forever to see her he needs to be here. I think I too need him to be here.

Meditating, praying and holding Inga's head at times calms me. So much care is required. Am I helping? This is so very hard, so difficult to witness my daughter's suffering and decline.

I bought her a decadent chocolate mousse pastry today. She isn't eating much and when I arrived with it she smiled and pointed to her bedside table to put it there for later. It was a dark chocolate mousse in a cup made of chocolate with whip cream on top, covered with shavings of chocolate. Here it is Texas in the summer and even in her room it is not too cool. So when she awoke from a nap an hour later, she reached over for it and it promptly started to melt in her fingers. Like the mother of a three-year-old I put a washcloth in her other hand as she started to devour it. Her grin showed how pleased she was and with each mouthful, there were more drips and more pleasure.

Then the gagging started. Coughing, spitting up and choking so much, she looked at me, pleading for help. My first thought when this started was, "Oh my god, am I causing my daughter's death? And then in the next instant came a memory of a dessert our family would eat at Bennigan's in North Carolina when the children were young called, 'Death by Chocolate.'" I was frightened and so was Inga. When I said to her that some Ativan might help, she calmed down and I called for the nurse.

Like giving birth, this dying process is long and arduous. She struggles and at times seems peacefully resting. I pray that her suffering comes to an end soon.

Inga continues to get up to go to the bathroom. A nurse offered her a catheter, saying that it would make it simpler for her. Inga said to her, "We'll talk about it tomorrow." Everything was for tomorrow. She thought when she felt better tomorrow she could deal with the tough things, like the Power of Attorney, writing her will, hospice care.

We brought Sam, Inga's Dalmatian, in to see her today, thinking that would be good for her. Inga smiled a little, yet didn't want her up on the bed with her. The staff all liked having Sam there and it was good for all of her caregivers myself included. Inga's strength wanes.

I am angry. My friends at home seem to be doing nothing. Some have asked what they could do. Have I told them? Where are the flowers? Where are the cards from them? No one seems to reach out and give that form of support. No email messages; they wait silently. I told them I brought my computer. They have been getting updates via "Inga's Healing Circle." Where are they? I don't know how to help myself. Oh yes I do. Breathe. And I need some sleep with the dogs in my little nest in the study at Inga's house. Tomorrow I will email friends my need for flowers and cards.

August 27, 2000

After contacting Liza, the mother of Erika's partner, and my email to other friends requesting support from them, responses started to flow in. I had absolutely no sleep last night after getting contradictory messages from Dr. Lucas and Dr. Warhoe. Dr. Lucas is telling us that Inga's death is imminent and Dr. Warhoe is suggesting a pic line directly into her stomach to feed her. At the same time, Dr. Warhoe was very direct and gentle as she told Inga, "Inga you are dying, you are losing your battle with cancer. This does not mean you have failed."

Fred arrived from North Carolina. Inga said he could come in for 90 seconds. Then she whispered to me to tell him "take off his shoes." On the waxed tile floors of the hospital room, most running shoes squeak horribly. He took off his shoes sheepishly and told her, "I'm sorry and I love you." She didn't respond. His time with her for that visit was up.

Breakfast time was at 12 noon. There is so much family distress. Inga tells me that she does not want to see her father and wishes he wasn't here. I inform Fred of Inga's wishes. Roy seems to befriend Fred. Inga told me that Roy was a special friend to her besides being her real estate agent. Roy is in his 50s; maybe he serves as a positive father figure for her. They had spent some time together on his property in the countryside. I did not understand her to say they were dating, yet I have such mixed feelings about him. He dotes over Inga and it is as if he is sucking her energy. He seems to be touching her in a way that is more than friendly support. She wants him to be near and wants him to do one of the hospital stay night shifts. Laura, Erika and I have been the only ones doing them up to this point and we agree for Roy to share this responsibility if Inga wants him to.

Jill's daughter Kayla is very cute and I appreciate her husband Alex who is helping in his own way. He took me over to his hotel so I could have some respite from the hospital and hang out by their pool while Kayla napped. The pool area was so noisy. I could not stand it and I wanted to nap. So I wandered around and found an indoor hot tub room in the basement where there was no one and fell asleep in the corner of the room. I awoke ravenously hungry and without my purse. So I asked at the desk and had a sandwich delivered to me by the pool and charged it to Alex's room. I wonder did I ever even tell him or repay him? I was then somewhat refreshed as I returned to the hospital.

When I arrive at the hospital, I have a run-in with Roy. I had left Inga's room for a few minutes and come back to Roy ushering Fred into her room. I came in and calmly directed them out. I reminded Fred and Roy that Inga had not asked to see Fred. Roy jumps in protecting Fred's rights as a father to see his daughter. There was no problem with Fred, he said he was sorry and he wouldn't do that again. However, Roy was giving me snarling messages.

I angrily stomp out of the room and down the hall. After I calm down, I go looking for Roy and we find an empty room in order to talk. I told him that I was protecting Inga, who is the only one who has a say in what she wants here as far as her visitors go. It is not OK to go looking at her while she sleeps; if she woke up, she would be furious. Inga doesn't need anything so invasive and damaging to her. I state that Fred and Roy overstepped a boundary and I expect them not to do that again. He verbally attacks me about boundaries and tells me I am such a cold person with all my rules. I tell him what he is saying is inappropriate. I don't deserve to be verbally attacked. This is my daughter dying. Not his. Inga has not said that she wants to have her father with her.

I remind Roy that Fred really has not made any amends with Inga. He only wrote her a little note on a small piece of scratch paper that was just pitiful. It asked, "Why are you so angry with me? I am sorry and want to see you. Love, Dad." I give to Fred, Stephen and Ondrea Levine's book, Who Dies, marking the sections "Unfinished Business" and "Forgiveness." I hope he will read this and be able to find within himself a way to reach out to Inga. Roy later apologizes to me and states he would not do that again and would continue to support Fred.

August 28, 2000

Inga continues her radiation treatment. I accompany her beside the gurney as she is transported to the off-site radiation center. She groans with the bumps and bounces into the transport vehicle. It is an exhausting trip. As we return to the hospital and are waiting, lined up with other hospital staff at the service elevator, one of the green-gowned employees asks in a loud voice, "Does anyone want a treat?" as he holds up a handful of candy bars. Inga's arm pops up in the air. He comes over to her with his treats and asks which one she would like. The one she points to is "Sweet Escape." Now isn't this the truth? Don't we all want this at times? Inga's humor again is a big relief for me.

Inga is now on a self-regulated morphine pump. She usually does not even have the energy to push the button herself, but one of us will ask her or she points to it. She has an unusual awake lucid time and stays up arranging and looking at her flowers after she goes to the bathroom. She asks me about taking a shower, but in the five minutes it takes for the nurse to arrive, she is back in bed and says, maybe tomorrow. "Tomorrow" becomes her mantra for anything that we ask her.

At 9:30 PM Fred, Erika, Jill, Laura and I watch the video taken when we swam with the dolphins last month in Mexico—so beautiful to see all of us so happy and playful. Then Inga calls out for more pain meds, bringing us back to the present time. After a short nap she wakes up and requests her "famous Jell-O mix." Tonight it is Haagen Dazs vanilla ice cream and green Jell-O because there is no red, which she prefers, available. She wants to do it herself so she is mixing and ordering us to get what else she needs for her concoction. Erika leaves now to go pick up her friend and partner Jeremy who is arriving from Seattle. Others leave and I make my little preparations for spending the night next to her.

August 29, 2000

Every hour I am pressing the morphine machine until about 5 AM when she awakes me with numbness in her left hand and shortness of breath. Nurse Sylvia offers oxygen, after a few minutes of that I see the panic on Inga's face, and I suggest Ativan. Yes, that is what she needs and she calms down. I return to my bed with the comforting frog, which is a purple velvet stuffed toy that Laura brought for Inga. A few days later Laura purchases two more, one each for Erika and me.

Around 6:30 AM, Dr. Fain arrives to make rounds and Inga is groggy and sleepy. She wants me to tell him how her night went. He tells her he will do just one more lumbar puncture to see if the methyl dextrate has worked; the previous test showed there was no change in the cancer growth in her spinal fluid. He tells her if the chemo has not worked there is nothing else he can do. I request that he do the procedure today, not tomorrow. He agrees to come back this evening after office hours. He orders acupuncture for Inga and also for her to see her psychotherapist, which she has been putting off. There is still a question as to whether she can leave the hospital, which Inga still wants. There will be a trial for Oxycontin for pain management to see if she can tolerate it without nausea and vomiting as previously happened. Also, they have to prove to the insurance company that they tried everything else, none of which works and therefore she needs IV morphine to control pain. Oh how I hate working in this bureaucratic system that never is here with the patient, my daughter, who is suffering in pain.

August 30, 2000

Michael Limmerick consults with us, the family. He is the palliative care nurse for the hospital. He tells us that we need to be a united front and that Inga's denial needs to be fragmented. He states clearly that Inga is dying and that it seems that she has been manipulating each of us to join her in that denial. We need to truly come together as a team.

Someone speaks up, asking what do we say when Inga starts going on about more treatment and such. I reflect for a long time on what it is that Inga might be able to hear. What comes to me is, "Inga's spirit will live forever and right now her body is dying." Everyone agrees that they will tell her in those words. Yes, Inga's physical body is shutting down. The cancer is aggressive and nothing can be done to stop it; it is taking over her body. Inga is dying. My thirty-year-old fighting spirit of a daughter is dying. This is agonizing.

We hold a team meeting and the truth about Roy and Inga comes out. They have been lovers. Now I don't feel crazy when I see him touching her in a sexual way. We all agree we won't collude with Inga's denial. We want hospice involvement and we know that Inga must agree. But Dr. Fain still hasn't told Inga that he can no longer do any treatment and that it is best she enter residential hospice care at Christopher House.

Maybe I need to back up a bit here. Since meeting Dr. Fain, I understood why Inga liked him so much. He was direct in getting treatment plans going, he always listened to what Inga wanted and he never talked about death. I asked Dr. Fain every time he made rounds if he thought the treatment was working and if he would make a referral to hospice. He would say things like, "Inga does not want to talk about it" or "Let's run this test or try this."

So when Dr. Fain made his morning rounds, I ask him to be direct with Inga as Michael has suggested and talk to her about hospice care. He agrees and I walk into Inga's room with him. Inga and he chat. Before I know what is happening, he is promising her something else to try and talking about the pic line into her stomach. I look at him and he turns away and leaves the room. I am furious. Who is in denial here? Outside of the room, I walk up—no, charge up—to him and demand why he had not told Inga the truth. Again, he defends himself and says when he returns from his weekend off he will try again. I am beside myself with anger. He is abandoning her, not telling her the truth and then walking away, taking the weekend off. I storm off down the hall just raving mad. How can this be? Not only is Inga in denial, but her doc is just behaving absurdly. How dare he? I walked into an unused hallway and wailed and cried and screamed. When I felt like I got my balance back, I was returning to see Inga and Dr. Fain stops me in the hallway.

"Carole, I am sorry. You are right; I too am denying that Inga is dying. It is so very hard for me too. She is so full of life and I can't face it. She is only a few years younger than me. I want her to live so very much. I haven't done the best for her. I must tell her she is dying."

At this point I started crying. Now I understand and I can forgive him and we hug. But we need a plan. He agrees to return after office hours for a team meeting with us first and then we all will go in to tell Inga together.

Laura has been asking Inga about seeing her father for a few days now and Inga finally agrees. She wants to be alone with him for a few minutes. When I return they are holding hands and Fred says, "She forgives me." It is now OK for him to be in her room. Now I must admit that Fred was loyal in his waiting for Inga. There were times I saw him just quietly reading or on his computer sitting on the floor in the hallway outside her room. He waited and waited and waited. All the team wanted reconciliation between Inga and her dad and now that it happened, there is a calmness and sense of relief. Her dad is officially on the team.

"Inga's Healing Team" meets. It is Erika, Jill, Fred, Jeremy, Roxy, Laura and I. Dr. Fain thanks us all for being here for Inga; he knows how important it is for all of to have support from each other as well as to show our loving care of Inga. He says he has had a hard time telling Inga that nothing more can be done and he is grateful that we will all do this together. We create a simple plan. First Dr. Fain will speak. Then Roxy will tell Inga some details of hospice care and request her to really hear this. Then we'll ask if she has questions.

We all walk into Inga's room and tell her we are having a team meeting with Dr. Fain, and there are some really important things to talk about. She says she is tired, and wants to have the meeting "tomorrow." No, we say, it must be now. So she wakes up a little and starts to prop herself up a bit in bed. Someone helps her with the pillows to make her comfortable.

Dr. Fain starts. "Inga, I know this is all very difficult for you, but I have to tell you everything. We have gotten back the last report on your spinal tap. There was no change. In fact, it looks like the count of cancer cells is elevated. The chemo is not working. You have a very aggressive cancer and we do not have any treatment. There are cancer cells spread all through your brain and spinal fluid. It is in your lungs and soon will be in all your organs. The truth is that the best care for you now is Christopher House, the inpatient hospice nearby. (a pause) I am so sorry." Inga's expression does not change; her eyes are glazed over. All of us are teary. The doctor asks her if she has any questions. Can I go home? she asks. He tells her that the best care for both her and her family is at Christopher House, the residential hospice. She needs a lot of care and he does not advise her going home for that. He tells her she needs to agree to go there. Then she asks, will I be in all this pain? Could I have as much pain medication as I want, even if it is maybe too much? We all know what she means. And Dr. Fain clearly tells her, "Inga, you can have as much medication as you would like; I promise you, you won't be in pain." Roxy then asks Inga if she is scared. She tells her how much we all love her and we will be with her all the time. Others speak out their love and care for her. She looks at all of us and then says that she wants to be alone to think by herself.

We all file out of her room in tears and sighs of relief with the entire truth spoken. Dr. Fain busily writes orders including a referral to Christopher House. We go off to talk and decide to give Fred the next shift staying with Inga while others go to dinner.

It's now 9 PM and Erika and I are driving back to the hospital when I get a call from Fred, who is staying with Inga. He is telling me Inga wants me and says he isn't doing something right. When I arrive back in her room, she is very upset because she can't remember her own telephone number. I tell her we can write it on a piece of paper and I tape it to her bed rail. "Isn't that pitiful that I can't remember my own phone number?" she says. Sadness washes over me as the reality of Inga's condition is made known. Cancer is attacking her brain.

She calms down and naps a bit. Then she says she wants us to read to her. Like a princess holding court, she is propped up again on her pillows. Each of us in turn tells stories, remembering events we have shared with her.

Fred tells her about taking her flying. On one occasion, he took her to camp via plane. She would smile at different parts of our memories, or even remind us to talk about "the time when ..."

I recall and share about our camping trip to Twin Sisters near Estes Park, Colorado. I have never been much of a camper, but she convinced me that it could be fun and a mother-daughter bonding time. So off we went one bright August morning with all our gear. We arrive at a campground and pitch our tent. Then off we go to hike the Twin Sisters Peak. It was a glorious day on which to take the moderate hike under the typical cloudless Colorado blue sky.

Then it became overcast as we returned and by the time we were at our camp site, Inga was chirping about cappuccinos. Now I love coffee too, but we are camping and didn't have the makings for such a gourmet drink. She kept insisting how great a special coffee would be right now and why don't we just run into Estes Park to grab a quick java. Now when Inga wants something she does have a convincing way about her. We hopped into the car and found a not-quite-perfect coffee spot but did enjoy our late afternoon coffee. No sooner had we finished and I was looking forward to heading back to our tent, than she got onto another kick. She saw a movie was playing in the local cinema that she really wanted to see. Why didn't we just take in that show which was happening in just a few minutes and we could still get back to camp before dark?

Now I am really laughing. For this is the furthest thing from a camping type of experience which I had in mind, but I could go along. Why not? It seemed like a movie I would like also. After we get out of the movie the sun is setting and it's getting a bit chilly. By the time we return to our campsite, Inga is freezing. She never was able to tolerate the cold, but I think it was 60 degrees out, not much less than that. I gave her an extra sweater that I had to put on along with her tights and pullover. She is still so cold.

I begin to put together our simple meal and am actually enjoying the sounds and smells of the woods. However, Inga is miserable. "Mom, I am so cold I don't think I can stand to sleep here." I'm surprised; after all it was she who wanted to come camping and it is she who loves it so much. So I ask her what she wants. She pleads to go home and sleep in our cozy and warm beds at my house. I laugh now and I still laugh about this. I hesitated some and resisted, but eventually gave in. We got back to Boulder about midnight. Our camping trip deluxe, sixteen hours together, and I'd say it still was a bonding experience. I'll never forget this story.

Inga laughs and corrects me about some of it as we went along.

Laura tells the story of how she and Inga met. Their husbands were both rock climbers and cavers. Being the left-at-home wives, they found comfort and enjoyment in being with each other. When Erika then started to tell a caving story, Inga stopped her, saying it's too scary!

Now Inga had another idea. She would write words on a piece of paper for us to have a contest. We each get only one chance and really only one chance to pronounce each word and then she will tell us the correct one. There are four to five words on the paper and then she says that she has more. I don't recall the words, but am reminded of her learning to read in kindergarten and the way she played school with her little sisters.

I was helping to fluff her pillows and she was getting agitated. She motions for me to move away from the bed. She gives Jeremy some instruction and he moves a few things and she sinks back and says, perfect. Then she says, "There'll be a contest every day and a prize will go to the person who finds the best soft, tasty, no sugar food that Inga likes."

She eats someone's Jell-O concoction, smiles and soon after throws up.

The stories continue and then Fred says he needs to leave. It is Laura's turn for the night shift and I ask her if it would be all right if I stayed too. I just want to be nearby. Laura and I create a mattress bed for the two of us at the left-hand corner of Inga's bed near the window. With lots of pillows and our two purple frogs, we both curl up and attempt to get some sleep.

August 31, 2000

It is 1 AM and I hear Inga stirring. I ask what she needs. She thinks she has wet her bed. I check and all is well. Then I help her to get to the bathroom. At 3 AM, I hear her tossing and ask if she needs anything. "Mom, I'm OK, go back to bed."

At 4:30 AM, I hear a knocking sound and jump up to see Inga spread-eagled on her bed with her arms hitting the side rails. I immediately call for the nurse, frightened because I know that this is a seizure. The nurse tries to talk to Inga, asks her what is wrong. What a dumb question; Inga is seizing and she needs medication. Inga is very agitated and tries to get up to walk to the bathroom, stumbling and pushing me away. I talk calmly to her and get her onto the toilet. She is then given some medication. Again, more flailing of her arms and entire body. Laura leaves to summon Fred, Erika and Jill. By 6:25 AM they all arrive and there is no change in Inga's level of distress. She continues to be highly agitated and throwing herself around in her bed. She does not seem to understand what we say to her. I ask a nurse for more Ativan and when she returns with the injection she says, "This may cause respiratory distress." We all look at each other and then at Inga in such distress and say to give it to her. Still no change after 30 minutes. We take turns touching her and trying to hold her in bed. At some point Inga looks directly into my eyes and mouths silently, "Help me." My heart feels like it is breaking as I go out to find a nurse and tell her Inga needs more Ativan. At first the nurse says, wait a minute, just calm down, I need to call the doctor for the order. Ten minutes later I am back to the same nurse and she says she hasn't reached the doctor yet. I yell out, "My daughter is suffering in there and she needs more medication, GET A FUCKIN' DOCTOR NOOOOWWW!!" I am furious. She wants me to calm down and I tell her I will calm down when she gives Inga more medication. So she huffs off into the room saying how much risk she is taking to do this without the doctor's order, but she will go ahead and give her more Ativan.

Chaplain Gary arrives very timidly. It is as if we have to take care of him. I ask him to say a prayer with us and can hardly hear what he says in the back of the room. Roxy arrives now and it is so wonderful to have her strong calm presence. She is a wise woman, knowing, and acts with mindfulness and much compassion.

On one side of Inga is Erika and on the other is Jill, holding and cradling their sister in bed. Then Inga pulls up and turns herself around in the bed and I am holding her head with each of her sisters at her side and Fred touching her too. I feel like we are in a birthing process. How long will this go on? She pushes and kicks with her feet and I feel her head "crowning" in my hands and into my entire body. Each person present is sobbing deeply, as we take turns, since all of us simultaneously would be too overpowering. Is this what dying is like? I pray silently for mercy, for release from this excruciating process.

Chaplain Barbara arrives and she is very helpful as she recites from memory a psalm after asking permission from us. She stands behind me with her hands on my shoulders and at times her entire body supporting me both physically and emotionally. How can this be happening? We are witnessing the death of my first-born child. It was only thirty years ago I was birthing her into this world—how can I now be birthing her into death?

Michael Limmerick is on the scene by 8:30 AM. The regular hospital staff is now returning to work. He informs us of Inga's status. She is not in the active dying process now. It can be days still. He supports us to take a break, go out to eat and leave her for a while. He says Inga needs time alone at this point on her journey. He walks us into the hallway and talks to us for a while. Now there are more meds given and he says that she is a bit more relaxed now. The nurse will be cleaning her up and he walks back into her room. I follow. He urges me to leave and I insist that I need to be with Inga too.

He relents and I stay back as they talk to Inga, telling her what they are doing as they insert a catheter, which will relieve any bladder pressure she may be having. They are respectful as they bathe her, then put on her favorite clean shorty pajamas. When they step back, I go up to her and tell her that her "team" is going out to breakfast and that we'll be back soon. "I love you, Inga, and hope you can rest comfortably now." She doesn't really respond outwardly, but I sense she is drowsy and will nap now. She seems more peaceful.

Michael pulls me aside as I am leaving. He chats a bit and then tells me that I really shouldn't get angry at the doctors. They are doing all that they can. I remember noting in my mind that this is not the time to discuss this with him. What right does he have to tell me for what and with whom I can be angry? I am angry that Inga is dying and I am angry that Inga did not get the medication she needed early this morning. I also need to let go of that anger.

We all head over to Madeleine's for some breakfast. Fred does decide to join us and I tease him that we need to have him come along so he can pick up the tab. He had been reluctant to come along saying that he wasn't hungry and didn't want to eat. Perhaps my humor was helpful in the moment. It is already over 90 degrees out and a very bright sunny day as we stroll the two blocks to the restaurant. I can feel myself breathe in the daylight; have I awakened now from this very horrific nightmare?

At 12 noon we are all back at the hospital and a representative from hospice arrives and the transfer arrangements are made. Is Inga awake enough to know consciously what is happening? She did agree to being moved to hospice and the time is now set for 4 PM today. I ask to ride with her in the ambulance. There is such a strong urge for me to care for her, to protect her somehow. I was told it was against the rules for me to ride along, but they allowed me to come anyway. They hooked her up to some EEG machine in the back and I told them that she has DNR orders. They didn't even appear to hear me, although one of them finally did look up to acknowledge what I had said.

Christopher House Hospice has a very nice garden area we pass through to enter. Her room is very large, filled with light and homey in a way. Erika and Jeremy are there already, arranging some of Inga's things, her flowers and thoughtful cards sent by many. As the nursing staff gets her comfortable in her bed, we tell her where we are. She is taken off the IV meds and fluids and hooked up to a portable morphine unit. It is discreetly tucked away bedside her bed. There is a more relaxed feeling in the room. The nurses are incredible as they introduce themselves to her and tell her exactly what they are doing. At this point she is not awake at all and the nurse tells us in order to make her more comfortable she will be monitored to get as much morphine as needed so she will be peaceful and without pain. How can I describe the relief I felt? Finally she won't suffer any longer. I am relieved not to have to fight with the hospital staff. I can be me, her mother, besides being her advocate.

Jeremy creates a decorative sign *Inga* for her door and adds pictures: Inga kissing the dolphin from our trip just five weeks ago, Inga running a triathlon just a year ago, Inga as a young girl grinning at the camera (she loved to have her picture taken), Inga with her dog, Samantha, Inga running on the trails of Texas that she loved. The staff really appreciated seeing Inga in her very vital and active life. They were even going to suggest to other families to do this. We put on her bed a favorite Indian blanket given to her by her friend Barbara. Inga is resting more comfortably now. I feel more rested.

Jeremy and Erika leave to go for a swim and dinner. They bring me back a delicious "Kirby Chicken" and then they take over the shift as I now need a break. Back at Inga's house I tidy up, which is a calming and grounding ritual of sorts for me. I email messages and read the ones that had come in. I feel the extended support of folks from "Inga's Healing Circle" all over the country.

September 1, 2000

At 7:30 AM, the ringing phone wakes me up. Erika calls to say the hospice staff thinks the end is very near. Inga's breathing has changed to the characteristic "death rattle" and other signs are indicating it will not be too long now. Jeremy will come pick me up.

Inga seems so peaceful, yet she is not really there. I sit and talk with her. I cry as I read from Stephen Levine's book a passage called, "Who dies?" The preparation for death meditation comforts me. I asked Inga's permission first, saying that I know this is my thing but I hoped it would help her too besides all of us gathering to say goodbye to her. We did make calls to let everyone know it was OK with the family for people to visit Inga. And many came. I do get annoyed with some, random irritations, from loud talking to Fred playing computer games in the room. I want to control what is happening, I recognize my urge and let it go. I want to take care of her. I hold the vaporizing mist mask against her face so the elastic band will not be needed. I give instructions on her bathing and change of clothing. They even wash her hair and she is so beautiful. Her short curling reddish brown hair makes her look like she is ready to dress up for a night of dancing. How is it that she is dying? She just looks a little fatigued, as if she had just been out for a long bike ride.

We have another team meeting. Roy states that there is nothing more he can do and so he has decided to leave town with his niece for the beach as he does every Labor Day Weekend. What is he thinking? "If you want to be part of this family, then you will stay here this weekend and be here for Inga's death," I announce to him. He thinks about it and says yes he will stay. Inga had said in the past week to all of us, Laura and Roy are like family to me, and I want you to treat them that way. We talk about an Inga Van Nynatten Memorial Fund to be established, and asking that donations could also go to Susan G. Komen Foundation, Austin Breast Cancer Resource Center, or to QuaLife Wellness Community in Denver. We establish a schedule for the main care team and also some basic agreements about visitors.

There are many sweet moments sitting with Inga, and many sad moments. I tell her how much I will miss coming to Austin to see her for Thanksgiving. Inga was planning a big Thanksgiving celebration in her new house. She was always making plans for the future. Laura has a lot of difficulty seeing Inga dying, as do many others.

We have created a sacred space here in this room with flowers and silence. We read to her, "letting go into the vastness." Spending time alone in the meditation garden and in the small stain-glassed chapel is supportive. I feel grounded outside in the rose garden through my senses and feel comforted by nature and the gift of earth, trees and flowers.

Roxy comes to take Erika and me for manicures. I do not want to leave for too long, yet I also need time away. We decide to grab a quick bite to eat. It is overly stimulating at Hoover's and I just eat my quesadillas and leave to wait for the others outside in the parking lot. Erika soon joins the others and then me.

Back to Inga's room and hearing her rattling breath. The doctor this morning said it would only be a few hours. Oh, our Inga would never do it like the doctor said. Patience, Erika says, Inga wanted her to have patience. So here is an opportunity for practice. The gift of patience is patience.

I want to wait; I am glad the others have left. It is hard to be around all the commotion. It is hard to be around the mothers and their young children. Fred asked me if I have ever met his son Aaron. How funny he is! Of course I have never met him, when and how could that have occurred? Candy, his wife, never even said hello to me and I feel my avoidance of her. I do not want her near Inga and feel my anger at how she treated Inga in these past six months. Not now, Carole, let it go. Maybe tomorrow, I am saying it like Inga, later, maybe tomorrow.

Inga did not have any life insurance. Her boss Marta said she declined it after she found out the money for it came out of the National Park Service budget. She preferred for the money to be spent on trails. In addition, it is how she denied death. A wave of lack of concern for us comes up, not so much for myself, but for Erika, who has been caring for her now for an entire month and many weeks in the past two-and-a-half years of illness.

How sad. Moreover, so much learning and letting go. Unconditional love has no wanting, just waiting and being present with what is in the moment.

It is late and we are all exhausted. Erika and I will spend the night here with Inga. There is a pull-out couch in the room. We try to sleep but sleep never comes. Listening to Inga's breathing—it stops in hesitation for a long time, then restarts. We pray, whisper, and get up occasionally to walk in the garden.

September 2, 2000

At 3:30 AM, Inga stopped breathing. The nurse had just come to reposition her. Then silence. No more rattling, no more breathing. No more Inga. She was gone. There was no sign or white light or anything, simply a cessation of breaths. Erika and I cried and held her and encouraged her on this part of her journey. Then we read the after-death meditation from Stephen Levine's book, *Who Dies?* This helped me and I hope it helped Inga's spirit find her way.

We prepared her room by lighting candles and covered Inga with her favorite shawl from Indonesia that her friend Barbie had given to her. We played music with sounds of birds. This was a first since Inga always wanted silence.

Inga looked so peaceful and incredibly beautiful. Her mouth, which was open for the past 36 hours with breathing, now relaxed into a broad smile. I patted and fussed with her hair. Her skin shimmered with an opalescent glow.

Fred, Jill and Candy arrived and we, the family, all hugged and cried. Goodbyes were said to Inga. Roxy, who I love dearly, arrived. Peggy came. Laura came. We read aloud again the meditation after death.

Jill told us the dream she had just before she was awakened by our phone call. "I see the figure of St. Christopher, you know, the magnet that Grandma always had in her Volkswagen when we were kids. St. Christopher is the guardian saint and protector of those who travel. It was St. Christopher there walking off with Inga."

We had talked about who would be there to greet Inga, since she had not known anyone besides her dog Rosa who had died. And we believed there would be a guide to help her to make the transition from life to death. Now we knew St. Christopher was helping her.

It was time to make arrangements with a funeral home. We knew that we just wanted a simple cremation and asked the nurse if they had recommendations. She gave us a list. When we told her that we did not want any formally dressed black-suited men coming, she suggested the first on the list.

At our team meeting, we called All Faith Funeral Home. They would pick up Inga's body and would wear "Dockers and plaid shirts." Since it was Labor Day weekend, they would refrigerate until Tuesday. Roy had not arrived yet. Erika talked with him and let him know it was time to come. He arrived at 6 and All Faith arrived at 6:30. Oh, my god, how can this be happening?

Bill introduced himself and was very kind with us. He did indeed wear Dockers and a bright plaid shirt. Erika and I wanted to stay with Inga while she was prepared for transport. He advised against it. He told us he would wrap her in plastic as the law required and this can be quite traumatic to be viewed. However, we insisted we needed to be with Inga in this part of her journey also. We put a photograph of all of us on our Mexico trip in her hand along with an iris, and placed a washcloth over her face. We removed the Indonesian cover on her and replaced it with her favorite comfy blanket that she had curled up with throughout her illness, given to her by Marta, her boss.

I sobbed in the arms of Inga's day nurse Carolyn as they wheeled Inga out. The deep tears of sadness came from my belly; they appeared in waves. I called friends back home, left messages, and talked to Liza.

We all went out to breakfast at Kirby Lane. Exhausted with dark circles under my eyes, I ordered something to eat and shivered from the cold air conditioning. Roy went out to his car and got blankets and sheets for us to cuddle under while awaiting our food. I love having this extended family and I am so tired.

We return to #9 Christopher House to clear out Inga's things. It is hard, yet we want to get this finished, taken care of so we could leave this place where Inga died. We want to be at her home where she lived.

We return to the house and I sleep for an hour while others go out for errands and such. When I awake from my nap, the power is out. I report it, but they tell me no one else on the block is out. Is this Inga playing with me? On the other hand, is this a symbol of the darkness and sadness in our lives now that Inga is gone? Spirit works in mysterious ways and I embrace whatever it means.

Details. Details. Arrangements need to be taken care of. Someone must write an obituary, the chaplain must be contacted for the memorial. I call my boss Naomi and she is very helpful. She is strong for me as I flip-flop between numb emptiness and raw, jagged pain in my heart.

September 3, 2000

Now, twenty-four hours after Inga's death, I am completely exhausted as we visit the Wild Basin Wilderness Center. This seems to be a perfect spot for Inga's memorial. Things do fall into place nicely. Laura has written the obituary and taken it over to the newspaper. Fred and his wife Candy will take care of the food for the memorial. Jeremy, Erika's boyfriend, will do a photo display board of Inga's life and will put together a program for the memorial. We decide to rent tablecloths rather than use paper or try to gather some from friends. Keep it simple and easy.

Erika is stressed out about money. There are more financial problems to be dealt with. There is no equity in Inga's house and she left a $7,000 student loan outstanding. She never wrote a will, only told Laura that she knew Laura would know what was right. She signed a will but we find out from an attorney later that it is not a legal document. So what happens to the house and car?

I am at Inga's home alone from 2–6 PM today and fall into intense grief with much anger. Erika at first thought she wanted to give Inga's diamond earrings to Roxy. I disagree with her. Liza, Jeremy's mother, calls and generously offers her support and willingness to come to Austin. I don't know if that's what I need now. I feel so confused and angry that Inga died. She was not supposed to die, she was supposed to be a miracle, she was supposed to live. Anger helps give me energy and I sure do need some.

The obituary gets misprinted. And I am angry about that. I am revisiting anger at Fred again and my perspective of the ways in which he was not the good father I wanted for her. I am angry with his wife Candy who also didn't act in ways I wanted for Inga's sake. As I was driving on the freeway today a big Texan car with a driver in a big Texan hat cut me off in my lane. I was so mad I gave him the finger. It took much effort to know how to do that with my left hand. I really have never done that before. It was very satisfying.

September 4, 2000

Today we were at All Faith Funeral Home to sign papers and make the final arrangements for Inga's cremation. Fred came and that was good.

Actually Candy wanted to come too, but Erika talked to them so that she didn't. Fred volunteered to pay the funeral cost, which was a big relief for Erika, who has been taking so much responsibility for everything. We chose a recyclable, biodegradable box for Inga's ashes. We imagined Inga would like that and then were also relieved of the stress of having to find something suitable.

We then went to lunch and met with Chaplain Barbara who will officiate at the memorial. Laura and later Jill joined us. Lots of stories came out again. Barbara took notes and wanted to get the facts of Inga's life straight.

The family and other team members were going to have dinner tonight at the Texas Land and Cattle Company. First the family would gather at the house and have a drink together. This could also be a time that family members would choose something to remember Inga by. Erika and I had picked out some things for family members already which seemed appropriate. We took pictures together. Then we went out to the restaurant. Inga's favorite steak dinner in the past few months had been on the menu, called "Silver Spurs." So I ordered that. It was a small filet mignon and it was delicious.

September 5, 2000

I take an early morning walk by myself when it is still tolerable. By noon the temperature has soared to 107 degrees as we pick up the white tablecloths and head over to set up for the memorial service. I love tending to the shrine. There's Inga's photograph taken in Mexico on the beach, three candles, purple irises, and dirt from a special healing spot in Chimayo, New Mexico.

About 75 people attend the memorial. Inga loved the heat and it was a record-breaking 112 degrees during her service. It was touching to hear all the stories from the people in Inga's life. Dr. Warhoe, Inga's radiation oncologist, came and Allen, Inga's ex-husband amongst many others I didn't know. A beam of sunshine moved along the shrine throughout the program. The healing candle melted wax all over the white tablecloth. Life is messy! This death was messy. Chaplain Barbara tells the story of the white rock from the book of Revelations, because she had been finding and giving away white rocks throughout her life. Since a week before Inga's death, I had been hanging on to the white rock sent to Inga from a friend of mine who lived at Findhorn in Scotland. I feel the comfort of its smoothness and warmth. There were so many people with so many stories of Inga's life and high-spirited nature. There were some people who didn't even know Inga had cancer. She really did not want to be labeled "the cancer patient." Even a massage therapist whom she saw several times didn't know and was shocked to hear she died of breast cancer. Inga was so young, so vibrant, desiring of life and all that it offered her.

A photographer friend of Inga's arrived and he offered to take pictures for me with my camera. He quickly finished the roll of film. With the closing song, "That's Right You're Not From Texas" sung by Lyle Lovett, many of us got up and danced. I think this was shocking to many there for it must have seemed out of context at such a sad time, yet it was a big release for those of us who had been grieving for weeks and months, a way for us to get through this time. Besides, Inga was a person who did shock others, so we were living her legacy. Fred told me later, "You'll dance for Inga and I'll run for her."

In the evening we all went to the hotel where several family members were staying and swam in the pool. I felt some connection with Aaron, Inga's one-and-a-half-year-old half-brother, who is so full of life and love. Inga would have smiled watching me with him. He even kissed me good-bye.

A day later, people started to leave, first Jeremy, then Fred with his wife, kids and parents. Erika and I are left to deal with paperwork, household stuff, Inga's clothes and mementos. We both felt feverish and sick so we just hung out at home together watching videos. One of the neighbors brought us a fried shrimp and catfish dinner. Inga would have appreciated this kind gesture as we did too.

Later I am looking through a box of Inga's clothes in my makeshift room and find a soft blue sweater. Crying quietly I hug it, wishing Inga were in it. I hope Erika doesn't mind if I take this one. I'm sure she won't. There are so many clothes and I hope that Erika can get some cash selling most of it. Laura comes over and tries on some clothes too, deciding what she would like.

I read one of Inga's journals. There is nothing really about her feelings, unlike my journals, which are an emotional warehouse. I notice my frustration and anger again. If only someone were here to fight with; I just don't want this to be true. My daughter Inga is dead and there was nothing I could do to stop that from happening.

Inga, please come back and fight with me—just for a few minutes or seconds. I plead for contact with her. Inga could be and was a difficult child and teenager at times. And then eventually we were able to work through many conflicts, some sooner than others.

I remember when she was sixteen, she chose to live with her father and had many battles with him. She used to tell me that it was I who needed to make the marriage work. Then one day she invited me to have lunch with her in a very nice Chinese restaurant. After we ate she told me that she had some things to tell me. I can't do justice in this moment to how she said it, but it was an apology and a request for forgiveness. She said she understood now how it was with her dad and me. She told me I really was the very best Mom ever and how much she appreciated the friendship that I offered too. Would I forgive her for all the awful things that she said to me in the past? And of course, I did. My heart is full remembering that time together as I hold Inga in my forgiven heart.

September 8, 2000

It is now six days after Inga died. This becomes my reference point, the hours, days since Inga died. My life is forever changed.

Errands, business at the bank, papers to review. I sign Inga's name where she was unwilling. Erika and I then go to eat migas and gingerbread pancakes at Kirby Lane. There truly are wonderful restaurants in Austin to keep me nurturing myself with food. I am thankful for this. Then we go to the hospital to order a copy of her medical records of her last stay in the hospital. I have a strong need to read it, to know everything was done for her.

We go home to sort through belongings. Am I taking too many things home with me? I want to remember Inga. How can I not? I want to feel the softness of her blue sweater and remember us laughing together about her complaints when it was so cold out, even when at 50 degrees. Inga's pink childhood teddy bear was her comfort for so many years; how can I not want to take it?

Inga's cremains sit on the kitchen table along with pictures of her, flowers and a candle. It is so hard to imagine her ashes in the small square box. Sometimes I just think she will dash in the door like she always did and ask me how I am today. I have had no dreams since she died. I want a comforting dream message. I don't feel my spiritual guides around me. I have Erika and I am so grateful for her complete availability and love. I feel so empty and alone.

September 9, 2000

I am sitting on Inga's rug, packing and preparing to return home to Boulder. This is difficult; I want to be in my own space and I also don't want to leave this place of Inga's. I also don't want to leave Erika with the piles of things to do. I keep thinking that my life will be different, never the same because of this and I'm feeling so lost as to what is next. I'll take the advice I gave to Erika as she was asking the same question. She was supposed to start graduate school this week and she withdrew her acceptance into the program. I suggested she go home, rest, grieve and contemplate what is next. The answer will come. I didn't at the time append my words with "trust me," but I want to do that now.

I arrived home in Boulder late in the day and was greeted by my friend Clara who was delivering a basket of goodies and flowers to my back door. She said she only meant to drop the welcome basket and not disturb my privacy, but I needed someone right then and she came in. I am worried about going back to work and financial matters. My heart aches and I am concerned about my own health. It was a little miracle that she was right there when I needed someone to talk to. Thank you, Clara.

Erika is now off driving to Atlanta to take Trixie, Inga's adopted Dalmation, to her new home with Jill and family. Then Erika will be off to visit her dad in Wilmington, North Carolina and then she will drive to Boulder.

We did decide to do a memorial service in Boulder in early October when Erika will be here. The memorial funds have started to build to almost $4,000 and I really want to use some of the money to mark a place on the Boulder Creek path to visit and remember Inga. I started contacting the city about who to talk to in order to place a memorial bench. Also, I am looking for a site for the memorial service with little success. Early fall in Boulder is just beautiful, my favorite season and with Inga being such an outdoors person, it only seems right for us to be outside. I picture a sunny, cool day with leaves on the ground. But where is this place? Flagstaff amphitheatre is too large and it is pretty well booked up too. Can I trust myself to find a special location for the memorial?

September 13, 2000
Dream Journal Entry
I have small rabbits in a bag. I cut an end off the bag in order to let the rabbits out and then see a decapitated rabbit. I am shocked and horrified. I did this—how could I? I thought I was so careful. The body of the rabbit starts hopping. I helplessly put the head onto the body. I am horrified. Can I put him back together again?

I do feel helpless most of the time. The horror of Inga's death plagues me.

An angel arrives. His name is Gary Lacy and he is one of the original planners of the Boulder Creek path. He has worked for the City of Boulder for twelve years. Inga met him a few years earlier and by chance, someone in the County Greenway Planning Department gave me his name as I was inquiring about placement of a memorial bench along the path. Gary met Inga in Tucson and later she contracted with him to come to Texas for consulting on one of the projects she as a trail planner was working on.

Gary and his wife Leslie and their two children invited us to have Inga's memorial service at their home and garden on Boulder Creek. Now the date can be set. It will be October 8th at 2 PM. We plan to share stories, music, laughter, reflection by the creek and food. Of course there will be chocolate, Inga's favorite food.

Gary also knows how to work the city system so that we can place a bench along the Boulder Creek path. He advises me to look for the perfect spot. My friend Myrna Bottone goes walking with me to help find the site. It is a rainy day and it's comforting for me to be with her. I do find a wonderful place under trees which looks downstream. It is high too so there is a sense of spaciousness and I love the sound of the water rushing by.

The lesson here is for me to trust myself and my process. Where I envisioned the memorial to be is where it shall be. I never said "trust me" on this. Will I ever?

Today I started my own grief group. I visited with my officemates Chuck, Toni, Mary, Patricia and Terri. They were fully present as I told my stories, grieved and tracked my process. We agreed to meet again. What I really needed was a support group in which I tell my story and others serve as witnesses and share their loving presence. This is exactly how they served me.

It is clear that I need to take time off from my work in the world for now. Grieving Inga's death is my full-time job and I have come to know this as my only truth. QuaLife has been the biggest part of my world, so another loss is hard to reconcile. I feel I have just come to a place of skill, security, and a sense of confidence that I am making a difference in the world. A part of me just does not want to let go of working at QuaLife and yet I know and do trust that the highest good of all will be served by my taking a leave of absence.

September 24, 2000
Dear Inga,

It's been twenty-two days since you died. It feels both like it was yesterday and that it was months ago. Sometimes I just can't believe I will never see you again on this earth plane. I can't believe, don't want to believe and know that I won't hug you again and be prodded by you to go out to eat or go out for coffee and something decadent. I can't believe, don't want to believe that there won't be Thanksgiving dinner at your new house as you were looking forward to. I can't believe there will be no phone calls from you in that excited voice of yours exclaiming, "Guess what?" or "Sit down, Mumford—this is a big one." I miss already the future we aren't going to have together. I miss that I won't have little Inga grandchildren. I am so sad that the BIG miracle wasn't there for you. I wanted it so badly.

It snowed yesterday, Inga, and now the white blanket accumulated on the leaves of the trees is starting to melt and drop to the ground, making loud plopping sounds. I look up and see the picture taken of us at my graduation from Naropa in 1992 and remember how proud you were of me and how proud I was of myself too. I have two copies of the same photo in my bedroom, one I took from your house in a sweet little frame. We both were so happy then. I think this is going to be a very long letter and for now, I will stop and continue another day.

I will need some structure in my life. There is so much I want to do and haven't the energy yet for. I am still struggling with my decision to take a leave of absence from work. I wonder what you would say about that. Help me if you can by sending me signs as to guide me. I don't know what is best for me now.

I love you, Mumford

Inga started calling me Mumford when she was in high school and not yet driving. I was what she called the chauffeur and should have a proper name for that role, thus she named me Mumford.

September 25, 2000

Dear Inga,

My body feels lousy today and my body drags down my spirit too and my mood. Feeling depressed despite the fact that this weekend I made the best decision for me at this time. I am taking a three-month leave of absence from work. It was a struggle, not the whole decision, but walking away from the interns and the mentoring program that I built from scratch. I know deep in my heart I can only take care of me now and mentoring seven interns would be too much. It would also restrict my freedom and all the wonderful possibilities that may come my way with time off, like traveling for six to eight weeks or going on a very long retreat. So what do you think about this; do you think wonderful things will come my way as I open up space in my life?

I feel you are in agreement. But what is my slight hesitation? Guilt; yes, that's it. Why didn't I take more time off to be with you, to take you to the healing waters of Lourdes or the Commonweal Center? Did I offer? Do you feel that I let you down in helping you to fight your illness?

No, I hear from inside or afar. There was only one time last January when I was sick and said no to you because I couldn't get out of bed. Did I ask you to forgive me for that? I think, yes I did. And you said you were angry. I heard you and still asked you to forgive me. Did I do enough? I think maybe I did. I must forgive myself now over and over again. I am so sorry. Yet I hear there is nothing for me to be sorry about. I did the best I could, which was more than enough.

My jaw aches as I write this which makes me wonder what am I holding back there. What haven't I said to you, Inga? I need to say some things to you out loud. And I resist in this moment. And I know I will do it. I feel so exhausted emotionally, mentally and physically. Resting today, this is what I need. I practice forgiving myself for the belief that I didn't do enough to help you.

I still await a sign from you that you are OK. I hope in time to hear from you.

Love, Mumford

September 28, 2000
Dear Inga,

This morning I had a deeper insight about my denial, about my deep desire to keep you alive through the mess and denial of your life. Right now, twenty-six days after your death, I choose to hold you in my heart with your deep undying sense of hope and faith that everything will work out. This I trust about you. Yet, I want to trust in me. I want to face what I deny and open to all the beautiful possibilities life could possibly hold for me. This is my memory of you. I miss you and please let me know you are OK.

While browsing in Boulder Bookstore for a book recommended to me by another bereaved mother I happened upon Kubler-Ross' most recent book, The Wheel of Life. *I started reading it on the porch in the late afternoon sunshine and then again before bed. I cannot put it down. I am so grateful for finding it. Elizabeth lived her life loving all that she did every day. May this also be true for me. At two in the morning, I finally put it down after devouring her stories and the unfolding process of her life. It gave me hope about my own life. May my journey be guided so that I will know and trust what is next when it is the right time.*
Love, Mumford

October 1, 2000
Dear Inga,

It is almost the one-month anniversary of your death. There are moments that I just do not believe you are dead. It is unimaginable. Erika called today pleased that the garage sale went so well. Friends helped a lot, she collected $900, and there are still some items for which she will be paid. That is a relief, for now she will have some money to live on for these next months. You told Laura that you wanted her to have Sam, but she does not have a place suitable for that. I think Erika needs Sam and vice versa. Your little sister has been such a support for you. Did you really thank her?

I am taking pretty good care of myself. I rest, read, take walks, get massages, journal, pray, visit with friends, hold Perry and feel him purring—this comforts me. Yet I feel at a loss as to what I really need and want. Do I know? I get butterflies in my stomach thinking about what is next. Living day by day is not easy for me.

Choosing to love myself through this is important, giving myself space and freedom to grow and heal and even take some risks.
Love you, Mom

October 2, 2000

This is the one-month anniversary of Inga's death. I could not sleep last night and finally at 2:30 in the morning I pulled my comforter onto the floor and fell asleep there. My agitation has gotten worse. All the little things grate on my nervous system: people who don't return phone calls; music blasting at my appointment with my hairdresser; my physical aches. My knees are burning and tingling. All of the normal stimulation from the world is just too much for me. I feel as if I am continuing to be bruised from my outer world, a reflection of the deep inner bruises residing in my heart.

October 3, 2000

I get up after sleeping twelve hours, except for a few brief arousals. One was my calling out to Inga in a semi-sleepy state. A shadow moving awakened me. When I opened my eyes, I asked, "Is that you, Inga—are you alright?" She said (or my mind said), "I am OK and I am always with you. I am the air you breathe." I could not remember the rest. There was more. That brief moment did appease me on some level, but I do not really feel the OK-ness.

There are blocks to my knowing she is OK. It is my anger. This fascinates me. How do others deal with it? I have been teaching and counseling others on anger for years now. All the earthly events keep bringing my awareness back to anger. It is the bottom line. I am angry; no, I am furious that Inga got breast cancer. I am angry, enraged that she died from it. I let out a groan, a sigh. And now what? I am not actually feeling it—the rage, that is. I know it is there simmering, stalking, smoldering, crackling, waiting for me to truly be with it. I am relieved and anxious to meet it. On Friday I have an appointment with my colleague and friend Janet, then I have an EMDR session scheduled. There is time, space and opportunities for healing.

October 8, 2000

Today turned into sunshine for Inga's memorial at 2 PM. My friend Myrna picked up my mother from the nursing home and brought her. At 87 my mother needed assistance with walking, but Inga's death affected her terribly. It was a memorable time with music by Susy and Roy. Laura Scott, my art therapist friend and colleague, did an exceptional ritual guiding everyone in creating mandalas and then we burnt them. Jennifer McKewon's grounded spiritual guidance brought all of us into a beautiful sense of connection.

A message from Inga's sister Jill was read, since she was not able to attend this memorial.

I am sorry that I was not able to attend this ceremony. I don't know if I know very many of you there but I wanted to share some of my own feelings about Inga …

*I have known Inga my whole life. She was there the day I was brought home from the hospital, very proud to be a big sister. And, she played the role of big sister very well. She told me **what** to do, **when** to do it, and **how** to do it. And I suppose a lot of who I am, I am because of her. She was my role model, my teacher and my friend. She taught me lots of things that I have carried with me through my life, and will continue to carry with me until I die. Among the things that she taught me, some stand out more in my mind. I will always remember that I learned my love of dogs and all animals from her. I learned to respect the earth and everything on it from her. And I learned that you must suffer to be beautiful. Inga, you have suffered so much … and you will always be beautiful to me.*

I will think of you every day that I look at a tree and remember the name of it. Every time that I do something good for the earth, I will hope that I did it the way you would. And every time that I take a photograph of something beautiful in nature, I will see a part of you there. You will be with me always.

The following excerpt was read from Inga's journal, dated May 5, 2000 and composed at a workshop in Port Townsend, Washington.

Things I Have Learned Recently
-Friends don't always need to know each other's history, only what is real at the moment.

-*When you make a real friend, it's almost like falling in love.*
-*Banana slugs are really ugly.*
-*Men will often not know that something is on their minds, but their actions show otherwise.*
-*Eating sweets is more satisfying before I do it than after.*
-*If someone is difficult, get to know them, then they won't seem difficult, only human.*
-*I don't think well when I am cold.*

The story of Inga's life, written by Erika, was read.

Inga Van Nynatten was born in Brussels, Belgium on July 27, 1970. Her parents, Fred and Carole, were living abroad while Fred pursued his medical degree. When Inga was 11 days old, she made her first of many transatlantic crossings to return to the USA for the summer. Her sister Jill was born in 1973 in Brussels too, while Inga was attending a French pre-school. Then the family moved to Wilmington, North Carolina where her dad was starting his medical internship at the local community hospital. Five months later in 1974, Erika was born.

School was a breeze for Inga; she loved it and was active in everything. She played the violin, though her mother encouraged her to practice in the garage because she sounded so screechy. Tap, ballet, baton twirling, model-ing, swimming, and science were somehow sandwiched in there. Inga ran the Rotary Run mile in 9:51 when she was eight years old. She built a maze to test the abilities of Erika's pet mice, created magic shows, and did home schooling so that her sisters would be properly prepared for preschool. Then there were the Barbie dolls with designer clothes, and the custom-built doll-house from fabric and wallpaper samples. There was never a dull moment for Inga; she was always finding a new activity that she approached with passion and vigor.

In describing Inga, all her family said, "INDEPENDENT!," "STRONG-WILLED," "ASSERTIVE" and "FUN." "Trust me" were her favorite words. Where Inga was concerned, rules never applied. We are cele-brating the life of a true free spirit.

Inga loved animals of all kinds. Dogs, cats, rabbits, amphibians, snakes, especially boa constrictors. Once she and her friend took one to her dad's medical office to get an x-ray as a pregnancy test for the snake!

When she was fifteen years old, Inga decided that she needed to start working and earn "real" money. Her idea was to sell clothes, in a men's clothing store, because who could do it better! She managed to talk her way into the job (a year earlier than the legal minimum age) and made enough money to buy herself a completely new wardrobe. As an added bonus, she had enough dates to wear all her new clothes. Not that Inga ever lacked in the boyfriend arena!!!!

When she graduated high school, she convinced her father to buy her a car. Not just any car, but a 1965 Mustang convertible that needed a lot of work. Two months, two junk cars, and lots of repair bills later, she had the car of her dreams, only to find that it was not really reliable transportation to and from college, and she sold it for a sturdy Volkswagon.

Her undergraduate years were spent at North Carolina State University, where she majored in zoology with the intention of becoming a veterinarian. While she was finishing her degree, she changed her interests to include landscape architecture, urban planning, and greenway development. Living in Boulder for several months solidified her feeling that every city should have a trail like this wonderful Boulder Creek Path. Even while finishing her zoology degree, she began working for Greenways Incorporated, in Raleigh, NC, developing community parks and trails. After graduating, she continued to work there until she moved back to Wilmington. There she had a barefoot wedding on the beach in 1995. Before her wedding, she also got her first baby, a beautiful Dalmatian puppy that she named Samantha (who you see here with us today).

Texas was her next destination, where she moved to go to graduate school with her husband, Allen. She worked on a master's degree in Urban Planning at the University of Texas at Austin, and began her career at the National Park Service, Rivers and Trails Program.

Her marriage ended in 1997, but she had already become a true Texan. Many excellent steak dinners had already eroded Inga's vegetarian beliefs, and both she and Samantha loved the desert heat. (It was a record-breaking

*112 degrees the day of her memorial service in Austin on Sept. 5, 2000)
Inga stayed in Austin, working at the National Park Service and pursuing
her interest in photography, salsa dancing, running, and swimming. In
January 1998, she made a presentation at the first International Trails and
Greenways Conference. It was titled "Closing the Trail Loop: Building
Trails with Recycled Products."*

*In March 1998, her sister Jill gave birth to a beautiful baby girl, Kayla
Rose. Two weeks later, Inga was diagnosed with breast cancer. She and her
family suffered through eight months of chemotherapy, radiation, and
finally surgery in December 1998. Inga's style was to not tell people that she
was dealing with cancer. She said, "I want people to know me as me, not a
cancer patient." During the early months of 1999, she thought she was
cured, and advertised this by completing the Danskin triathlon twice in the
summer of 1999. In October and November, she and Erika went to Mexico
and Guatemala to travel, a plan they had been working on since her diagnosis. However, after returning from her trip, doctors found a spread of the
cancer, to her chest and bones. She had more radiation, more chemo, and
refused to believe the numbers. "There are 1% of these cases that have a
complete remission. I will be one of those," she said.*

*In April and May, with a new head of hair and a reduction in the size of
her tumors, she was again unfailingly positive. The reaction that she had to
a new chemotherapy was very good, and she interpreted this as a remission.
She told everyone that she was done with cancer, and she started making
plans to buy a house. "I need something to look forward to," she told her
astonished family. She bought her first home on July 1st, 2000.*

*For her 30th birthday (the end of July), she went with her sisters and
mother to Isla Mujeres, Mexico and had a great time. She had given herself
a break from all the drugs, and she was feeling good. She ate fish tacos,
floated in the 80-degree water topless, ate guacamole on the beach, snor-
keled, danced 'til 3AM, shopped, swam with dolphins, and had a henna
tattoo of a lizard wrapped around her belly button. But when she got home,
the pain in her back increased. Soon the diagnosis was made: The disease
had not been beaten; a new tumor on her spine was pressing on her sciatic
nerve. To keep her spirits up, she bought a new car, and decorated her new*

house. Despite aggressive treatment, throughout August, her health declined rapidly. The cancer kept spreading, until it had scattered throughout her entire brain. Finally, there was no treatment available.

On August 29th, three days before she died, she had a surprisingly lucid period of hours. Her family and best friend were in her hospital room, and she ate two Haagen Dazs bars. They laughed and told stories until 2AM. At 3:30AM, she had a massive seizure, which set off a period of agitation and struggling. After four hours, she went into a semi-comatose state and was transferred to hospice care. At the hospice house, she slipped into a coma. The next day, the doctors were sure her death was imminent. She lived another twenty hours to prove them wrong. Inga died on September 2nd at 3:30AM with her mother, Carole, and her sister, Erika, by her side.

Inga was always a fighter, and never wanted to be known as "the cancer patient." Many of her colleagues and most of her acquaintances never even knew she was sick, and she wanted to keep it that way. When she had reconstructive surgery, the scars were planned to fit underneath her bikini bathing suit. Doctors' appointments were necessary and took a lot of Inga's time and energy, but if she could rearrange them around her salsa lessons or work commitments, she would.

She always lived life to the fullest, enjoying every moment. Some of her favorite memories that she wrote in her journal include: "Seeing my first moose along the Snake River," "Crying on my best friend's shoulder and then going out dancing," "Eating sun-warmed raspberries in the fields of Montana," "Walking in a fresh snowfall at dawn in perfect silence."

Inga crammed a lot of living into thirty years. She will be greatly missed by everyone whose hearts and minds she touched.

It was a beautiful time for reflection and remembering Inga. I felt so good to be held, hugged and surrounded by my Boulder friends. We ate chocolate cake as Inga would have liked as we continued to celebrate her life by looking at photos and sharing memories.

Release

The next phase in walking the grief labyrinth is to step onto the path. This is an act of trust. Whether it is tracing your finger on a lap sized labyrinth or taking physical steps walking a full sized labyrinth, this is time for movement forward. I recommend taking your time, going slowly, and noticing sensations, thoughts and feelings as they arise.

Reviewing and reflecting on my journey with Inga, her life, her battle with cancer, my life of losses, her death and my early days of grief, I enter the labyrinth, releasing and letting go of memories and emotions as they arise. This is a process of surrender over time and it has been very challenging for me. I return over and over again to letting go of all the reminders of the pain she endured with her cancer. I practice over and over again choosing to release rather than hanging on. I find even when I am not actually walking the labyrinth I make the choice to release in many forms. This does not come easily for me and I know how difficult it is for others. Yet when I practice and actually do let go, it makes a difference in loosening my attachments to feelings that hold me back. At times, I feel more relaxed and peaceful.

During this process I discovered that thoughts would come up that surprised me. Other losses in my life would appear. I had many thoughts and emotions about my childhood, teen years and my early married life. Grieving work is complex, for it brings up collective losses. It seems impossible to grieve a single loss at a time. The boundaries of grief do get blurred.

The labyrinth walk itself, taken one step at a time, offers the practice of reconnecting with your body through movement without holding on. Grief work is very demanding physically as well as emotionally. The very act of moving your finger or your whole body through the labyrinth is healing. The intention is to walk while releasing. One needs to let go of any self-judgments that may come up about "doing it right." Releasing with gentle awareness is the guideline; this is not a gym workout.

I discovered many ways to release rather than tighten my grip on what came up both in the labyrinth walk and beyond. My intention is to share my path and hope this will inspire you to find your own.

Join me walking and releasing through the labyrinth.

Release Survivor's Guilt

Survivor's guilt strangled me as a parent. My children were supposed to outlive me, not the other way around. It is unimaginable to outlive my own child. A parent's job is to protect their children from harm, so I fell into being consumed by guilt. I had breast cancer, as did my mother, and now I had passed this ugly disease on to my daughter. I was guilty as charged. Even strangers pointed at me as the cause of my daughter's cancer. And I took it on. I blamed myself and I knew it wasn't healthy to do this. Yet it was all I could do.

When my older brother died at age twenty-nine of Hodgkin's disease, I felt guilty too. Why did he get cancer and not I? I wanted to help him and I felt helpless. The summer before, we had driven cross-country to Phoenix so he could look into the possibility of moving there for his health. His lungs were riddled with tumors and the climate seemed to help his respiratory system. After his death, I questioned whether there wasn't more I could have done to find treatments for him.

I have long thought about guilt as a disguised emotion. Yes, we must take responsibility when we have done something wrong or have made a mistake. However, the true emotion driving guilt is anger. This anger towards oneself must be addressed and looked at directly. Anger towards the child who died can seem overwhelming, yet it needs expression also and a means of being released.

A key to dealing with survivor's guilt is looking at it directly and working with one's anger. The energy of anger stored in the body creates blockages, which affect one's physical health as well as emotional health. Simply walking or slow jogging with the conscious intention to move anger can be extremely freeing. One can walk the labyrinth with a focus on guilt and anger. I addressed this over and over again walking the labyrinth, by painting, talking with other parents, shouting at God and in my journaling. I was able to release anger as I walked on the labyrinth path. What is most important is to make the choice to address this issue. Professional counseling was extremely helpful as well. I don't need survivor's guilt; I refuse to be consumed by it.

Release the Dark Side

The back, dark side. The shadow speaks. In Jungian terminology the shadow is that part of us we fail to see or know, that part which we are unconscious of. It is the denied part of the self.

Self-disgust. Shame. I don't feel good about myself today. Inga wanted to live and I gave up hope. She begged me to not give up. "Get these pills into me, no matter what," she would say. "They kill the cancer that's killing me and I know this chemo is killing the cancer. Make me eat food. Make me swallow these fuckin' pills."

And I didn't. I couldn't. I see her limp, cold body, her glazed, pleading eyes. And I moan. What kind of mother am I who couldn't keep her daughter alive, keep her safe? I am so ashamed of myself as a mother, as a human being. How dare I judge others' actions when I didn't do what Inga wanted me to in order to keep her alive?

I could have insisted on a stomach plug. I see Inga's sad, pleading eyes. Help me, she said out loud and with her eyes. And I don't know if I did. I have asked her over and over again. She always responds with, "I'm OK." How about today, Inga? How are you? Did I help you enough? Did I protect you? Did you feel abandoned by me?

I feel so self-loathing.

Mother, Mother, Mumford. Listen to me. Hear the unhearable. I am OK and I am with you now. I wish I could hold you and hug you. I want to bring to you the love and peace I know is in your body. I am in your body. In your heart. Don't turn me away. Listen. Please listen. You were a perfect mother even with all your imperfections. Especially in my final days on earth. Please don't doubt me. Trust me on this. You know I know my truth.

There is much I didn't know in my earthly form, but I know I was surrounded by your love when I was sick and dying. Please tell Erika and Jill too. Even Dad. I felt you all loving me and caring for me and holding me tight, not wanting to let me go. You all did your very best. You were the best you could be. I appreciated all of you. I was shocked by it all, I couldn't imagine death as divine love or death as being able to take me away from all of you. My body gave out and nothing would have changed the outcome. I am OK. You must be OK too. I see you with much joy these days. This book seems to create pain for you and it will bring more than that if you let it. You don't understand the greater plan with it and that is difficult for you. Walk the labyrinth and let the book come to you. Writing will start to flow even more. You will receive much more peace and a time of grace. Call on all of your support people. Name them Team Carole. You brought together Team Inga for me and now it is the time for your circle of support. Go ahead write their names. Watch the clouds; they keep changing. All is well. I love you completely even when you loathe yourself.

Release Losses from Long Ago

It is the spring of 1979 and I am thirty-six year old speedster. I am on the fast track of life, mother of three, wife of a physician, founder and board director of a cooperative preschool, computer systems analyst, cook, chauffeur, and general social life manager extraordinaire. Today I am driving the normal speed limit on Oleander Drive in Wilmington, North Carolina on a lovely day after dropping off my children at school. I am going to my job at the police department where I am working on a computer project for parking ticket management.

My life is tightly organized according to everyone else's needs and there is no time for me except for moments like today when I drive alone to work, listening to the radio as I plan my dinner menu and my after-work chores.

Wham!!! There is a bang and sunglasses shoot off my nose. What happened? I am at a dead stop, but I never hit the brakes. Someone ran into me. I am stunned. Fred arrives and he tells me to lie flat. I laugh. I have places to go, things to do, what is he saying?

My car is not drivable, it is totaled, and I feel totaled. Nothing will ever be the same. I would see the world now not through the lens of darkness, but through the light of day, of reality.

While I was recuperating from my whiplash injury, a lump was discovered in my right breast. My husband said to go and see my gynecologist immediately. He was very concerned because of my history of breast cancer. My mother had it and her sister died of it when I was just four years old.

I went to my gynecologist immediately and he referred me to a surgeon. I don't remember the surgeon's name, but I remember his face and demeanor. He was an older man with round, smooth-skinned cheeks and his silver hair was neatly brushed. His glasses gave him a very authoritative look. He seemed very concerned, said he would biopsy the lump right then and called for his nurse to assist him.

The metal tray was wheeled up close to me with a white cloth covering up the instruments. I want to say the instruments of torture. Yes, that is what I remember. I was given several shots of Novocain. My body trembled in fear. I didn't say I was afraid but everything in my body spoke that truth. Then the cold metal went against my small breast and he said I would feel some pressure and that would be all. He told me to relax. No way, how could I? I think they just want to say something. How dare he? He hit the arrow home. I felt a crushing, stabbing, bruising, horrific painful sensation. It is almost over, he said as he put a stitch in to hold together the skin where he entered and violated my breast.

The doctor rushed out of the room without a kind word. Did he ever say he was sorry that the procedure was so traumatic? No he didn't. He rushed out of the room because I was crying and he had others waiting to see him. The nurse who followed up was sterile, antiseptic, as if she were pouring alcohol on my open wound. She said it would heal quickly and I would get the test results in a few days.

Later I found out what a priority rush was given to my biopsy and to all of my care. Well, not to *all* my care, to my physical care. I was a doctor's wife and they wanted to cut whatever it was out of me really quickly. It was only a few days later when the surgeon called me with the news. Or did he call my husband first? Probably so. It was cancer. In the same week I was fit into the surgeon's busy schedule. I was told how fortunate I was to have found this so early, as it was a very small lump. Because of my small breasts and quick response from the medical world, this could be taken care of immediately.

I was not thankful; I was in shock. It was like a bomb had exploded in me and there was no time to get my bearings. Everyone else knew exactly what needed to happen, but it was my body, my history, my mothering breast. I had no time to recover before an additional shock wave hit—over and over again. They all said you will be just fine. We caught it early, it's so small. But they removed my entire breast, not just the pea-sized cancerous tumor. They took my breast, my handful-size breast and my nipple. My tender, childlike, innocent breast that was always with me, that I watched grow during puberty. The breast that first felt the stirrings of my sexuality. My breast that suckled my firstborn child. My breast that was mine. They had no right to take it all without asking me. They didn't ask me. They told me. They didn't give me treatment options. They didn't let me say goodbye to it. They didn't offer to hold me while I grieved losing it.

I had been in the hospital several days when my surgeon told the nurse to change the dressing and that it might be time for me to look at the scar if I felt ready to do that.

When he left the nurse followed his orders, but with no kindness. She was hurried or had seen it all, or am I making excuses for her? She told me that it didn't look so bad. She said since I had such small breasts there wasn't much missing tissue. She told me it was the large-breasted women who have a hard time. I was shocked again. I did look and got another shock. Whose body was I looking at? There was no empathy from that nurse. I was dismissed. I was told what I should feel and that I was lucky.

In the next week at home, it happened again. My mother-in-law came to talk to me in my bedroom when I was changing my clothes and she saw me breastless on one side. She saw the scar where my breast had been and she said, "Well, that's not as bad as I thought it would be." She didn't ask me how I felt about it or even what I thought about it. My mother too had asked so matter-of-factly when she was told it was cancer, "When will they remove it?" She didn't ask me about me, only about it, the cancer, and how quickly it would be gone. Then life would be the same. That's what seemed to be the underlying message. Let's get back to our routine, our normal—skip over grief—emotions, feelings. Let's get our factual, scientific, controllable, pretend life back.

It would never be. I was not the same. Nothing would ever be the same and before I even consciously knew anything at all, I knew deep in my heart of hearts that a new pathway was opening up for me to journey on.

Six months after the first breast was removed a lump was found in my other breast. It wasn't a big surprise. Statistics say a recurrence is pretty common. Everyone looked on the bright side. It would make reconstructive surgery easier. I wouldn't be lopsided any more.

I was training for a 5K race at the time and my attitude turned to "let's just get this over with." I didn't want a biopsy this time but chose to go straight for surgery. A biopsy would first be done while I was under anesthesia. Then at least I wouldn't have to deal with that trauma. It was as I thought it would be, cancerous, so off came my left breast.

The day after the operation I was walking in the hallway pushing my IV pole when my gynecologist caught up with me and asked how I was. I told him, "I'm great, I am out walking, so I can go home soon and maybe still do the race I had been training for." He kind of backed me up against the wall and waited a few moments, looked me straight in the eyes and said very slowly, "How are you really feeling? No woman loses a breast and does just fine. You need to grieve."

That was Dr. Bashford. I remember him and those few minutes very well. I wrote him a letter several years later to thank him for his insight and directness with me that day in the hospital hallway. He was the first person to use the word grief with me. As it turned out, when I contacted him he was no longer practicing Ob/Gyn medicine. He had gone back to get certified in psychiatry. He had moved from bodies to minds, hearts, emotional lives and psyches.

Dr. Bashford woke me up to my vulnerable self. My naked, pure heart of sadness. The bigger suitcase of grief that I had carried my entire life now had a name. It was not until five years later that I really started to process it. To embrace it like a lost friend. At that point I found Rubenfeld Synergy and Ilana the founder was my mentor for body/mind integration at her center in New York City.

That reoccurrence of cancer in my second breast really got my attention. It made me realize that people die from cancer, and caused me to focus on how I was living my life. The fact was that if it came back in my other breast it could also come back someplace else in my body. In my eye perhaps, like my mother, in my lymphatic system and lungs like my brother or in my liver, colon, pancreas, kidneys … Somewhere it could be laying down its deadly cells that would destroy my healthy cells.

I was afraid I was missing out on my life. I decided to make a list of all the things I wanted to do before I died. I started back at journaling, writing out my thoughts and feelings, something that I had done very actively before I got married and started a family.

The first item on my list was to play. To play with my children. While I took wonderful care of their physical needs, feeding them nutritious meals and helping them with schoolwork, driving them to their gymnastics and swim lessons, I knew that fun was just not part of my life. Playtime got eaten up by responsibility.

I co-founded a cooperative preschool when my youngest daughter Erika was ready for preschool and I couldn't find one in town that I thought would suit her needs. The one we started had much enrichment provided by the parents, who shared their skills and talents on a regular basis. I loved to do art projects with the children, having collected everything from buttons to items from nature—pinecones, sticks and small rocks. I would help them to create fantasy collages. This was fun for me and I wanted more and more quality time not only with my youngest but also with all my children and our family as a whole.

I always had wanted to work with clay, not particularly to make pots and containers, but to play with it in my hands and sculpt shapes. So art classes were put on my list. I wanted to feel the sensation of wet clay next to my skin. I wanted to *feel* physically as well as emotionally. The earth seemed to call out to me.

I wanted to stop working in the business world and stay at home. I wanted to study my dreams, which had always been prolific, but which I had never taken time to look at more seriously. I wanted to let go of parts of my life, as I knew it and have time to just sit still and reflect on my life. And I got it. The auto accident woke me up. I stepped into a time of many losses and conscious letting go. I stepped into unraveling the tightly held ball of my inner grief.

Release Not Being a Good Enough Mother

Tears well up as I look at Inga's photo and I feel my commitment to her mixed with great sadness. My mind battle tries to keep me focused away from my feelings and grief. The thought arises that somehow I am not a good enough mother if I don't tell this story and write more, that my memory of her is not honored if I don't do this. I also think of the times I didn't support her as I believed a great mother would have. I didn't live up to my expectations for myself. I was not a good enough mother.

Give yourself a break, Carole. Love yourself. Let go of those endless mind thoughts and judgments about yourself. You love Inga, now love yourself too. And respect your process; remember what you were saying to a client yesterday: "You know what is right for you. Rushing ahead of yourself won't do you or anyone any good." So I need to take my own advice to heart.

I want to honor my process of grieving and writing and living my life. This is enough for today. I need to release those "not good enough mother thoughts." What serves me well is to respect where I am and what does work for me and let go of the rest. I cry for my daughter, I cry for myself, I cry for all the mothers. Sometimes I sob and the judgments fall away.

Release My Mumford Role

Inga called me Mumford. She would say "Mumford, I need a ride to the mall. I need more socks; someone has taken mine. Mumford, I need crackers; there is nothing to eat. Mumford, take me to the track. I need to be there in ten minutes." Inga always knew what she needed. She always seemed focused on the next boyfriend, meal, movie or cool idea. How inspiring she was. How exhausted I was. Too many demands, too much filling up the time we were awake. Or were we awake? I wasn't awake in my body or senses most of the time. I barely chewed my food or had the time to hop in the shower.

The time for being together with all her wants and needs are gone. Gone forever. I am no longer her Mumford. I no longer am pregnant with her desires, her needs, her priceless ideas—unless this book is really her wanting something from me still. I chuckle thinking of her on the other side, continuing to push me into things. No. I want to write this book. I need to write it. It is important that I write it. I need to unleash the images of our past and fill pages with my remembrances and reflections. I need to review our life together until there is nothing remembered left unwritten and all the images and words blend into oneness. I need to write until I am finished and let it all go. I need to say everything until I have nothing more to say. And then still release it all. I am no longer Inga's Mumford.

Release By Cleaning Closets

I look at Inga's wedding picture and start crying in a familiar, broken-hearted way. She was married for only two years and had no children. Rearranging the pictures of Inga is probably not a good idea right now. Grounding myself by cleaning does seem to help. I never loved cleaning, yet the act of doing it serves me well. I attack the space under my bath-room sink with a vengeance. Inga loved to organize. She told me, you know I am a planner. I liked how her kitchen only had what she needed in it. It was easy for Inga to throw things away. Start fresh, she'd say. If you haven't used something for six months, get rid of it. So releasing was not a foreign concept for Inga.

I comfort myself by hugging the purple frog Laura gave me. I call my old office mate Patricia and ask about helping me to continue my personal grief group.

Erika and Sam have left for Seattle—another letting go. I cried twice with her and now I send prayers her way. I tell Inga to take care of her lit-tle sister and return her home safely. I normally wouldn't have any fears about Erika traveling. Nothing, no, nothing is normal. Inga died and the world doesn't feel safe or loving to me at all. I worry about my daughters Erika and Jill. As soon as I start to write, my body, my mind and my heart and soul ache. I feel the lack of God's presence. There is no basic goodness with me. I feel empty and alone.

I go to sit at my shrine and cry out, "Why me?" What am I to do with all this pain? Sit and be still, breathe, drink tea, and the pain lessens its grip on me. The phone rings. There is no one I want to talk with.

How did Inga manage all of her pain? She just did. I do feel guilty. Not for any one thing, just generally. I lived denying her possible death from that rotten disease. It was too painful for me then and it is still painful. I am angry she died. I am angry with her for dying.

Then I notice the warmth of the sun bathing my face. My breath moves more gently, deeper into my belly. The wave of grief starts to subside. Don't rush, there's no hurry. The elm leaves are turning a bright yellow. The seasons change. The colors and time alter the intensity of my grief. I tap into my need for forgiveness. I don't feel I am ready. I have let some of the pain go today. There is always another day and another closet to be cleaned.

Release Through Body Talk

This body, my body wants to move. I have no energy, just the thought. But I imagine the shrine room clear of cushions with the Buddha as my watcher. Play some music like Piazzola, "Adios Nonino." The ache in my throat is my guide. Where is the sound behind the ache? Where are you? What is that? It emerges. Quietly at first. Slow to move. Stepping out of myself as a way to step deeper inside. Go slowly—be quiet—make no sound—just turn off the music.

I was turned off back then. I ran away, which was the best I could do then. I did the best I could, running, running, doing, doing. The dishes, the shopping, cleaning, phone calls, researching, pleas for help. Who will help? God help me. God help Inga. This can't be happening. Aggressive. Aggressive cells. Aggressive treatment. Aggressive acting out. Augh—

The sound starts to trickle out. Then grows louder and louder. The screams from all those days gone by. The sounds of painful aloneness, being sick and alone. Abandoned by husband and father, friends. Who knows? How do any of them know? It is buried. She is buried. The scream buried in the cells, my cells. I embody the scream. Stop. Don't scream. Stop. Let her show herself. What will I come to if one scream awakens another scream—a stream of screams that will never stop? My anger awakens me to louder screams, awakens me to the many who suffer. So many screams. So much anger, so much suffering. So many daughters who will not be at their mothers' death beds. How could you have died, Inga? It isn't right. "Where are you, Inga? Where are you?" my gut exclaims.

Release My Inner Critic

She grits her teeth, a snarl appears and then there are the screams. Stop, you wicked believer, she says. You don't know anything. You keep rambling over and over again. No depth, no feeling, no nose, no eyes, no ears. "Listen." Listen, baloney. You don't listen. You sleepy-eyed sloth. You arrogant, mischievous little imp. That's what you are. Imp for important. Self-important, self-absorbed. Stop. Stop all your nonsense.

You go so often for the sweet escape. You drink cappuccinos and devour Australian ginger biscotti. You don't know the route to authenticity. Be real. Sipping coffee or a glass of wine. Escape routes take you off to view snow-covered mountains. Blue sky. Perfect world of nature. Now you go look into your heart.

You slip into thoughts of being useless and yes, you are. No one wants to read about this. Life, life is a sweet escape. Inga knew. She wanted a sweet escape. Now you too want a sweet escape, to float on a cloud of illusion. You run from your grief like a scared little girl who believes death doesn't really happen to thirty-year-olds. You eat sugar to find the sweetness of life. You believe as absolute truth what Woody Allen says, "I ain't scared to die; I just don't want to be there when it happens." You avoid and ignore the bold headline news of reality. You haven't transformed. Dead is still stark cold nothingness in your heart.

My inner critic advises me today. She seems exhausted. Maybe a rest would help, so I send her off for a pleasant trip to the beach while I now choose to step into my grief journey. She will come back renewed, and perhaps bear some news of what I might need to pay attention to next.

Release Murkiness

Today the creek is muddy. I imagine the warmer weather is melting the ice and snow at higher altitudes. Mudslides bring a murkiness to the once-clear water. I am not feeling very clear myself today.

One day within a few months of Inga's death, I went to the supermarket feeling really lousy. When the cashier asked me in her chipper voice how I felt, I told her how I really felt. "I am miserable. My daughter died of breast cancer a few weeks ago and I feel horrible." There was nothing murky about me. I know it may have been more than she wanted to hear, yet it was too hard for me to pretend I felt otherwise. I imagine she was shocked and I also think she will remember something more than the sad woman in the line who told her how life sucked.

When I engage with others with both my emotional and rational self, it is possible to discover peace and greater intimacy. I long for more connection with people as I imagine many others do. We all want to be kind to ourselves and others. Yet we stumble, drawback, and hide our hearts. Sometimes we don't just risk sharing our soft places and our grief. I let go of being alone in my grief by communicating the clarity, not the murkiness, of how I was feeling.

Release What I Forgot

What did I forget to tell her? Is it really that I forgot? Or did I just not want to hear her responses? Or did I forget because I am just not that bright? Or did I ever never forget to tell?

Hmm. Which route is today's route to honesty, to letting go of my avoidance and ignorance and moving into being authentic with my entire heart, mind and soul?

I did tell Inga she was not a planned baby, I just got pregnant. It happened again and again. Conception came easily to me.

Did I tell her how depressed I was when her father then left me to go off to medical school in Belgium and refused to take me with him? No, I am sure I didn't tell her that. I didn't tell her how sad I was, so lost and alone. I felt so rejected. We were in a serious relationship, her father and I. I wanted him to get his acceptance to medical school even if it was abroad, thousands of miles away. I was thrilled for him when he got that letter. Did I tell her that?

I was living in Milford Connecticut at the time in a little beach shack right on Long Island Sound. My brother had just died earlier that summer. Did I tell her about that time? No, I didn't. Carl was so young when he died and I thought that I died too. Oh, I didn't tell her any of this. I didn't tell her about the dream I had. The dream that came to me on the third night after his death. I can't believe it, I didn't tell her any of this. I remember it so clearly, the dream, my waking up to life, my terror of death, my walks on the beach alone. And then Fred was leaving too. At least he wasn't dying but it seemed like he was. I said, "Let's get married. I will work and put you through medical school."

I forgot to tell her.

Release the Rose Garden

There is a lovely rose garden out the back door of Christopher House Hospice. Not so many blossoms, but being outside there is comforting. This garden is a hot house. The heat is oppressive. A dying daughter is oppressive. It is hard to breathe when the life of my firstborn child is ending. I want to be outside, but the only time I can relax a little and go to the gardens is at night, when the air has cooled a few degrees. Stillness there permeates my bones.

I want to run away. I thought about running away back then as I still do. How can I revisit the gardens of Christopher House and not go back inside, through the living room, past the small, blue stained glass-walled chapel? There I continued to plead with all the gods for a miracle. Let me take my daughter home to her house and the groaning air conditioner, home to her dogs Sam and Trixie. Back safely home, where death could not find her.

In the hallway, there is a nursing station. Further down the hall are three men in black suits and white shirts and ties. They are life vultures, predators, waiting for one of the families to say goodbye to their loved one, so they can step in and whisk the body away.

I am about to step into Inga's room and I hesitate. I will stand outside and look at the photos there on the door. There is the one with the dolphin kissing her cheek taken just five weeks ago. How could she be there in the water and now lying in this hospice bed soon to be taken away? How can this be? It just cannot be happening. I will not go inside. I will go back to the garden, keep walking, get into her car, and drive to her house. There she will be making dinner, fussing about something that needs fixing. She will be spilling flour on her apron and the countertop. Making a *real* mess, unlike my messing around beside her dying body.

Wake up, Inga! Wake up, Carole! This must be a bad dream.

Release Helplessness

Holiday season is just around the corner. This is family time and I am questioning. What do I have to be thankful for? I am at work at QuaLife and thoughts of Inga and her death weigh heavily on me. I want to go away. How can I get through the holidays? I can't stand the thought of the festivities. Last year right after Inga died I spent Christmas in Puerto Vallarta with my friends Dave and Linda who were spending the winter there, but this year how will I manage?

I pushed my doubts away until one day while talking with a colleague at work, the topic reappeared. Bob asked me directly how I was feeling and if I was making plans for the holidays. No, I told him, I just want it over with. I am feeling incapable of dealing with anything associated with Christmas and I just don't know how to even talk about it. Yes, that was it, I did need to talk about it and was feeling lost getting started.

Sitting down to have a cup a tea with Bob, closing the door to the office, I began to sink into the heavy darkness of my grief once again. I do want to be thankful for life and I really just don't feel it. I don't know how to cope. I feel a sense of helplessness and despair. I don't know what I need or when I need it. I want to hide, disappear. I don't want a holiday. I don't want to pretend. I don't want to smile or be pleasant. I don't want to talk about it.

After listening to me for a very long time, Bob made the following suggestion. "Let's create a program together, a grief retreat day, to help you and others who are grieving prepare for the holidays. It can be a time for getting away from the glitz of the season to be supported wherever you are in your grief. What do you think?"

I immediately felt a shift occur. My body felt lighter and I felt energized. What would this day be like to best serve me? I started a list. I wanted massage, music and a way to practice stepping into my grief and also back out of it. I wanted to talk about Inga and the holidays of the past. I wasn't sure I wanted to talk with my family about this, yet I did want to talk. I wanted hugs. I wanted to remember Inga in some very concrete way and started to think about an art project. I didn't need to figure out all the details, there were very capable staff who would do that. I wanted help to focus on me and my plan of coping for the holidays. I wanted to be nurtured with food and tea and not need to do anything.

My need to escape was lessened. Talking did help. A glimpse of hope was appearing. The Good Grief Retreat Day was to be born in November 2001. It was very helpful not only for me, but many others as well. The program would then continue annually for many years and remains a reminder to me that grief needs space, time and good listeners. I am thankful for Bob as well as all the staff who contributed to that very first program and all those who have carried it forward. Helplessness was transformed to helpfulness.

Release Thinking

To think or not to think. I used to think a lot. My mental neurons fired fast, frantically and furiously. Supermarket lists, plans for the upcoming birthday party or family dinner, budgets tightly wrapped in fishnet wire, the pantry organized and full of canned goods … the trash needs to go out on Tuesday, don't forget the clothes at drycleaners on Friday and whose homework is due tomorrow? I used my mind to add up grocery items as I placed them into the cart so I wouldn't go over my budgeted amount. It was also a game of sorts. Who needs a calculator when I have full functioning cells in my head? It was my kind of brain aerobics. Drop the cents, round up or round down, keep the tops all spinning and I would make it through my day pleased to have taken care of all my family's needs and have a cup of coffee, two or maybe three. Caffeine sure kept me going and it was my drug of choice. Coffee, chocolate and a thick layer of sugar-coated anything. Especially Dunkin' Donuts. Yes, my mind knew the plan. My mind ruled and she was queen for decades. She loved being in charge, ruling her subjects and the environment, until one day the lightning bolt struck. Cut through anything my mind had ever neatly arranged before.

He said, "There is a lump in your breast." And I knew immediately it was cancer. First thought, not best thought.

I felt numb, felt nothing until the doctor jammed a biopsy knife into my breast. Then all my damned up tears, all the pushed aside feelings broke through. The doctor scurried out of the room abruptly leaving his nurse to clean up my puddles. I didn't know what to think anymore except that I could die like my brother, my aunt and countless others. I left the medical office in a daze and went to pick up my youngest daughter at her preschool. I confided in one of the parents who was also my friend. I cried some more. Where had my list gone? What should I do next? My husband and the surgeon decided to act quickly. I let them decide. Remove the breast as fast as possible. Three days later I was lying with an IV in my arm—not thinking, just hoping, praying, crying and observing the world from the underbelly of my turtle self.

Release Regrets

I held and touched Inga while she was dying and after she died. I felt she was well cared for by a multitude of professionals, family and friends. We did the best we could to honor what we thought her wishes would be after she died. However, I do have regrets about her after-death care. We chose a funeral home. They didn't rush us in any way, but they took her away too soon. They didn't suggest any alternative ways of caring for her then. And now I know there were options.

Several years later, I took a job as a spiritual counselor/chaplain with a small local hospice in Boulder. When my first patient died, the family chose Natural Transitions, an organization that provides education and support to families about a home funeral. They believed after-death care is sacred work and that, as was the custom in olden times, the family should take care of their loved ones both during and after death.

The body was transferred to the son's home where the grandson's bedroom was converted into a special place for his grandmother's wake. Here a team of us and the family bathed and anointed the body. I was very moved to be invited to partake in this ritual. As I was rubbing fragrant oil on the dead woman's feet, I felt blessed by the spiritual essence in the room. I cried in regret that I had not been able to care for Inga in this way. The ritual created the space for me to say goodbye to my patient. I was left with a lasting sense of connection with her spirit. There was so much love and peace in that room as different people came to pay their last respects and quietly leave. In the living room just outside, others were laughing, eating and telling stories about her.

I regret I didn't have a wake for Inga, in the home she loved and wanted so badly to return to. I must let go of my not knowing and what I didn't provide. What I do know is that it was a missed opportunity and I did the best I could in the circumstances. I choose to release my regrets and let my children know what I want for my after death care.

Release Beauty

I bought a bouquet of flowers to place on the countertop in front of my computer. I am house sitting in a magnificent place and I replaced a straggling poinsettia there. The new flowers weren't very special except that today a yellow tulip blossomed. It has my full attention as it leaps out of the mass of other flowers. It seems to say to me, "Pay attention." So I do. Well, isn't that what retirement is all about? I have time and I notice things more than I used to.

A friend of mine once said he liked to watch the progression that fresh flowers made right in front of his eyes. They are beautiful when freshly purchased, when some are still in the budding phase. Then there is a middle stage when they come into their full bloom. Then they start to wilt and dry out. As they start dying, some flowers are more dramatic than others.

They do all die, relatively quickly. But this yellow tulip I hope will live forever. This is what I do. I hope to hold on to all of life's beauty. I get sad
thinking ahead to the days of the flower's demise. But then again I can
come back to the present and enjoy what is here now. The tulip seems to
be reaching out to me, the petals extending beyond its natural circumfer-
ence. I am grateful for this tulip. I am grateful that spring is here again. I
am grateful for new life. I am grateful to be noticing what I am releasing.
Ultimately, everything, including great beauty, dies. Inga was beautiful.
Inga died. And I am letting go, very minute steps at a time.

Release Uterus Grief

Arising from the depths of my body, a wail waits. I suddenly realize it is
my uterus sobbing. My uterus holds Inga's memories of growth, contrac-
tion, and aliveness, as it was her first home inside of me. It was my uterus
that helped birth her so naturally and until this day more than five years
into my grieving process has not claimed its despair. Where is Inga? How
can it be true she is no longer on this earth plane? How very sad.

The monologue I presented last Saturday brought much aliveness into
my heart and mind, but not in my uterus. How could I ever even think it
would? Yet the part of my body that speaks now is my uterus. It calls out
for attention, affirmation, respect and supportive listening.

I ask my uterus to tell its story. Tell its grief.

*I am a loner, and no one, you especially, ever looks toward me for wisdom,
advice or consultation. Your heart gets all the focus. Yet it was I who
brought Inga and her sisters into full maturity. It was I who protected them
and found them and watched over them, a guardian given no gratitude. I
have a voice too. I hold much heartache from Inga's death.*

*So listen closely, show up, and do not stray. A castle is what I am, a palace.
Where else would be as fitting a place for the soul of your first child? You
wanted only the best for her and I was the provider. I did not absorb any of
your fears or doubts about being a single mom. I created a spiritual, loving
home for infant Inga. She loved being with me and wanted to stay as long*

as possible. That is why she was three weeks later than her expected due date. She came to me with her very own doubts and fears. She knew this visit would be brief and she preferred her womb home to starting her life adventure.

Inga adored me and I her. She was an eternally shining light of love and sweetness. She filled me up. She talked gibberish with me and I never let her down. My sadness is all that I am full of now. No joy has trickled down to me. Not yet that is. Where are the happy stories? Where has her humor gone? I have not seen it yet. No nonsense, I need a nap. Enough grieving for today. That is what Inga would say.

Release Rattlesnake Tale

The wind was blowing, spreading enough rain for me to snuggle into my bright purple parka. Hands in my pockets since I forgot my gloves. Who would think gloves in mid-April? Teller Ranch lies out in East Boulder, with cows, bailed hay and maybe some calves. I really wanted to hike there to see the newborns, the young ones and their mamas caring for them. Those young ones were thirsty or were they hungry? How would I know? I wanted to know. They were drawing me into their world. There were only a couple of calves off in the distance. The fields were empty, and only cows roamed the corral.

My friend opened one of the gates and said wait. I hold my breath now thinking about that moment. There coiled in front of us was a magnificent rattlesnake. I think the snake too held his breath, poised to strike if need be. However, he was too sluggish as he awakened to spring on this much too cold and windy day.

I have never seen a rattler up close in the wild. I felt no fear. I was shocked by my relaxation, awareness and sense of being privileged to be in his presence. I would love to find an explanation for my fearlessness that day and I also will let go of wanting it.

Wake up! Snake said. Wake up and pay attention. Don't make me bite you. There are too many sleepy-eyed toads to be had and my blurry eyes can't see straight. You are clearly walking into my territory so go quietly and let me rest here in the sunshine. Find your own sunny spot to clear the way to greater understanding. Transform your thinking and find your heart. Don't hang on to what is not yet formed. Healing comes through laughter, as well as tears. This is my true tail (tale).

Release Painful Memories

I remember driving to the hospital with the air conditioning blasting and still feeling hot. I need a sweater because they apparently treat germs at the hospital by freezing them. Inga sleeps a lot now, her whispering voice pleading for relief. She wants distraction, just as I do. Yet that is all there is—distractions. Nameless nurses checking IV drips, temperature, vital stats, they say. What is vital? Knowing she is not dying yet. Or is she really dying but no one says so? Her spinal fluid is a main highway carrying cancer to every organ in her body, including her brain. Yes, her brain has tumors scattered throughout. Cancerous cells are marching through her tender young body. More unhealthy cells than life-giving cells. There is a battle going on and Inga's body is losing. There is no time for a living will. Inga refuses to make out her real will. She doesn't have life insurance, something she doesn't believe in. She believes she will live forever.

I just can't shake these painful memories. The stabbing truth of those cells taking over her vital organs. Nothing helps today. Walking one step at a time, the coolness of the floor under my bare feet brings me back to my house, the barren trees outside my window. I feel empty and lost as I sip my tea, remembering and releasing. Remembering and releasing is my endless path.

Release the Long-Ago Past

When I was a little girl and I cried, the tears were silent, muffled, almost dry tears. I had a little bathroom, a toilet and a sink, both blue. There I found privacy. I could sit there and feel. Later I smoked in that tiny bathroom with the window open. Oh how I loved to smoke there. I recall the choking sensation as I swallowed the pain. They would yell so loudly. I didn't want to hear them. I covered my ears with my hands to block out those screeching sounds. My chest curled around itself like a knotted rope. I didn't breathe; I waited. The door slammed. The car's motor roared and the tires squealed. My father was gone or was it my mother? One of them left and then there was silence. Thank goodness for the silence. A small puff of air filled my lungs but the knotted rope in my chest remained as a souvenir of how my family functioned. It is the way I recreated my own family scene many years later.

The walk-in closet in my bedroom had a window, an outlet for the smell of sweaty shoes on sunny days. I remember rummaging through the closet looking for things I had stored in boxes or for the change of season clothing I had shoved way in the back.

Today I recall my mother changing her clothes there. How terrible she looked without her bra on. Her flat chest with protruding ribs and form-less shape horrified me. I would never want to look like she did. She was like an alien from outer space. Her broad back looked so normal, but when she turned around, there was nothing. Her chest was like her back. The photos of her in swimsuits when she was younger revealed her true identity. Who was she now, reshaped in such a bizarre fashion? I wanted my real mother back. What was she like before the surgery stripped her of her womanly breasts? How did she cope with her strange new formless-ness? But then, how did I? I didn't. I was so very angry. The piercing anger was relentless long ago, fury that the softness of my body was removed. I feel accepting now, so I do believe I have released anger's grip on me. I have grappled with it and taken responsibility for my helplessness against its power. I have embraced the part of me that has known anger best. Yes, the best way to release anger is to embrace it first, then, open-armed, send it on its way.

Release Secrets

To tell the secret or not to tell. I do have a choice., whether it's a very tiny secret from yesterday or one hidden in the cobwebs of time. Then there are those secrets born in my genes, carried down from my family, my mother and her mother. The taboo topics, like sex and cancer buried even deeper into the cells, masking the words as if it were an apparition. I can't speak it or write it, for then it would be real and pretending is so much more my training. Just like during toilet training, I knew what I could speak about and what I shouldn't say. Just put sex and cancer and all the thoughts and feelings about them into the trash. I didn't talk with my mother about cancer while she was still capable of carrying on a logical conversation.

I did talk with her about another family secret. She denied it happened, but she did listen to me. She didn't want to believe me. She said my father loved me so much, I was his favorite. Why would he hurt me? I reminded her of his drunkenness, when he wasn't himself. It was then that he acted in inappropriate, sexual ways with me. She didn't run from taking responsibility for being absent in her protection of me. She didn't stand up to him. She said she was very sorry. She lived through my telling this secret.

We never really talked about cancer—her cancer, my cancer, my brother's cancer, Inga's cancer. Not the reality of those times or how we felt about them. Where did I tuck away all the unspoken cancer talk? Had to just get through those times. Each cancer changed my life, shaped my future, took me down an unpaved road leading to talking things out, getting help, journaling, listening to all my voices.

Inga's diagnosis sent me searching, but first researching the medical literature and resources I knew so well from helping others professionally. First get the facts; that's no secret. Then make choices from all the available treatment options. But Inga usually didn't ask for my advice. She was so independent.

There was the one time we went to an alternative health center on the outskirts of Austin. There they offered a cleansing diet and enemas to promote healthy living. The food served was all raw, organic vegetables and lots of water and herbal teas. They taught meditation, had group process and offered yoga classes. Inga asked her oncologist about the program there and he gave his approval. "If you are going to try something like this, now is the time. We've got you stabilized with no new tumors, your blood counts are good and I want you to take a break from chemotherapy anyway. So go for it if you want to."

We spent the afternoon touring the facility. It was a relaxing ranch-like environment far away from the city with a Southwest décor, classical music playing and a small pool. We spoke with one of the guests and also a physician newly on staff who went through the program for his own health six months before. He was so impressed with the results after his three weeks there that he wanted to return and did.

I thought this all looked good and told Inga I would join her, do the program with her. She said she had one silly question. "Does this mean I can never eat chocolate again?" She didn't hide her concern, make it her little secret. She could have just said that she didn't want to go there. When she was in her last days, she asked me if I thought she had made the wrong decision. Did she do everything she could to fight this cancer? Should she have done that cleansing diet program? I told her she had made many choices and they were her choices. I said, "Never be sorry for what has happened; you can't change the past. Just choose wisely now and relax."

Release Knots

My father was a seaman, a deck hand on a tugboat, a maker of rope knots and knots in my stomach. Do I really want to remember all my childhood distress with him?

I first said no to my father when I was nine years old. It was in a very well-known shoe store in downtown Stratford, Connecticut. My father wanted to buy me an expensive pair of shoes for school. He prided himself on buying the best name brands; a good refrigerator for him had to be a General Electric, not a Sears. Thus it was with shoes. I wanted shoes like the other girls were wearing. However, my father thought the sturdy, brown Mary Jane style would last me many more years. I did my best. I said no, I did not like them, but he did not hear me or chose not to hear me. Before I knew what happened he was paying cash for them and we were walking out of the store with those awful shoes boxed and carried in a great big paper bag. I was disappointed, but I didn't tell him. I was angry, but I didn't tell him. I was just not going to wear these shoes, but I didn't tell him that either. I already said my "no." I hid the shoes in their box deep in my closet and never said another word about them, deciding I would never show him those shoes on my beautiful feet. He never asked, I never told. The knot was tied and our secret agreement secured. Today this very old knot is untied, freeing and empowering me.

Release Escape Hatches

There was a pear tree that overhung the roof just outside my bedroom window when I was a child. My brother and I would climb the tree, picking fruit and challenging each other to climb to yet another, higher limb. Sitting on the roof early one evening to cool off from the house heated by one of my parents' regular emotional uproars, I realized I could escape the house by climbing down through the pear tree. I was free after all to go wherever I wanted! I did not have to stay in this volcano called my family home.

So when things got stressful I looked for my escape hatch. When Inga died, I looked for a way out of my suffering. I found temporary comfort in my food escapes, my short walk to Ideal Market, to buy a "long John" donut, crispy on the outside and stuffed with a creamy lemon filling, then slathered with a thick blanket of chocolate. A sweet something and a cup of coffee were my pacifiers. They calm me down, settle me. Knowing they were within reach, just like the limb of the pear tree, helped to manage my anxiety.

My parents fought often and loudly. I learned both to escape the explosive nature of their relationship and to recognize it within me. When I recreated my parents' relationship within my marriage, I hit an impassable barricade. I had to look at myself and my relationship with anger. The seeds of anger planted in my childhood were now mine to either nurture, pull out or contain with a white picket fence. I chose containment. My fence has a little locked gate, to which I have the key. Yes, my family gave me the key as well as the garden, but I needed to learn when to enter the garden, when to unlock the gate and how to relate with those on the other side of the fence.

I was angry with Inga for dying, for abandoning me. I was angry with her for causing me so much pain. I felt like a victim. I wanted her to live and I wanted me to live so I could hug her children. I was enraged at God and everyone who did not understand how unfair life was. I wanted life to be fair. I wanted what wasn't reality. The truth is suffering happens. Shit happens. But I don't have to step in it and then walk on my grey carpets grinding the brown excrement into the fabric. I have a choice about how I respond. This is the point of reality.

My father sawed off the pear tree limb while I was at school one day. He didn't know how it affected me, he was only pruning for the health of the tree. My escape hatch had disappeared. I became healthier along with the tree. I had to face my situation. I had to make a choice. I discovered inner resources, inner support. There was no big problem here. I had created what I thought was a good solution to my dilemma with the pear tree and now it was time to create anew. I learned there is another way to face grief besides pretending with a smile that all is well. I stepped into my fears and my grief. My broken heartedness softened me, it didn't strengthen me. Or it didn't strengthen me in the way it did my mother. My mother too lost a child and she didn't model grief well for me. She chose rigid strength. She asked me to be strong for her and with her. Her strength seemed to be holding an image to the outer world of managing well, pretending all was well when it wasn't. Her strength was hiding her grief from others. Her strength was in running away into her work life and shopping worlds.

My strength now took the form of a lonely tentacle reaching out into the world. I asked for help, I cried with others. I threw paint with fat brushes onto large white pieces of paper tacked on the walls of my art therapist's studio. I yelled at the heavens and crawled on my knees through the torrential storms of my own grief. I let go of my deep desire to escape. I learned to forgive myself and Inga.

Release My Father

I went home to visit my parents during the summer of 1975. My husband was doing a summer residency in Chapel Hill, North Carolina and I was frantic trying to entertain my three children in a very small two-bedroom apartment there. I could spend only a few hours each day sitting by the swimming pool, so I decided to drive north to Philadelphia to visit Fred's parents and then on to Connecticut to visit my parents.

My father had been an alcoholic all of my life. He would get "dried out" for weeks, maybe months at a time, but then he would always go back to his best friends, other alcoholics, and drink and drink and drink. As soon as I began driving, I would pick him up drunk in bars and take him home to sober up. Or I would drive him to the rehabilitation hospital if he was willing. During this visit, he seemed pretty sober. We even had a somewhat positive talk about my life and he wanted to know how I liked living in North Carolina. While the details of the conversation are very vague, the overall sense was of a closeness that I hadn't had with him in a very long time.

When I got the phone call soon after I left Connecticut that my father had died, I was quite shocked. He had seemed relatively healthy when I saw him. It was September 2, 1975. (It wasn't until months after Inga's death that I discovered that he and Inga died on the same date.) I told my mother I would get there as soon as possible and I drove again back to Philadelphia with my children and took the train by myself to Connecticut.

My mother was very hard hit by my father's passing. All of her victim issues came up. How would she support herself without him? It was a very hard time for me too. I lost a father whom I never really had in the first place. I encouraged my mother to sell the house and move to North Carolina where I lived. I thought it would be good for her. My husband and I had always thought that having all the grandparents in town would be very positive for everyone and especially for our children.

I was afraid to see my dead father. I cried briefly at the mortuary, but also felt so much relief. He had caused so much pain for our entire family that I was glad there would be no more phone calls about his drunkenness. I felt a hardness in me, a cool aloofness. It is the way I managed. Just a few people came to my father's memorial. His drinking buddies came drunk, but there were only a couple. He didn't have many friends, yet he had many when he was buying rounds.

My father died of a heart attack, but really it was cirrhosis of the liver and stomach ulcers that had become infected because of his drinking. My stomach feels tight and my eyes burn. It is hard to swallow the truth about the life and death of my father. My husband told me later after he read the autopsy report that if he had gone to the hospital he could have been treated and most likely would have lived. I read my mother's journals and she wrote she couldn't get my father to the hospital. She asked him if he wanted her to call the doctor and he refused, so she did nothing, even though he was vomiting blood and in much pain. He just wanted a drink, she wrote. I feel nothing. She probably felt nothing; she walked away. She let him be in his misery sitting in his lounge chair in the TV room over the garage where he spent most of his time. Tears are still not there. Jaw tension, a burning sensation in my stomach. What am I holding in? What wants expression? Jaw, what have you got to say, what are you holding on to?

Jaw says, "I am angry at them. All of them. My mother for enabling him to drink all those years. For her helplessness. I am angry at my father for killing himself that way. For drinking himself to death. He was killing himself my entire life. And I feel sorry for myself that I didn't have a father. That I had to father him. I wanted a grandfather for my children. I wanted him to help me build a bookcase or help me to move my furniture. I wanted him to tell me that everything would be all right. I am so sad that he died so young. He was 64 years old. He opted out really young."

Stomach and gut say, "I have always got to hold everything together. I don't let anything in and when I do it poisons me. I don't want him to poison me again, so I hold tight, hoping that it will all go away. The poison, the feelings of anger. I am so angry, like a lion who snarls. I am enraged that he chose not to care for me. I am so angry that he chose the life he did. I am so angry that he treated my brother so horribly. I am enraged that he didn't keep his promises to my mother and to me about staying sober. I won't digest this any longer. I squeeze it, push it out."

My body breathes and I feel relieved. I feel relieved not that my father died but that my body doesn't need to hold onto these feelings. What an amazing body I have that speaks the truth. I feel my power to live full out. Goodbye, Dad.

Release My Mother

I am my mother. No, I am not my mother. I cannot deny the reality of being my mother who nurtured me. She gave me my first mothering instructions, the rulebook on raising a child—her "to do" list of what would be best for me. I kept it for fifty years before examining it thoroughly. Then it was time for me to take charge, to take care of her because she no longer could care for herself.

Mother moved to Boulder when she was 84. She lived in a very nice assisted living facility with a private room and half-bath. She had a view of an open field where wildlife roamed freely and beyond were the foothills and the Flatirons. She did not complain very much, she was relieved to be finally in a safe, nurturing place where she could ask for a tuna salad and her daughter lived close by. It is how she wanted her life. Well, almost. She really wanted to live in my house. And that was not possible.

When her granddaughter Inga died, she fell over, literally fell over onto her back in the dining room, as if the rug had been pulled out from beneath her. She never walked again without assistance. She headed quickly downhill with incontinence, multiple falls, sleep distress with calling out for help, and lethargy. She needed to be transferred to a full-time nursing care facility. She wanted again to come to my house or for me to move with her into the semi-private room she was assigned at Boulder Manor.

She watched videos of her grandchildren and great-grandchildren. She watched game shows and occasionally went to activities organized at the home. Mostly she sat gazing off into space.

I was called in to be with her at the hospital emergency room one cold snowy evening in January 2002. The nurse said my mother was delirious with a 104-degree fever and had a bacterial infection in her blood from a cut on her leg. They called it a blood sepsis and told me she might not live through the night.

I sat at her bedside, crying and finally at my wit's end saying to her, "Mother, you can't die now, please don't die now, I can't bear to go through another loss right now." I broke Mother's mothering rules. I asked her to do something for me, to stay alive a little bit longer. I needed her to help me to hold the grief of Inga's death with her presence. I needed to take care of her as a way to take care of myself. I said goodbye to her with a squeeze of her feverish hand, kissed her cheek and knew she heard me when I said, "I love you." I added, "May you do what is right for you."

My mother pulled through, the antibiotics were working, her fever dropped and she became well enough to go home in a day or so. This amazed the nurses, but they did not know about our little conversation the night before.

Exactly one year later, Mother died peacefully in her own bed after refusing medication, water and food for five days. I was in such a state of appreciation for that extra year with her. We made peace in a way I never thought possible. Her rules became my rules, which became her rules. She exited this life on her terms. I dressed her in a favorite royal blue sweater and new matching blue hat. On her chest I placed a decorative silk hanging I gave her for Mother's Day, which said, I love you. The peach colored rose was a favorite of hers and I put one in her hand.

The nurses and I made a royal procession through the hallways, where she once roamed in a wheelchair. We went out through the door where she originally arrived into the glorious sunshine that bathed her now cool face. I kissed her goodbye for the last time. I told her how much I loved her and said her infamous parting line … Auf wiedersein. Till we meet again.

Release the Family Pattern

Jill called me today. She told me when was putting her daughters Kayla and Emmy to bed, Kayla was complaining because she had a scratch on her arm and it was bothering her. Jill reassured Kayla that she would be OK, her arm would heal, she would survive this. Then Emmy said, "You will survive. It isn't like you have breast cancer." Jill reminded them both that people who have breast cancer do survive, like Mormor (the name I took, meaning mother's mother in Swedish) and Grandma. Emmy then piped up, "But Auntie Inga had breast cancer and she died." Emmy started crying and crying. Her mother snuggled and comforted her. In fifteen minutes Emmy stopped, wiped her eyes and went to bed. It is a shame Auntie Inga didn't ever meet Emmy. She would have really liked her.

This incident demonstrated to me how much has changed in the grieving patterns of my family. My granddaughter was able to express her sadness and be completely supported by her mother. Not only did Emmy remember what she had heard about her Aunt Inga, she was also able to talk and cry about her death. She never met Inga, but she is not carrying the family grief in her little body as I felt I did at that age. I am proud of us all. The chains, which kept us tied to silencing our grief, have been broken. Jill encouraged and supported Emmy. It was safe for her to be herself and feel what she was feeling. Emmy did not have to regulate her emotions in order to take care of her mother.

My grief as a child was buried because I had no place to go with it. I withdrew into my secret world because my parents and grandmother were not available to be with me emotionally. My mother did the best she could yet I knew on a deep level not to bother her. She was fragile beneath her strong outer façade. She could not accept my sadness because it was impossible for her to accept her own. We can only offer to others what we have resolved and worked through for ourselves.

Release Sadness

Inga as a young child loved to be in the garden at her grandparents' home in Philadelphia where she discovered the world with much glee. She would find earthworms after the rain and let them crawl down her arm. Everything was wonderful to her then. She delighted in the world and with all beings.

I feel raw sadness in my entire body thinking of those days and her bright-eyed wonder at the world. It is such a contrast with her pleading look at me as she begged for relief from the pain she was experiencing days before her death.

There was nothing I could do to protect her from death nor protect her from the pain she was experiencing. And here I am, left with a raw open heart of great sadness. A great heart. A heart open to the world. A heart unafraid of touching sadness in the world. There is nothing to do except to be with it. And I am one with it. There are no walls, no boundaries, no judgment, no questioning, no answers. There is only one big heart of sadness which I share with everyone I encounter. Everyone's sadness is my sadness. I touch it and also let it go.

Back in the garden, the soil is turned, the weeds pulled out, the green beans watered, the new sprouts tended to. Inga tiptoed barefoot amongst the rows listening to her Bonma (grandmother), in awe of the treasures in the garden. Then the plants died at the end of their season of growth, they became mulch and compost for enriching the soil for next years crop. Did Inga see death there?

When her dog Rosa died, she refused to join the family gathering to mourn together. She seemed so unwilling to open her heart and her sadness with us all, unwilling to share her tears with us. She said she needed to do it her own way and she did. She sought out boyfriends who were her confidantes. I wanted to know her in her grief and never did. I need to let go of this wanting.

Release Doubts

My friend told me several weeks ago she was feeling overwhelmed and angry with her hospice support team. I offered to be with her in whatever way she thought might be helpful. I made several visits with her alone and then later with her mother. She didn't think her mother would welcome a visit with me, but she very much did. She was a very stately woman, almost like a queen holding court from her high bed throne. She listened to me while I talked about spirituality in my life. I spoke of the great love surrounding all the births of my children and also experiencing love in times of dying and death. She seemed to want to say something, but got lost as the sentence started to float from her mouth. She held on to my hand for a very long time and told me she wanted to talk with me more about spiritual matters. The last time I was with her, it was a Tuesday on my lunch break from the Spirituality and Caregiving Conference I was attending. I was with her for nearly an hour. I ask myself, was I helpful? Did I serve her? Did I say anything that brought comfort or peace into her dying process? I talked with her about Inga and wondered if she saw her or others who had died. I said they could possibly help her on this journey into the unknown she was embarking on.

I did a short meditation with her, inviting her to go into nature, the sunrise or perhaps sunset. I suggested she might focus on those scenes, especially the bright light of the sun. She said she couldn't focus well on anything. So I lit a candle at the foot of her bed and we both sat quietly looking at it for quite a long time. There was a deep sense of peace in the room. She held my hand so tightly as might a child who didn't want to take her first step alone quite yet. And I ask, did I do enough? Was I enough for her? I ask this both of her and also of Inga. I pose questions, reflect and feel so very sad. They died and I am left alone with my doubt and uncertainty about being a good enough helper, a good enough mother, and a good enough human being. It is time to let this all go.

Release the Tug of War

A visit with my hospice patient today highlighted a dilemma, an internal tug of war: being in-between two worlds, the land of living and the land of dying. My patient was most clear when she uttered these words to me: "I don't want to live and I don't want to die." It seemed as though when I asked her questions, she often replied with "I don't know" or "I'm confused" or "I'm tired." But when I just sat silently with her she found words, thoughts and feelings to express herself and she also appeared calmer. What a tough place for her to be, in the throes of grasping at life and at the same time wanting the freedom of not being here.

When Inga was in so much pain, I had a similar dilemma. I wanted her to be free of pain and I didn't want her to die. I couldn't bear her pain, nor bear my pain knowing the relief from pain might actually be death. How incredibly sad to stand at the threshold of saying goodbye to my firstborn child, wishing her relief from her suffering and knowing that her death was near. I saw an image of myself torn apart by this, as if both of my arms were being pulled off in opposite directions.. It was torturous. How did I survive that? How did I let go of each of the forces that were pulling on me? Not through a conscious thought, action, or decision. My heart wanted her alive and my head knew the pain itself, along with the cancer, was killing her. I was helplessly standing by. The cancer was in her spinal fluid and even chemo injected directly into the spine did not result in a lessening of the number of cancer cells. The chemotherapy was helpless just as I was. I had no choice, Inga had no choice, and her doctors had no choice. It was time to stop treatment and inform Inga that her death was near. There was some relief from the tension and at the same time a tremendous burden of guilt, sadness and remorse.

I think of this tug-of-war between life and death in my neighbor, who committed suicide recently. He did have choice and he chose death over life. He wasn't ill physically. I struggle with many feelings about the way he died at his own choosing. I ask what could have been going on for him to make that choice. Inga fought for life and I cannot understand his decision to end his life. I know it was very difficult for him when I sold my house. He even got angry with me, which was unusual for him. His family said they never saw him angry. I think that contributed to his pain. I feel such great sadness for his family.

Many grieving parents cannot seem to find any reason to live after their child dies. As someone said to me today when I shared the story of my loss, "I always wondered how my mother's death was affected by the death of my sister. I just don't think Mom ever got over it. Or does a mother ever get over her child's death?"

Is the death of a child something to be gotten over? Isn't it the same dilemma *as living with dying and grieving with living*? We have such a tendency to want to solve the "problem" of death or grief, but the real problem is our need to deny the existence of each. We see death as an enemy and yet it is one of the certainties of life. This is the biggest lesson I have learned. I no longer fear death; death is not the enemy. The following poem emerged spontaneously.

Living with Dying

Living with dying
Dying into living
Seeing the whole picture
Seems like the sky
Isn't falling after all.

Come dance with me
On this death floor.
Follow the grains
Step lightly
Gracefully
Sadness flowing.
No regrets.

Cheerful day
Tears tapping an
Expansive heart
Peaceful rest
The unknown guest
Awaits.

Release Damn Drugs

Drugs. Advil, Ativan, morphine. Inga always asked for drugs when she was in pain. She had many headaches while growing up. Was that a sign of what was to come? She was rarely sick with a cold or the flu, although I remember my worry when she had swollen lymph glands in her neck. Her father said it was just normal, but I worried about lymphatic cancer. My brother had swollen glands and he died of Hodgkin's disease, a form of cancer. But I couldn't, didn't, wouldn't ever let a thought of her dying come into my mind.

Back to drugs. She never did drink alcohol, but she did smoke marijuana with her boyfriend Rob when she was sixteen. Now Rob, he was into drugs. I was glad when she broke up with him. He put his fist through her bedroom door once when she locked him out. He was an angry one. Well I was an angry one too in those days. But I didn't do drugs. I liked to have wine with dinner, that was it. No, I did do medicinal drugs that her father got for me. I had such intense gut spasms and bloating. So he prescribed a muscle relaxant. And I took it. When I had migraine-like headaches, I took the heavy duty drugs that put me to sleep and I woke up groggy and headache-free. He wanted me to take anti-depressants, but I resisted that one. Drugs wouldn't fix my unhappiness. And I was right about this.

During the last week of Inga's life, she took many pain medications. She wore a pain patch, still had that Ativan too. It seemed to help a lot. When she was choking after devouring the chocolate mousse dessert that I bought her, Ativan calmed her down.

Inga did have a high anxiety level. She was scared about flying, even though she had flown with her father in small planes as a child. At one point after she had cancer, she discovered if she had one drink before take-off, she could relax. She found this in her own way as she always did.

We would push the morphine pump button for her because she didn't have the strength. At least she was in control then of that relief from pain. How horrible to be in so much pain. The mouth thrush was another thing. It was bad enough that she did not feel hungry, but the chemo caused all that mouth discomfort. It killed off the good cells in her mouth as well as the cancer cells in the rest of her body. How brave she was. How nobly she walked with drugs and sometimes not. How amazing she lived with all that pain and with all those drugs.

Damn drugs—they weren't always good enough. Damn drugs—there weren't any that could cure her of that damn disease. Damn. Damn. Damn.

Release Inga

I am wearing the turquoise bracelet I gave Inga many years ago. Today is Mother's Day 2007. Erika invited me to brunch with my son-in-law Jeremy, his mom and sweet, two-year-old Anna, who arrived, dressed in a gingham hat and dress toting a large bouquet of flowers. She is just so cute, a delight when she is not saying her favorite word "no" and also a delight when she is. This is another milestone, another Mother's Day without Inga. I miss her and my heartache has lessened. I enjoy the food and company but say goodbye as I know I must head over to Inga's bench along the Boulder Creek path.

The plaque on the bench has discolored. I need to polish it. A large tree was cut down and weeds are sprouting, not the iris we planted seven years ago at the dedication ceremony. The dirt has eroded around the bench's anchor supports. However, the creek's melody is still the same and constant like a really great friend.

I feel very calm. I ask Inga to come sit with me as I move over to the far left of the bench to give her room. I whisper silently, "Come talk to me, Inga."

Mumford, I do like Emmy, please tell Jill that I do. I really liked seeing you so happy today talking with both my sisters and enjoying Anna at brunch. You really have come a long way. It has pained me to see you in so much pain, so I am more relaxed now too as you have relaxed. See that froth there, the water stirred up as it falls over the rocks. That is like your spirit. When I died you were tossed around endlessly. Now watch those delicate bubbles as they break free from the turbulence. They are back in the natural flow of this creek. I see you traveling lightly. About your back, Mom, don't worry so much. You will be just fine. Soon you will be doing sit-ups, but not too quickly. Your work is right here, writing. And I am proud of you for that. Thank you for being so loyal to me, for not forgetting me or running away from your grief. You are the very best mother and I thank you for being mine. I thank you for it all. I have to go now. Take great care of yourself and just be yourself. I love you a whole lot. Oh and I like my bracelet on you. Remember how we used to trade clothes and jewelry? It is still happening.

Peace. I have found peace. Peace with Inga and her death. She won't always be with me in the same way. She will be real to me, alive in my heart. I do let you go, Inga, again today. I release you and I release myself.

My life is like a babbling brook. Sometimes I am trapped, a branch wedged between two rocks, and at times I am a bubble drifting aimlessly. In the spring when this creek runs high, the water is muddy with the creek bed and shoreline churned up. I have times of clarity and times when nothing is true except my murky existence—a very depressed state. The rocks or obstacles exist in the flow but need a beaver if a true dam up is to occur. I can choose to be beaver-like or move around the rock obstacles. I can choose to sunbathe and appreciate the sun's existence too. I found Inga's death unimaginable and terrifying. And I found gifts through living with her death and with my grief. Thank you, Inga, for being my firstborn child.

Receive

The center of the labyrinth is the place of receiving. It is the holy of holies. It is the center of my soul and the place I was seeking. After review, then releasing and letting go through all the twists and turns of the path, I do reach the center. Here I can rest, wait and receive. After letting go, there is actually space now for something new to appear. When in the midst of all the emotions of grief, the path seems endless. Reaching the heart of the labyrinth may bring a surprise. I have walked the labyrinth hundreds of times and each entry into the center is unique. Here are some of the many gifts I have received along my grief journey.

What have you received into your life since the death of your loved one?

Receive Dreams

My dreams became more regular after I stopped taking sleep medication. I needed prescription drugs for several weeks after Inga died to help me develop a more regular sleep pattern, but I missed dreamtime. Therefore, I began to sleep more and always invited my dreams to help me in my grief. When I felt Inga's presence with me through my dreams, I would usually awake feeling a sense of peace.

October 20, 2000
Dream Entry
There is a reunion of women who died of breast cancer. All their photo-graphs outline the page. Inga is there in one of the photos and I am so happy to have a fleeting glance of her.

October 21, 2000
Dream Entry
An old man came to me and said Inga's passing was OK that she was in a good place. I am really angry and push him away.

October 31, 2000
This is the Day of the Dead. It is 4:31AM and I have a significant dream.

Inga is lying on my bed to the left of me. I am so happy as I tell her, 'You're back.' She says, 'Do you think I have enough time for some sex?' I do not know, I tell her. I reach out to touch her arm. Erika is also there. I tell Erika 'Inga is here and you can touch her.' I tell Inga, Oh, there is so much I want to know. Do you like the plaque I placed in your memory on your bench?' Inga says, 'That's nice.' And I ask her, 'Do you know a trail will be developed in Austin in your memory? She says, 'I don't know right now, but that's nice too.'

I awake very happy and grateful for this dream as I write it down.

Later I have another dream.

Inga and I are at a wonderful house where you can open a large window and there's a pond. I want to put goldfish there in the pond. She is concerned that limbs may drop there and hurt the goldfish. I ask her about the other side. She says nothing but smiles.

My mother's father died before I was born. I never met my grandfather, but got to know him through my mother's stories. He inspired me to remember and write down my dreams. My mother told me when she was a little girl he would ask everyone to share their dreams at the breakfast table. While my mother did write hers often, I took to doing this on a regular basis in my teens. I never started to work with them though until later in my life, when I decided to take a dream class at the University of North Carolina. This awakened me to a whole new world, my unconscious.

When I was in graduate school studying psychology, I chose to commit to Jungian psychoanalysis and dream work for two years.

Jeremy Taylor is my dream teacher, whom I met in 1996. His profound and simple truths about the value of dreams ring true for me and I benefit very much from the power of the group model that he has developed. His basic dream work tool kit contains six basic hints for dream work:

1. All dreams speak a universal language and come in the service of health and wholeness.

2. Only the dreamer can say with any certainty what meanings his or her dream may hold.

3. There is no such thing as a dream with only one meaning.

4. No dreams come just to tell you what you already know consciously.

5. When talking to others about their dreams it is both wise and polite to preface your remarks with words to the effect that "If it were my dream …" and to keep this commentary in the first person as much as possible.

6. All dream group participants should agree at the outset to maintain anonymity in all discussions of dream work.

I registered for a weekend dream workshop to be held April 30, 2004 in Loveland, Colorado with Jeremy. I thought quite a bit about what dream I would want to bring into the circle of participants if I were fortunate enough to have my name drawn out of the hat. There turned out to be about twenty people at this workshop and five would be able to have their dreams shared.

After the first dream was presented on Saturday, we had a break and I started having a very strong urge to find one of my dreams to share other than the one I had already chosen. I reread a few dreams and marked a couple and the more I did this the more I felt this strong knowing that I would be chosen next. The more I trusted my felt sense, the more I knew the dream I would choose. Sure enough, my name was drawn and my knowing was affirmed. The receptiveness of the group waiting for me to start telling my dream is still palpable to me.

On February 17, 2004, I had the following dream, "Hallucination".

I walk out into my living room and kitchen area (which looks like it does in awake life). The grey counter top in the kitchen has white spots on it. I try to wipe them off and they don't come off. Then I turn and see all over my gray carpet messages written in white. I rub my eyes. This can't be true, I must be hallucinating. The messages grow larger and some objects appear too. I ask if someone else is there and do they see them too. I think I should go get my dream journal and write down these important messages and never do.

On the right lower corner there is a wrapped package that says "Open me". I know this gift is from Inga and I excitedly open it. It is soft and at first I think it's a roll of paper towels. But it is a scarf or table covering that is beautiful. It is golden with a dark royal blue inlay pattern. I spread it out and am just delighted. I try to read the other things written, but do not understand.

Later the room is now at QuaLife where I work in my awake life. I am on the third floor and there is a Christmas tree and I tell the dog to stop chewing on one of the decorations. I tell the boy who owns the dog that no dogs are allowed on the third floor.

There is a Muslim woman with a very decorative nose plug (on the left side of her nose). It is gold with a diamond in it. She says they will be praying today and that's all there is to be done. I am down on the first floor and meet Erika who will go in to pray. I want to go too, but decide not to.

Now I am running up the stairs and meet a man also going upstairs. I tell him, "I'll race you there." He starts running upstairs too. I tell him this is how I get my aerobic exercise.

I did not get much sleep that night, was awake at 2 and couldn't fall back asleep until 4:30. My neck, hip and back ached when I awoke and wrote the dream down. My journal had no additional notes or reflections about the dream.

I told the group that I actually had another dream that night too. Everyone said they wanted to hear that dream also.

This dream is titled "Scared Touching the Man."

There are many people, actually mannequins, who are in a circle. I touch one of them and he comes alive. I am really scared.

Individuals started asking me questions and then sharing their "if it were my dream ..." statements. The dream with mannequins could be looked at as dead people and one of them transforms. There is a lot spoken about activation of masculine energy.

The paper towels in the other dream were disposable and could mop up tears. Lapis or dark blue color in Native American tradition can be seen as representing masculine awakening (the feminine grieves) and lapis is the stone of spirit. The Christmas tree could represent the old religion and the Muslim offers new spirituality. I had been Christian in awake life and was moving towards the Buddhist way. There may be conflicts coming out through assumptions that I thought true and the dream offers choices. What I thought was paper towels is really a tablecloth. The Christmas tree can represent rebirth. The dog is the instinctual part of me and I tell him he is not allowed here. I could ask myself what are the choices and assumptions that I am making right now.

I remember Inga's last Christmas at my house with Jill and Erika. I remember her wanting a real live Christmas tree and I got one. Usually I would just decorate my houseplant, the Norfolk Island pine tree. I recall early in the week, I felt I had to talk to her about my fears of her dying from cancer. I wanted to hear her hopes and fears and communicate more about everything she was feeling. We all gathered in the living room. I was sitting on the edge of the sofa and she was sitting next to me. After I spoke, she got really angry with me and told me not to share my fears with her.

She didn't want to talk about it. "Let's just have a wonderful old fashioned Christmas with lots of presents and cookies." "Let's bake lots of cookies." So Erika and Inga went to the supermarket and bought pounds of sugar, butter, flour, chocolate chips, sprinkles, and sour cream. They got all the fixings for six different cookie recipes. I asked who was going to eat all these cookies. They replied they would take them to the homeless shelter.

The messages that came on the carpet were not all clear, but the one that really mattered said, "Open me." I knew it was from Inga. I heard her say "Don't make a big deal" and "Let's do the fun stuff." She has communicated with me now. Jeremy said this dream is like a veil being lifted between the two worlds. This gives me the opportunity to know Inga from where she is now.

I sit now with her looking at me through the photograph and my heart feels both full and empty at the same time. I ask her to give me some guidance in my life.

Receive Metaphors

A hand-painted silk scarf was given to me in appreciation for all the work I had done with LifeSpark. I helped to found this group when it began at QuaLife in 2002 to support those diagnosed with cancer through offering Reiki and Healing Touch. This beautiful scarf has a red, orange and rust colored rose at one end and a string of pearls uniting the leaves through the entire length. I felt honored and humble receiving this symbol of my life's work with this group. I had a slight flash of disappointment and sadness that our paths were going separate ways. However, I accepted the invitation to do a presentation tonight for their monthly meeting and explore life metaphors. At the event, they chose to present me first with this metaphor of appreciation to wear.

We were off to a great start because having this scarf draped around my neck was so central to tonight's theme. I chose the topic of metaphors because this is what I am so focused on these days. What a great group it was as we went around the circle, first checking in by naming an image or symbol which best described how each of us felt this evening. One person felt like an equilateral triangle, balanced and steady. There was a tree stump feeling grounded, a still pond, a pansy with one wilted petal, and an open door, among many. I guided them through a labyrinth walk in their mind's eye as a way to discover their life's metaphor.

Join in by walking your labyrinth now.

Find a comfortable position on your chair. Settle in. Experience the chair holding you and supporting you allowing you to let go and relax, giving yourself the opportunity to step into your inner world. Allow yourself to take a cleansing breath to help you to relax. Breathing in and letting go. Feel your muscles, your tendons and your joints relax. Whenever any thoughts come into your mind, just let them pass through noting, "Aha, another thought."

Now we are going to walk a sacred path together, the path of the labyrinth. This is a time to be connected to spirit, for us to be connected to a core of feeling in ourselves that makes our lives vital and full of meaning, that makes our lives a mystery evermore to be uncovered.

As you continue to follow your breath imagine yourself in a very beautiful place in nature. (Remember that at any time you can change my words in order to best fit your own experience. And if you are having trouble hearing me, just gently lift your hand and I will speak louder.)

So in this place in nature where you may have been to before (or maybe it is a brand new place you have never been to before), allow yourself to feel all the sensations of this place. The sun on your skin, is there a breeze, is it cool or warm? What sounds do you hear? Smell the smells of that place. Is there a fragrance in the air? Allow yourself to take in fully the textures of this environment. Notice if you want to take your shoes off and be barefoot there or what shoes you are wearing and you want to keep on. Notice what kind of clothing you are wearing and if you feel too warm or cool. It is all quite fine. This is your journey. Look around turning slowly 360 degrees and look for a labyrinth. It doesn't have to be in great detail. You will know it is there because it calls to you. The center place calls to you. Notice what is there in the center. Maybe you can't quite see it. But you know it is there. You sense it. Perhaps it is a plain rock or maybe it is a shrine. Or maybe it is a misty environment. It is the center of your labyrinth.

And when you feel ready allow yourself to move closer to the place that feels like the entry point of the winding trail that is going to lead you to the center. You stand waiting there or perhaps you choose to sit. And you spend a few moments first reflecting on your intention for this walk. Or maybe you pose a question you would like the answer to. You review your life right now. Maybe you ask what is my life metaphor? Feel all the sensations, notice all the feelings as you stand on that threshold.

There is no rush. Spend as much as time as you would like. (silence) Soon I will ring a gong that will symbolize the start of your walk into the labyrinth.

Now you begin to walk into the path, feel the contact you are making with the ground one step at a time. When thoughts come up just let them go. Continue at your pace. Notice any emotion arising. Are you remembering someone who is no longer with you? Feel yourself being led along this path. The only place to go is forward. No need to do anything but follow the path. It will lead you to the center. (silence) Return always to your feet on the ground. Let go, noticing and then releasing. Noticing and letting go. No place to go. Feeling yourself getting closer as the path twists and turns. Then you are almost there and at your own pace you notice what it is like (gong) to step into the center, the place of receiving.

You have reached the center and you feel yourself settle and open to receive. Allow whatever comes to you. It is just perfect. It is for you. (silence) Turn around facing all directions and see if there is anything there for you to pick up and take with you on your journey back. Breathe into this place and all that you receive. See if there is any symbol, very concrete, that comes to you. (silence) So with gratitude (gong) you leave the center and return on the same path.

Back to where you started. This is the same path from which you came. And perhaps you feel different sensations as you walk away from the center. Maybe you want to move more quickly. Or maybe you want to stop to observe the place around you. Maybe you feel like dancing or singing. There is no special way to return. Whatever way you return is absolutely perfect. Simply follow the path once again taking with you that which you have received. (silence) You can feel in your body, in your heart and in your mind the gift from the center place.

When you find yourself at the threshold where you entered, take some time to make that transition to just being back in that special place in nature. Walk around aimlessly, perhaps taking a drink of water, and then very slowly start to come back to this room. Notice the contact your feet are making to the floor of this place. Notice the contact you are making with the chair and take a deep breath and perhaps even a yawn wants to come out. Gently start to wiggle your toes and then your fingers. Maybe you want to stretch and readjust yourself in your chair. (gong, gong, gong)

I direct the participants to meet with one other person to share their experience. My suggested format is as follows: The person talking and sharing his or her story of what happened for them speaks in the present tense as if it were happening right now. Share your feelings, sensations, thoughts and any insights you may have had along the way. The person listening just listens in the beginning, not interrupting. When the person completes the story, then ask the following. What surprised you? What did you receive in the center? What is the symbol which seems most powerful to you? What is your life metaphor?

When the group reassembled, I suggest the following. Consider taking any image or symbol from your journey and prefix it with "I am." For myself when I was guiding this process I kept getting the image of a golden container, a bowl with a broad pedestal. Using this image, I am surprised by it being gold, not something I am normally attracted to. I also feel there are gifts inside the bowl and I see the group's images from the opening check-in there. I feel myself expand and the simple phrase flows. "I am a golden container overflowing with gifts." This is my life metaphor.

Receive a Golden Ring

I title this dream "Golden Ring."

I am on vacation with a group of people. I am attracted to one of the men. I learn later that he has a wife. Together we pick up fish for dinner. I walk into his house with him. On the stairs I tell him I noticed the many compliments he gave our dance teacher. His wife seems all right, but I question whether she suspects something. I tell her traffic delayed us. Later I am looking for my ring and a piece of lost clothing. The ring is golden and has an unusual shape. There is a plain band and on it, an empty cone-shaped receptacle. This was Inga's ring and I tell myself I should not have been gardening with it on. At least I find it, but the diamond is missing.

I reflect on this dream and the powerful ring symbol. It inspires me in the following awake dream state of active imagination. (Active imagination is a Jungian concept embracing a variety of techniques for activating our imaginative processes in waking life in order to tap into the unconscious meanings of our symbols.)

Was her hair golden? I do not remember. What was she wearing? It is so confusing, getting only a glimpse of the other world, not finding in my memory bank of treasures the fine-textured details to fill in the desire, my longing to discover what lies there while I am deeply asleep. She lost her ring and I have found it. The gold did not sparkle, but it caught my attention in the sand. It could have been just a bottle cap, but I have a propensity for picking up objects on the beach. As I hold it in my right hand examining it, there is a delicacy to it. It will not fit my finger, although I do not even attempt to try it on. I can see clearly it is a much smaller size; it is for a thin woman, not for my firm, rounded fingers. What is so unusual about the ring is the cone structure attached to it. Like an ice cream cone with the pointed end resting on the base of the ring. I imagine the heat has melted the chocolate, but no, it is a ring. There was a diamond there at one time and it is no longer set in its cavernous mount. I want to look for it, so when I find the owner I can return this ring intact.

As I look up at the miles and miles of sand and water with no one in sight; no one is looking for a lost ring but I. Now that is it. I am the ring. There is no seeker of lost rings; there is no one but me ringing the truth of my existence. I am round. I am whole. I know what I am. I have been someone else's property, valued, maybe even treasured, but now I am lost. I am injured. I have lost the most valuable aspect of myself through no fault of my own. I bury myself in the sand searching for my completion. How can I be whole without my jeweled essence? My diamond is not the rough one first discovered in my underground home. This diamond has been polished by my years of life itself. Is there wisdom hidden in its lost facets? Who am I without it? Who am I without a part of me buried?

Despairing, I start to dig into the sand using my cone now as a shovel to clear the path as I search and sift and sniff and grope for my gem. Granules slide away revealing more granules and an occasional shell from the sea. I ask my neighbor the ocean when it will be reaching high on this shoreline. Can you help me wash away the sand? Can you help me find what I am looking for? Ocean responds, "I will join you and bring you a scallop to help. Perhaps her pearl will fill the void you are lamenting." No, it just will not do, I need my diamond back.

I ask the diamond, "What do you represent in the dream?"

I am Inga and there was a time when nothing would comfort you, even the pearls of wisdom of many well-intentioned friends. You only wanted me alive and in the flesh.

"What message do you bring to me at this time?"

You are feeling delayed, not moving as quickly as you would like and the ring is a reminder. You are committed as with the symbol of the engagement ring. A part of the ring is lost, as you sometimes feel lost in your grief process. The true jewel you are searching for is out of sight, but can be found. You are not distressed in the dream; you did feel there was hope. You did not lose the entire ring, only the diamond. The message is to continue gardening, tilling your soul soil, seeking balance with others and self and allowing your dreams to support you.

I return to my dreams for guidance and inspiration. I place Inga's turquoise bracelet next to my bed along with my dream journal and ask her to come to me in my dream life to assist me.

Receive Vivid Awakeness

I had two dreams last night with Inga in them. I am disappointed with myself since I did not get up and write them down immediately. The first dream was reassuring. I only remember the feeling of gratitude for her coming to me as I requested. I was certain I could wait until morning and write it down, but didn't. The second dream is a disturbing one with a powerful violent image of a chain saw. I awoke frightened and confused as I wrote the title "Chain Saw Cutting through the Bathroom Door Where I am Hiding."

I am with a young woman I don't know. We are looking for Inga. At first, Inga is with us in this very large public building, not a home. Then the lights go out and I must report there are strange things happening here. I am in danger and scared. The young woman and I run into a bathroom. It does not have a doorknob or lock just a round hole where the knob would eventually go, as if this bathroom is still under construction. I hear the roar of a chain saw cutting in the distance and the sound is getting closer. I lie on the floor, bracing myself by putting my feet against the door to keep it closed. The woman with me is hiding under the sink. The saw is getting closer.

I will need the help of my dream group with this one but I contemplate this dream's imagery. The chain saw reminds me of murders and violence. It certainly got my attention and I did not stay asleep, but got up and wrote this one down at 6:30. Seems I needed violence to cut through my laziness. There is a sense that Inga was the one with the chain saw, she was trying her best to wake me up, to tell me something, but I do not know what. There is nowhere to hide from her and all that she is representing in this dream.

Since I did ask her about my book before I went to sleep, the door may represent some blockage I am having. The young woman with me may be my editor Liz who is not helping me to keep the door blocked, yet she is hiding too from the chain saw. Bathrooms represent cleansing and releasing. What do I need to release about Inga at this time? I hear immediately my dependence on her. This writing is my hard work, not hers. I see her smile at me.

I go into this bathroom to hide, not to use it for its normal function. This reminds me of the little bathroom in my childhood home where I used to hide and smoked my first pack of cigarettes. Is there something I am ashamed of or feel guilty about in my waking life sending me to hide out? I do feel self-indulgent in my current life style. I am not working in the traditional sense. I live in a beautiful house, which is not mine. I just bought a new used car that I love. I am not worried about money even though my financial advisor says I need to be earning something because my retirement savings will not last my lifetime. I have no formal writing training and yet I am writing a book. I love dancing Argentine tango. I have a business class frequent flier ticket to Buenos Aires in September, and another trip planned in November to vacation in Puerto Vallarta. I have really great daughters, three incredibly wonderful granddaughters and one more grandchild on the way. Life is good, so good that I feel the tug of guilt. Is it alright for me to feel so good when Inga is dead? Can I come out of the closet with loving my life? Yes, and I needed this dream to awaken me to these vivid pleasures with Inga supporting me.

Receive Bee Wisdom

I needed to put my reading glasses on to get a better look at the black spots dotting my bedroom carpet. What are these critters? Yes, they are corpses. Yellow jackets, wasps, bees, whatever you want to call them. Maybe a handful or a dozen at most, but they are dead. Am I confused or what? As I vacuum them up I try to figure this out. There is not an obvious trail to an open window or crack along the framing of the door. I fall asleep still confused.

The next morning while watering the house plants, I enter the office, where I rarely go, to discover multiple piles, not just a few, but dozens of dead bees along the doorway to the porch. In the adjoining bathroom there are more, maybe a hundred dead ones along with numerous others swarming on the window in the shower. Now I am really confused. They too seem confused or dazed. They pose no harm to me, hardly noticing me. They seem drunk with their useless efforts to get to the land of honey. The glass window barricades their vain attempts to reach paradise.

I heard about the plight of bees and insects driven off-course by our modern day wireless world which is filling the winds with electromagnetic waves. What am I going to do? Just shut the door on them and wait for them all to die? No, my confusion does not win out. Thus, I begin my personal rescue mission with a glass votive candle holder to catch them and a CD envelope as the scoop to move these homeless beings outside. Often I catch only one at a time and then sometimes I manage three or more sleepy ones all in one fell swoop. Now even more clearly, I can see where they came in through the bathroom air vent where several seem trapped. They must have been very confused as they hatched and went for the light inside rather than outside.

So what is this metaphor about? Confusion does not defy death, nor does denial cure any problems. Capture what still has energy, set it free and just don't worry about anything. Death happens and life goes on.

A day after the inward movement of bees seemed to end, I saw a bee convention of hundreds swarming just outside the window where many had been trapped inside. I watched in awe. They seemed to be telling me thank you and paying tribute to those who had not made it out this season. Blessed be the bees for they pollinate and truly are the forerunners of creation.

Receive Surrender

Can I control something today? Yesterday I could not control anything, but the jury's still out about today. I want more meaning in my life today or at least some sliver of understanding. Inga was my firstborn and she is dead now almost seven years. I had no control over that outcome. I had plenty of choices, but what I wanted was a full life for Inga, a life filled with everything she wanted. She was supposed to be a happy 60-year-old tending to her crotchety old mother. I cannot control anything. I can fantasize. I can hope for better circumstances in the world. I cannot control the meaning in my life. Will I serve anyone by bringing myself back to my breath, back to my grief labyrinth, and by helping to create a place where there is acceptance of death, dying and bereavement?

"I cannot" is not the same as "I will not." I am not helpless in my life. Every day is new. Today I am not in charge. God is. Basic loving kindness is in control. My decisions are not mine to evaluate, to benefit my feeling good, better, the very best. When God is in high command, Buddha is her right-hand man. There is a marriage within of my selfish, warring parts that know only the limitations of their solo adventures. Today I can relax, there are no problems to solve, only the immediate sense of non-reality to avoid while coasting on the road of non-control.

In a dream a few days ago, I was piloting a very small, narrow airplane with an extremely wide wingspan. It didn't have an engine, but I was told that I had damage under the right wing from too much throttle. This plane was a glider without an engine yet it had no gas, no need for a throttle. To me, the lesson was that I am not in control of anything. I have become more silent, listening rather than speaking over and over again my story. When I step into trying to make something happen, revving my engine, I only hurt myself, limit my ability to fly free. I do choose yeses when no's are not my refuge. I choose to love the controlling part of me that still is part of my being. Surrender does not come easily, yet I do choose its wisdom and value my dream reminders.

Receive Intuitive Knowing

I attended an all day Intuition and Healing Workshop with Judith Orloff today. Judith is a psychic first and a psychiatrist. I have done several workshops with her and receive affirmation that my own intuitive knowing and psychic ability is strengthened in her presence. She was doing some focused work with a woman in the audience when she took all of us on a guided visualization. It was there I saw a vision of my umbilical cord as it is still connected to Inga. The cord was white and quite thick, attached at my power center around my navel and it led out to nothingness. It was waving, searching for something to attach to. I know that I must sever this cord to free myself. This will take practice and patience.

Later at home I continued to ask for a miracle, a healing. That's what Inga wanted and what we all hoped for. There were many healings in different forms, just not the big one of a longer life on earth for her. I think about the cord that I detached today and all of a sudden I see and hear the image turn into a headset, earphones to listen with. I invite listening with Inga. Now I think of this as bizarre, but don't let my judgments interfere with the reality of what is going on.

I hear Inga tell me, "Love yourself, no matter what. I loved you, Mom, and always will now. You must love yourself always." I feel more peaceful. I tell Inga I do love myself and will follow her advice. I invite listening with Inga in the days that follow and receive many messages.

"Mom, you did everything you could to help me. I am happy now and did everything possible in my life. Now you go for it. Live what your heart wants. I love you too."

"Mother, there is so much love around, take it. I didn't know it, but you can. You are so loved. I love you. There are so many special surprises that will bring you happiness. Have faith, **trust me** on this. And write this down so you will always remember."

"You are a circle of hope and faith. There will be a time when unconditional love will really be known to you. He is out there too; you can have a special relationship with a man. So do what you are doing to care for yourself. Keep it up, Mom. I love you."

"Don't ever be afraid that you didn't do enough for me. Don't ever be afraid that what you are writing is not important or useful. I am at peace, more peace than I have ever known or that you will ever know in your life on earth. I know now what I never knew on earth. There really is love everywhere. You are in the midst of it; breathe it in, breathe it out. Touch everyone with it. Mom, I am so proud of you. Keep your meditation practice alive and keep dancing. Keep writing. Writing isn't a job, it is an art. It can be like putting colors on paper with gigantic strokes. You love to do that and you may grow to love writing too. But until the love grows into a pattern that softens the edges of sadness and struggles, then just pretend. You heard me. Just pretend that you love to write and the writing will teach you to love it. Trust me on this one too. Everything is a circle. Everything comes around to love."

Receive Poetry

The following poem, with no author or source was dated 4/27/2000. It was found on Inga's computer and her work colleague emailed it to me. I have researched it on the Internet and found it in Stephen Mitchell's book, *The Enlightened Heart.* I can only assume that it held special meaning for Inga. It now has special meaning for me. I feel a sense of peace knowing Inga did have a relationship with her spiritual self. This gives me hope and trust too that Inga is in God's hands now and always was, as am I.

The Odes of Solomon

My heart was split, and a flower
appeared; and grace sprang up;
and it bore fruit for my God.

You split me, tore my heart
open, filled me with love.
You poured your spirit into me;
I knew you as I know myself.

Speaking waters touched me
from your fountain, the source of life.
I swallowed them and was drunk
with the water that never dies.

And my drunkenness was insight,
intimacy with your spirit.
And you have made all things new;
you have showed me all things shining.

You have granted me perfect ease;
I have become like Paradise,
a garden whose fruit is joy;
and you are the sun upon me.

My eyes are radiant with your spirit;
my nostrils fill with your fragrance.
My ears delight in your music,
and my face is covered with your dew.

Blessed are the men and women
who are planted on your earth, in your garden,
Who grow as your trees and flowers grow,
who transform their darkness to light.

Their roots plunge into darkness;
their faces turn toward the light.
All those who love you are beautiful;
they overflow with your presence
so that they can do nothing but good.

There is infinite space in your garden;
all men, all women are welcome here;
all they need do is enter.
From *The Enlightened Heart* by Stephen Mitchell

I read a notebook of Inga's poetry which she never shared with me. I am struck by the depth of her soul expression. I wonder about her fears, which were numerous. Did she know at some level that she would die young? Why was love so tormenting for her? Her writing was beautiful. I am touched deeply reading it. She inspires me to write poetry.

Untitled

An ice cube
which does not melt
immunity to heat
has given it strength.
No amount of fire will melt it
A small amount of warmth
brings a light from within.

Do not try to melt the ice cube.
It will mean more if
you simply warm it slowly
from the inside out.

For rapid melting
may make the water evaporate.
                    Inga Van Nynatten 04/03/89

Wasted Time

A fist
breaking barriers
of finite reality
What a waste!
Instead of clenching
unwind
relaxed pleasures
of weak bonds
growing stronger
rather than
strong bonds being torn
by our own minds
wasted on distant stars
and painful stairways.

I want to pick lilacs
be free to laugh
at the sun
to run and feel the wind
as all creatures do
to love and hate,
fear war
and respect nature
And in time,
When I no longer do these things

to die.

Inga Van Nynatten 01/06/89

Where are you?

Peace is with me
Peace is right here, right now.
Muddy creek gushing
Sounds melting into oneness
Where are you?

I am with you
She whispers
Here by the trail
In the sunshine
In the water
Falling on itself.

Carole Lindroos 07/2006

Receive—Understanding
Denial of Death

The denial of death is so natural. Disbelief in death is the norm of our everyday lives. To deny that death comes to each of us is to believe that we are in control of our destiny.

When Inga was born and I would hold her in my arms, I thought about this miracle of life, this child as a gift. She was special and she was only mine for a short time. I don't know where those thoughts came from. It seemed that I knew on some deep level that she would die young. At the time, I thought about her growing up, going off to school, eventually leaving home for college and then getting married and having a home of her own. I thought of her as independent, with a will of her own that would take her out of my arms and into the greater world. I never thought about her dying. That was unimaginable. I was scared sometimes that she would be sick or in pain.

She did have an accident when she was two years old. She was playing and running in our apartment and fell into the radiator and cut her forehead. We took her to the emergency room. There was no denying she felt much pain. She cried inconsolably and I was terrified. The doctor said she needed a few stitches and I still feel a bit of sickness in the pit of my stomach when I recall that moment. Inga couldn't sit still (nor could I) even after getting two injections to numb the area. Her father held her tightly and still couldn't get her still enough to put the stitches in. So they put her in a straightjacket. Horrible as it was, it worked and was the only option at the time. I stood by frozen, still and worrying. I think I wasn't breathing either. When it was done and Inga calmed down a bit we were walking to the car and I fainted. The crisis was over so now it was my time. I have learned to sit down and monitor my low blood pressure, but that time I had a falling down fainting experience.

Denial is a powerful mechanism. It kept me in action when all of my internal forces wanted to shut down and escape the situation. Denial got me through Inga's stitches and twenty-five years later denial got me through her cancer diagnosis and through her death and dying.

Denial continues to be my helper, my internal confidant. When denial is in charge, there is disbelief. Inga's phone call back in March 1997 came just two weeks after the birth of my first grandchild, Kayla Rose. How could this be true? Inga has breast cancer; she is only 27 years old. I was stunned by the news. I felt light-headed and the world around me seemed surreal. All my senses were blurred. It was not that she had cancer that tore at me; it was wondering if she would die from it. Why were those thoughts there? My mother and I were both long-term survivors, yet cancer and death are irrevocably intertwined. It is a disease that can be fatal. My aunt died in her 40's of breast cancer; my brother died of cancer at age 29. I had worked with many cancer patients over the past ten years and many of them died.

Not a conscious choice, but a choice nevertheless, the denial route helped me to function. It helped me to stay cozy and protect my vulnerability. It helped me to work through the normal functions of my days. It helped me to not have to face the terror of my own child's death every minute of every day.

Here are entries from my journal that speak of denial.

The weight of those feet, whose feet, my feet. The heavy, solid, seemingly huge but not so very large toes seem to be glued to the surface of the floor. It is a hardwood floor or it could be the earth. Brown, rich, nourishing, nutrient-filled Mother Earth. But my feet can't move, my feet are glued there, impossible to take a step. They say I am grounded, I say immobilized, solid like a concrete wall, hard like the rock of Gibraltar, an immoveable object. Where can I go when I can't move? Nowhere. No place. Just stay put, be good right there on that spot. No breath, no energy flowing, only the will to survive.

Or maybe it is the earth that just spoke. She says you must stay, you must live. You must be something, somebody when I am not. She didn't stay put. She died. Inga left her heavy body behind. She traveled or is a traveler to that great unknown. Where has she gone? Where does that trail lead? Will I recognize it when it is offered to me? Or will I stay frozen in eternity, defying the natural course of life into death? Where will I rise above this immobilization? Where will I travel to see the great journey of the beyond? Where will I find her? Just breathe. Come back, breathe movement into that lifeless body of yours. Melt the sadness of all that has passed before you and all that you long for in the future. Be here now. Now be here. Right now.

I remember when I was a child, thinking I would grow up and be an adult who could leave my house. Leaving was my obsession, my saving grace. When I sat on the roof outside my bedroom window by the old pear tree, I planned my escape. I didn't need to grow up first. I would pack a change of clothes and my piggy bank savings, climb down the pear tree and hop the Barnum Avenue bus. I would get to Bridgeport train station and take the next express to New York City. Oh, how I loved the big city, the tall buildings, the bustle on the street, the finely dressed ladies. Radio City Music Hall shows delighted me. Could I grow into being one of the chorus line girls? Oh, the places I would go. I had enough money for lunch at Horn and Hardart's Cafeteria. I could get lemon meringue pie for twenty-five cents via the turnstile. Yes, I had enough money but then there was no more. What would I do then? How would I eat? Where would I sleep? Back with a snap, a harsh wakeup to reality, sitting on the roof outside my bedroom window. Never got out. Not back then, except in my daydreams. My body sat frozen still on those warm summer nights.

A breeze tickled my fanciful thoughts. My brother yelled up to come on down to play catch. Maybe later, I yelled back. I was busy, I had plans to make, places to go, new horizons to view. Catch and toss. Choose what is mine, shake free of what isn't. New York City, now that is mine. Paris, that's mine. London, that's my kind of town.

To remember the escape is not to remember the place, the painful, chaotic, blasting, barbaric, awful place. Not on this trip. No, I have a choice, that's for another time, another day, maybe tomorrow. Inga always said, let's talk about that tomorrow. Today I play dress-up. Today I play and plan. Today I dream the great escape. Today denial is my best friend.

Anger

Present in my grief, not hiding in denial, not running for pacifying agents, not lost in food, alcohol or drugs, I met anger. Anger brought me some aliveness and energy. Anger is not to be mistaken for anything else. It is not blame. It is not craziness.

To be present when anger arises is quite a challenge, even in all the little ways. At our hospice staff meeting today, a colleague was trying to play an inspirational CD recording and couldn't get the player to work. Someone went over to assist her and it turned out that it wasn't plugged in. She was holding that plug and I piped up, "Is this some kind of metaphor for you?" She responded by playfully sticking her tongue out at me.

I start with this example from my life because I almost lost the lesson in it. I had received her response as an expression of irritation with me and had immediately pushed it away. I don't even really know that she was mad at me, but I took it that way and also rejected it. That is one of my coping mechanisms. In grieving I have experienced many who have avoided or ignored feelings and also those who have given me angry responses in varying degrees to my sharing the death of my daughter. Even friends or those whom I wouldn't expect to get that from have pushed me and my grief away. They have used their anger to keep me at bay and to protect themselves. They haven't wanted to face their own grief nor mine. But anger sure does get a negative label stamped on it.

When my hospice patient raised her voice in response to a caregiver's questions, she was telling them indirectly that she had had enough. I asked her when I first met her if she was angry because of all the losses she had had. She replied, "I don't get angry. I never get angry." In approximately ten minutes of continuous questions on my part, in my attempt to get to know her, she raised her voice at me and said, "Oh, I don't know. That was long ago and far away." She sounded frustrated and angry with me. Her voice got bigger, louder, and she responded with emotions she didn't recognize as hers.

I imagine that many people have turned away, changed the subject, stopped in their tracks and tried to calm her down. I believe expressing anger provides an avenue for her to find her way in dying. With her agitation comes an unsettled quality, a kind of stuckness and distress. With expressing her anger comes some settling in, calmness and even an opportunity to heal.

Energy does get locked into the body with this distress and there are times that grief just doesn't move. Perhaps there are those who bypass this, but I know I certainly did not. Being angry helped me to get moving again. I did grief art therapy for about a year. Most of my paintings expressed red hot anger. I would cry through most of my sessions, but the anger found its place with lots of very large brush strokes on big pieces of paper. I felt relief as my entire body expressed my rage through the brush and the paint.

Another one of my hospice patients expressed his anger often with all of his caregivers. I asked his daughter if I could do an art intervention to help him to put his anger into a creative expression. She agreed. I brought him to the art table one day with a four-inch brush, two colors and a circle ten inches in diameter drawn in the center of the white paper. The first thing he did was to dip the brush in the paint and then put it in his mouth. I quickly tried to stop him, fearing that the paint might be toxic. He bristled in anger at me and wrestled the brush free from my grip. I gave in and just let him be. He painted his nose yellow, tasted the paint, which he grimaced at, then proceeded to put color on the paper. His anger was shocking to me, even with all the years of experience I have had in counseling. His anger gave him some control in a world where he was dependent on others for all his needs. Later he painted on the paper and smiled in delight with what he was doing.

Anger is a natural response to loss. When one observes a two-year-old who has something taken away from him or her, there usually is a reaction, a scream of anger. Many parents stop their toddlers and may even tell him or her that it is not OK to be angry. While I aspire to holding a larger view, one that embraces anger, I know that I can fall short. I have also seen many parents in the current day be calm and encourage their children with all of their feelings. I think this is a very healthy development. In schools, there is also more being taught about death and dying. My daughter Jill called me one day to say that my granddaughter who was six at the time asked her what it was like to be dead. What would our world be like if birth, death and grief were core curricula in the schools?

Inga recognized anger. She was angry she had breast cancer and she was angry with anyone, myself included, who expressed any concern about the gravity of this very aggressive form of cancer that she had growing inside her.

I took her for a second opinion with a well-known and respected Denver breast cancer oncologist. He reviewed her charts and told her his opinion. "Have surgery immediately. Don't wait. This cancer could spread easily into the tissue around the breast. Dying from this disease is not pretty. You must be more proactive in your treatment choices." Inga stopped him and loudly asserted, "Don't tell me I am going to die from this damn disease and furthermore don't you tell any other woman that. You are not helping me at all by saying what you just did." She was as adamant with him as he was with her. He apologized and went on with some other comments. Inga later told me she was glad she flew off the handle with him and asked what I thought. She also really heard him and anger was her first response to his breaking through her protective denial.

Anger has such a negative reputation. While I personally and professionally know the damage it can cause psychologically, it also has great merit. It helps move people through the denial and shock phases of the grief process. It also informs us of what and whom we love and value. Anger points us to places that need healing. It educates others. Anger brings energy into our bodies. It mobilizes us. It protects us and our vulnerabilities. It covers over sadness. Anger can be a doorway to greater intimacy and connection with others, as long as it doesn't scare people away. Anger is a gateway to change.

Depression/Sadness

When I was a little girl, absolute strangers would come up to me and say, "Don't be so glum, smile and you will have a better day." Now 50+ years later I smile much more, but my natural relaxed facial expression is one that looks sad. It tells the truth of my inner world. I still am a bit leery of people who are always smiling. Don't they know what is happening in the world? Don't they know every day brings a multitude of losses and sorrow to people all around them? We are constantly letting go of life, as we know it. Yesterday will never be relived. My granddaughter's first jump off the side of the pool will never happen again. We take photos to relive memories. We plan trips and events for the future. But today will never be again. Maybe that's a good thing. Each day we live a day closer to the end of our life. We live into dying, whether we face it consciously or not.

We live our lives grieving, which includes sadness, anger, denial, bargaining, peace, joy and sorrow. This is a gift from Inga to me. I have faced and lived through the worst death imaginable to me and yet I do smile. I continue grieving and tears come easily to me. So does opening my heart to others' pain and joy.

Sadness is immobilizing at times. When my tears were just under the surface or protected by my anger, I felt frozen and stuck. I knew I was in pain and I couldn't experience relief. It was as if a heavy, dark blanket weighed me down. Sometimes I felt like an ice sculpture, trapped. Slowly tears would come, first with a stinging sensation in my nostrils, a tightening in my throat and often an eruption like a geyser. Sometimes my sadness was a gentle light river of tears that bathed my cheeks and dropped onto my sweater. My good friend and colleague Myrna Bottone called these tears "holy water." She was my mentor in practicing being with my tears. Tears are to be respected and valued. A sense of relaxation occurs when I fully embrace them. Sadness and depression are a vital element in grief.

Receive Empathy

One of my mentors, Cheryl Clements, died two weeks ago. I didn't know her personally very well yet I always think of her when I pour Epsom salts into my bath. She once said at a gathering of bereaved parents, "You know, you can just dump the entire box into your bath; it really helps to cleanse the toxins of emotional waste." This is another self-care reminder and she was really big on that, as I am too. Cheryl was the very best grief counselor in Boulder; she will be missed. I last saw her dancing tango this past year and was pleased to know she shared my dancing passion.

I attended her memorial service today and was very touched by her father's sharing at the very end of the service. He said he wasn't sure he wanted to speak but found that he needed to. He described with much emotion being at Cheryl's bedside when she died. Then he said, "There needs to be a law that no parent can outlive their child." I would vote for this. Of course there wasn't a dry eye in the audience. I went to speak to him afterwards and found healing in the hug from this man whom I will never see again and had just met. He knew empathy. He was an example of the kind of man who can be both strong and gentle at the same time. Kind and caring, confident and tenderhearted. As he even said, "I am a rock and now you will see me a pebble."

Receive Self-Forgiveness

I have been thinking again a lot about guilt today after a session with one of my clients. She had been tormented by the thought that she did not do enough for her partner when he first became ill. He died months later and if he had not died, her behavior would most likely not have been an issue.

During some active imagination, I rediscovered my own feelings of guilt with Inga.

I am carrying my granddaughter and a mountain lion appears. I put myself between the lion and her. I snarl as I face the lion and yell at him, "Here I am. Do what you may, but you can't have my granddaughter. You can't have my daughter. You can't have Inga."

I burst into tears and was right there with a real lion, but there can be no more "lying." No more lounging around not facing my own guilt. I must be real because those monstrous feelings of guilt are there in me. I didn't do enough for her. I took some positive actions, but I did not go down the ideal nurturing mother road. It is time to face those flawed, avoiding, self-centered and uncaring parts of me. I did not make time, drop everything and dash down to be with her.

Inga telephoned me, reached out to me when she was first diagnosed. She was terrified and she wanted me to help. She did not say it directly but she wanted me to comfort her. She needed me and I failed her. I did not tell her that I would be down there as soon as I could book a ticket. I do not know what I said, but my offer, if indeed I made an offer to come down to be with her, was a hesitant one. She was diagnosed a week after Kayla, my first granddaughter, was born. I had a trip planned to Ohio to be with Jill and the new baby. I should have gone to be with Inga. I did not. How can I forgive myself for that?

Then there is the question of resources. Inga utilized traditional medicine, for which she had health insurance. She also found acupuncture and massage to be helpful. I sent her money sometimes for that, but did I really do enough financially. I think I depended on her father for that. My feeling was, he has more money than I do; let him step up to the plate. Moreover, he did. Yet I feel guilty that I did not do more. I could have given her more. I went with her to the health spa to inquire about their three-week dietary program and lifestyle change. I offered to attend the entire program with her, but did I give her some incentive or insist? Inga did not want to give up chocolate and sugar. Why didn't I convince her? Why didn't I offer to buy her something if she did it? How controlling of me to think like that. But was she thinking clearly? Did she know the program might have saved her life or lengthened it? She died and I feel responsible.

Mothers are supposed to keep their children safe at all costs. Mothers protect their children from harm, from danger. Mothers put their children's needs ahead of their own. What kind of mother was I that I left things undone? I feel guilty that my genes carrying a predisposition to breast cancer were passed on to her.

Like thorns buried deep in my flesh, these guilt feelings are making their way out of me. There is a line from a Buddhist teaching that speaks to me. "That mind of fearfulness should be put in the cradle of loving-kindness and suckled with the profound and brilliant milk of eternal doubtlessness." The guilt of all those things done and left undone has been surrounded in fear and there is a choice, a place of laying them down to rest surrounded by gentleness and kindness. I have no doubt that there is freedom for myself and all who encounter their guilt, their "lions" of the past. When guilt appears, I have an opportunity not to be driven by my self-perceived failures from my past. I can face any threat wholeheartedly with the strength of my healed wounds.

When my client told her story, I suggested she consider forgiving herself. She said she did not know how. This is a matter of practice and I have returned to forgiveness many times. Forgiveness may come more naturally to some, but it has not for me, so I must keep practicing. Sometimes I think we just need to "fake it until we make it." This may sound glib but I do think we need to go through the motions of forgiving even when we do not feel it so we can move in that direction. I am not proposing to jump into forgiving someone else before you are ready. There needs to be space for anger and understanding. Most important is to forgive oneself. So one might practice by saying to oneself as I have done …

I forgive myself for all the things I didn't do.

I forgive myself for all the words I didn't say.

I forgive myself for being uncaring.

I forgive myself for what I didn't know.

My own forgiveness has taken many practices and forms. What I tell myself keeps evolving and these thoughts have brought a calmness and acceptance.

I forgive myself for the belief that I didn't do enough for Inga.
I forgive myself for any angry words that I expressed at Inga that hurt her in any way.
I forgive myself for my stubbornness.
I forgive Inga for her stubbornness.
I forgive myself for not loving others enough and especially Inga.
I forgive myself for not loving myself enough.
I forgive myself for being fearful when Erika left today.
I forgive myself for my humanness.
I forgive others for their human ways.

A forgiveness meditation is included in the appendix. Read it slowly out loud to yourself or to someone else. Or you might want to record it and listen several times, until you notice a shift in your feeling state. I have used this meditation in leading workshops over the years to help others discover their own forgiveness. Walking the labyrinth with your full intention to forgive yourself is helpful. Be willing to receive the gift of self-forgiveness.

Receive Offering Forgiveness

Sunshine warms my left arm as I watch the sparrows greedily searching for crumbs. I have a luxurious thirty minutes now at my favorite coffee shop with my notebook. I want to finish this book. I surprise myself by thinking I want Fred to read it. Last night I dreamt of him, his younger self. He was going out for a run and he turned to ask me if I had forgiven him yet. I replied, "You haven't read my book yet; you will see when you do."

Forgiveness of him buzzes like an annoying bee around my head. How do I feel about this? Do I forgive him for how he was with Inga in the last few months of her life? Do I forgive him for being the absent father that he was most of her life and now still is with Jill and Erika? I get irritated when he forgets their birthdays and their daughters' birthdays. How can I really forgive him, and let him go to just be himself without feeling jerked about by his behaviors? How long will I hold on to him this way? Why do I? I am so tired of rehashing this, yet I must.

I am angry he did not come to my brother's funeral when we were dating. Now that was 38 years ago. Where has this anger been hiding? I am still disappointed, sad and angry with him for not supporting me when my father died 33 years ago. This remnant of grief curls its head up to reach into my heart. I lost Fred before I ever married him. I lost him emotionally, but then again, I lost myself emotionally long before then.

So I can return to the labyrinth to walk and release Fred and my anger with him and make the journey once again. It is almost Mother's Day and he is facing the death of his own mother. I would like to help him, but he wouldn't want to talk with me. We don't ever talk. I can do *tonglen* and *metta* practice for him, for myself and for his mother. In *tonglen* practice, when we see or feel suffering, we breathe in with the idea of completely feeling, accepting, and owning the suffering. Then we breathe out, radiating compassion, loving-kindness, freshness—anything that encourages relaxation and openness. It is a way to embrace rather than reject the unwanted and painful aspects of experiences, overcome fears and develop greater empathy.

Metta, a word in Pali translated as "loving-kindness," is a meditation tool that permits one's generosity and kindness to be applied to all beings and, as a consequence, one finds true happiness in another person's happiness, no matter who the individual is. While there are many versions of the practice, the following is the one I use. "May I be safe and free of danger. May I be content. May I be filled with loving-kindness. May my journey unfold smoothly." I would repeat the previous four lines many times and then turn to replacing the "I" with others, such as Fred and Bonma (his mother).

May we all be at peace. May we all be forgiven and forgive. May our unspoken goodbyes release us from the grip of anger.

I light a candle on my shrine, contemplate forgiveness, and follow my breath. Then I pick up my finger labyrinth, rest it on my lap and place my index finger on the entry place into the labyrinth. I reflect on memories of Fred and Inga. There are so many ways I feel he let me down. Not showing up on time to swim and gymnastic events for the girls. Not calling Inga to find out how she was feeling in the final weeks of her life. Am I willing and ready to forgive him?

As I start my labyrinth journey, my breath immediately seems to become fuller and more relaxed. I see Fred's face and I let his image melt away as I come back to my contact with the base of my labyrinth, its silky surface and sudden turns. Breathing and letting go, tears come. I feel sad about how our relationship dissolved. I want to forgive him and I want to be at the center already. I release these thoughts. Back to my breath and the base of my finger making this journey. A wave of regret surprises me. I wanted to be more effective in helping Fred to reconcile with Inga. I wanted them to know and accept each other. I regret I was so unable to make any changes between them occur. How could I not get through to him so he would understand and feel in his heart what the right thing to do would be? I was helpless, am still helpless. Let it go, Carole. Feel the rhythm of this walk—the curving, unknown path I have walked so many times yet whose center, still place I am still so uncertain of getting to. Did I miss a turn? Where am I? Am I going out, not in? I question myself. Let that thought go. Be with the journey, Carole, breathe into your arm, your hand, your finger. Yes, that's it. Oh, at last, what a relief. I have landed on the three small stones marking the center.

Here I am to receive. There is a surge of energy within me, as I feel myself be forgiven. Yes, I am forgiving myself. I feel washed, cleansed within and without in love. I am free through love and self-forgiveness. But what about Fred, can I forgive him now? I know I will as I return through this path. I don't receive forgiveness towards him, I just offer it, practice it. So I start my mantra as I return on the path I came in on. I forgive you, Fred. I forgive you for all the times you acted unkindly towards me and towards each of our children. I forgive you, Fred, for all the birthdays you have forgotten. I forgive you, Fred, now and in the future, for all the lack of attention you paid to our children and grandchildren. I forgive you, Fred, for not being who I wanted you to be as the father of my children. I forgive you for all the love you left unspoken. I forgive myself and I forgive you for our inability to protect Inga from death. I choose forgiveness. I choose love, not anger. I do forgive you, Fred.

The rain has stopped and the sunshine through the beaded window of tears awakens me. Everything looks brighter; I feel expansive, more peaceful and lighter. I sit silently for a while with my labyrinth in my lap. How grateful I am.

Receive Fragrant Tea

The fragrance of chai delights me. Life is a mystery of changes. I never used to drink tea in any form. In a few days it will be June 6, which would have been my 37th wedding anniversary. Fred and I got married officially in Antwerp, Belgium in the old courthouse downtown. I had the feeling of it all being like a childhood game of "let's pretend we are getting married." I made a dress of dark blue and white silk, which draped nicely over my very pregnant body. I was due to deliver in just six weeks. My hair was very long, reaching to my mid-back, but I had put a barrette in to hold back the sides, allowing my glowing face to really show. I was radiant, partly due to the unusual heat and the excitement, and mostly due to getting married to the man who I loved so very much. The anticipation of giving birth to our first child took me over into what felt like an adventure, the very reason for which I was born.

The few people who gathered were Fred's relatives and their friends. If it wasn't for the occasional kicks from the baby I would have thought I was dreaming. I didn't understand much Flemish, but Fred said, I'll just let you know when you should say "Ja" or yes. He teased me about not knowing what I was saying yes to. In our marriage vows he insisted there be an agreement for me to have iced tea (sassafras was his favorite) ready for him at all times in the refrigerator. And he was serious about this. We were young and we were in love.

However, I married him to please his mother. It was actually she who asked me to marry him. We were sitting after dinner one night and she turned to me and said "Carol, if my son here would ask you to marry him, would you?" (My birth name was Carol; however after I was divorced I returned to my maiden name Lindroos and added an "e" to Carol because I was not the same Carol as before my marriage.)

And I said yes. That decided it. All these years later I wonder if anything would have turned out differently, if Fred had popped the question to me all on his own. I have no regrets though. I am thankful for my life with him and I am thankful for my life without him.

Receive Ritual Gifts

In the middle of the word "spiritual" is the word "ritual." A ritual is an established form of ceremony that gives symbolic expression to certain thoughts and feelings. Most rituals for me are naturally quite spiritual.

In a ritual, one creates a small event in order to reflect on bigger events in one's life. I have small rituals, such as reading an inspiring book with a cup of tea, or tossing white rocks into the creek near Inga's bench in order to remember certain times from the past. There are also bigger rituals, such as weddings and funerals or memorial services.

I have utilized rituals in many forms in order to renew and refresh myself. A ritual can release bound-up energy and feelings in our psyche and help us walk in balance and reverence. A ritual can be done for transformation. It is not a goal, but rather a process to help us move through our grief and live more fully.

In 2003, I turned sixty and wanted to celebrate this birthday in a special way, as a ritual. Nothing seemed to jump out as something worthy of marking this special point in my life. For this entire year, I also was traveling to San Francisco almost monthly for a professional training program, End-of-Life Counseling. This was run by Frank Ostaseski through the Zen Hospice along with a group of well-known teachers in the field of death and dying: Ram Dass, Rachel Naomi Remen, Norm Fischer, Ange Stephens, Frances Vaughan, Charlie Garfield, and others.

During our April training weekend, we all went to Grace Cathedral on Saturday afternoon to walk the labyrinths there. The one outside was beautifully placed amidst a small park and garden. Before I entered I reflected for a moment and the question I posed was, "What shall I do to make this 60th birthday special for me?"

Rounding one of the many curves and corners, I arrived in the center and the thought popped into my head that I should go to Chartres in France and walk the labyrinth there. The entire trip to Paris and wherever else I might go could be like walking a labyrinth. I would take my small hand-made finger labyrinth with me and walk that daily. I would have a minimum of plans and awake each day open to what the day might bring. I remembered friends who had a small studio apartment in Paris and I decided I would contact them to see if it was available to rent. I had enough frequent flier points to fly abroad business class. After all it was my 60th. I have an old friend who lives now in London. Maybe I would stop there on my way to Paris and Chartres. It all unfolded like a very beautiful gift. I felt so much peace. I felt close to Inga, as if she were smiling with me, in me and around me. She would be proud of my trusting enough to step into this gift and return to the world with it.

Later a few of us gathered and started talking about our experiences in the labyrinth, when two homeless men came over and asked us why we were there. We told them about our EOL counselor training and that we had come to walk the labyrinth, as it was a metaphor for walking the path of life into death, into the unknown. One of the men said he had a friend who just died and he knew a lot about death. He asked if we would like to know his view on death and dying. Of course we all responded positively. He then pulled out a Ziploc bag from his pocket and offered each of us a piece of the contents of the bag. He wouldn't say what it was; only that it was safe and it was his way of teaching about death.

Some of my friends hesitated, but I felt drawn into this experiential learning and went ahead and took a piece. Others declined. When I put it in my mouth I made a face, a grimace and some sounds of disgust. But I kept chewing. He said, that's death—at first you are repulsed, but if you can keep chewing on it, you can swallow it, and it is really OK.

Wow, was I impressed. What a great way to teach. What he gave out was crystallized ginger. What a lesson. I trusted my intuition that what he was giving me really was safe and that there was something of value to receive from him. I was very appreciative of the lesson.

When I can stay open to receiving, there are many gifts. The contemplative gift of the labyrinth always holds something for me, even if sometimes it is only boredom or a smidgen of doubt. Sometimes it is a bigger gift, like my birthday trip. Often it is a joyful state, or a simple, calm abiding. The labyrinth is a powerful tool.

Receive the Mother Lineage

My mother was a writer and I didn't want to be like my mother. She loved to write poetry and short stories, but was never able to devote herself fully to it. No wonder I have been so resistant about writing. Mother played the piano so I didn't want to play the piano. I wanted to dance. Mother lived her life through me and I needed freedom to live the way I wanted to.

When I was pregnant with Inga, she wanted me to come home, so she could take care of the baby and me. It is what she knew how to do. When I refused her offer and wrote her that I was going to live with the father of my child, she was angry, but never told me directly. It was not her way. So I ask myself how and when I have expressed anger to my daughters. I reflect on the times that I have felt anger with them and wonder how I found the natural dissolution and resolution. Do I respond and act emotionally differently than my mother? I do think so.

I have had many advantages to support me that my mother never had. I have been educated, learned skills, utilized stress reduction coping tools. I have had years of therapy, I would guess about ten years worth off and on over the past three decades. I have friends whom I talk to in depth. I have had practice in conflict resolution. I have had jobs, and colleagues who have stood up to me honestly. My mother didn't have those kinds of opportunities and resources.

So what has changed in my mother lineage? A lot. More important are the things that *haven't* changed, those things I share with my mother. Those aspects I honor and respect. A generous spirit, a love of surprise, and thoughtfulness. A love of people and nature. My mother loved looking at the clouds and seeing shapes and animals. We both are courageous, strong-willed and determined. We both have held the belief that every-thing will turn out OK, a positive attitude about life.

My mother knew much tragedy and she was always hopeful for the best outcome. Yes, I want to pass that along. She believed in people, especially her family. She always said I could accomplish anything that I set my mind to. I have my mind and heart set on writing this book. This is the mother lineage. Now I want to prove her right. She was a writer and now I am a writer.

Receive Baby Memories

She was a tiny, pink, crying beauty. How was it possible that this was what, who was growing inside me for nine months? I never saw a baby close up before Inga. How could that be?

I was twenty-seven years old and no little bitty toes had crossed my path or rather, I hadn't crossed theirs. I lived a grown-up life, a life with people in suits and high heels. Yes, that was a very long time ago when suits were still fashionable. The workday was my kind of day. I was a systems engi-neer. I loved drinking coffee and smoking cigarettes as I thought out prob-lems. Their problems, those suited male problems. Get smart, make money and definitely drink coffee, lots of it. Can go a long day leaded up with the real stuff, but then along came a vacation.

I went to Puerto Rico with a female friend over the Thanksgiving holi-day and she invited some cute guys at the next table over to play cards, a game we used to play during lunch at work. One was really handsome, but shy. Ding, ding, those damn bells went off somewhere in my heart. They got my attention and I kept saying yes. Yes, to Thanksgiving dinner in the officer's mess or whatever it was called. Yes, to swooning, that is what I did. I swooned when I saw him in his Navy dress whites. Yes, I would go explore the island with him and by the way, yes to ditching my best girl-friend.

I said yes to writing to him after we parted sadly a few days later. I said yes to a ski vacation in Stowe, Vermont and yes to visit his folks in Phila-delphia the next month. I said yes and yes and yes over and over again.

So the no he said to me four years later was a shock. No, he did not want to father our child. No, he did not want to get married. No, he had to finish medical school. No, he worried that the baby would be a distraction on his mission, his goal to become a doctor. All my yeses then collapsed into my NO to him.

I would have this baby here where I was working in Stockholm and raise the child myself. It is a progressive city and I had aunts and cousins who would help me.

The baby was a girl, an amazing creature. She was a precious gift. How could I even have had one second thought about possibly not meeting her? She arrived on a very hot day in Hôpital Brussels amidst a group of encouraging bystanders, doctors-to-be, nurses and yes, an obstetrician too. They were cheering me on with "Poussez, poussez," yes, oh yes, I got to meet a most amazing little one. She was my precious gift for thirty years. She was named Ingaborg Anna Leni Van Nynatten.

Receive a Paranormal Experience

I have had many out-of-the-ordinary experiences. I have always been uncritical of them and watch out for them. They happen all the time, but I guess I am not always available to receive their lessons. One particular day I was open; grief had opened me to the paranormal.

It is a warm day and since I don't have any time restraints, I am heading down to Inga's bench, which sits facing downstream on the Boulder Creek Path. I am walking upstream to reach it. I am dragging along, not hurrying, feeling a bit depressed and I want some time to just sit and think about and be with Inga. The bicycles whiz by and those darn skateboarders make quite a racket. I hesitate just at the small wooden bridge, hoping that no one is sitting there already. I feel relieved to see the bench is vacant.

The trees shade this small cove and I stop just at the entrance and make a small bow as a gesture of honoring the space. The bench is warm from the sun. As I sit down, I hear a woodpecker (or is it a flicker?) in the tree just ahead of me. What is striking is not *what* I see, but *how* I see him. He is pecking away in an ordinary way, yet I have this inner knowing that the bird is ill. Inga was ill. And that woodpecker is ill, very ill.

I talk to the woodpecker. Do you need help? I wonder where one goes to get help for a woodpecker. I tell the bird I want to be of assistance. I feel so very sad. Back when Inga was sick, I wanted to help her. I thought I knew all the things that could help her. Then I ask the woodpecker to help me. Now I catch myself. How can a woodpecker help me? Help is surely what I need. I am sitting talking to a woodpecker; now I have really lost it. I will talk to my therapist about this next week.

A walk is what I need, so I tell the woodpecker that I am leaving for awhile, but that I will be back. I walk for fifteen minutes and when I return I find the woodpecker perched on a rock just a few feet from the bench. I start crying when I see him. I know he is sick and maybe even dying and I want to assist him. I ask him if it would be all right for me to sit next to him. And the answer I get is, "Please, yes." I take a deep breath and get up very slowly and sit down beside him. After a few minutes, I know that I must reach out and touch him. First I ask permission. And the answer is, "Please, yes, touch me." So I very slowly place my hand on the woodpecker's head and back, gently stroking it. I cry and at the same time feel very calm and peaceful. I thank him for allowing me to touch him and tell him that I hoped it helped him as it certainly has helped me. I slowly get up and walk away telling him that I am going home to get my camera, if that would be all right to photograph him. I didn't wait for his answer as I was now back to my ordinary way of living and thinking.

When I return the bird is gone. I smile, knowing the profound nature of this experience, which was not to be recorded on film, only on paper and in my heart.

Receive Forgiveness Revisited

I am preparing again the monologue I had written and performed last fall. Why did I say yes to doing it again—revisiting the sobs and cries that leave me feeling skinless? Yesterday I had an hour-and-a-half rehearsal with the director Kirsten Wilson and my piece went to a new level. There I connected with the raw sadness of Inga's absence. I sit now at her bench. Where are you, Inga? What do you think about my monologue? My neck is so stiff, as if I am straining. I ask my neck to speak its truth.

Yes, I am a neck. A neck full of tension. I am a neck that is not limber, not flexible. You turn your head and do not even pay an iota of attention to me. You want to always look good onstage. I guess that is natural. You are a woman, after all. You have beautiful women friends. Inga always wanted to look good too. She wore very cute hats to hide her bald head. Although I think she looked great with no hair or very little hair. I am tired of looking my best. I get pulled around, whipped out of shape with those auto accidents and here you are just inattentive. I hate that you don't notice me. Pay attention to me! You are just a little kid in grownup clothes. You play sometimes, you dance a lot, but always in those very high heels. Maybe it is fun sometimes. You feel special click-clicking along. What I want is less pressure from you to look good, or look a certain way. I want you to acknowledge all that I feel, we feel. The grief, the joy, the amazing gratitude.

What a wonderful day this is! Sometimes I urge neighbor jaws to grit those teeth, to grin that mouth of yours. I push and prod her and she knows well how to do that. I invite your hands to strangle me. You wanted to strangle her many times when she was a wee one. How could you have even had that thought? You never touched her that way. You simply strangle yourself now. Inga, did you forgive her? Did you forgive her for all her harsh ways with you? Have you forgiven yourself?

I sit and contemplate that. Yes, I do choose to forgive myself. I choose love. I choose love. I choose to let go of anger. I have done a lot of that. Oh, I am so grateful for all my letting go.

Inga, I know that you know what I am doing. Are you with me? Please be with me. Here I go again, pleading. Is there anything you need from me? "Forgiveness," she says. What did you do? "I died. And I know how painful that is and has been for you. You brought me into the world and then I left too early. I am not there for you. To play with you. To help you find a new hairdo or go shopping with you. I am not there to support you in your life. I am so sorry I left you so early."

Inga. Inga. I do forgive you. I forgive you thoroughly and completely. I forgive you and I love you. And I still want you to be with me. I feel you with me now as I write this. Thank you.

Receive Amore Armor

On my left foot below my big toe is a large callus which hurts when I touch it. I ask this part of my body to talk to me.

I wear a shield, a suit of armor; no, not amore. *How did love jump in here?*

I am very small and to the side of your foot. I don't get in your way. I don't even cause you much pain when you are dancing in those stiletto heels of yours. I stay pretty hidden; there's no need to pay attention to me. I burrow deeper and deeper inside. You don't really want to know what I cling to, do you now?

Yes, I am honest, pure truth—raw, vulnerable truth. You don't want to know. I can tell. You just want me to go away. Melt my armor, soften the callus, clean out the debris and get it over with, like a skillful dentist removing the decay in a rotted tooth.

I am rotten, holding what I hold; I cling to this truth, tuck it deep in your big toe pocket and scurry inside. No way am I telling you. You are too kind to everyone you meet out there. Are you kind to me? Would you be kind to me if you knew my secret? Just move on, ask the rest of your body to be truth sayers, but not me.

Haven't you ever withheld? Time and time again you withhold from people close to you. You claim emotional exhaustion or just are too busy. You claim to be unaware. Yes, you do have your routine. What seems neat, tidy, easy. Who said life is easy? Who said life is safe?

She died and you weren't able to save her from that. She did expect you to, you know. She wanted much more from you than she ever asked. And she asked a lot. But she didn't ask you to save her. She withheld that. I am withholding something else. You can beg all you want, but you won't ease it out of me. Your wrist will be worked to the bone and you won't find out what I know. I have got this over your head, not under your foot.

OK, I'll tell you. I am a reminder to you. You are not in control of your destiny nor anyone else's. You are helpless to save anyone, yourself included. So best you just let go and let be. Forget where you are dying to get to. Forget believing that you'll make money again and will be able to afford your own home. Forget trusting the process. Be a Buddhist; form is emptiness, emptiness is form. Be formless, forget forming anything. I am not to be overcome and melted into nonexistence. I am not real anyhow.

Step out into the emptiness and step out again. Live with all the anxiety that arises, but don't feed it. Love everything. Love me even when you don't get what you want from me. Love the space between us. Love the pain of my armor. Love the burning tears that want their escape. Love the ache in your wrist for writing so fast and stumbling along the way. Love the annoying ones. Love the mistakes. Love the missed opportunities. Love the flies who have mistaken you for their breakfast. Love the wasp even while you swat him away. Love the times when you couldn't find love in your heart. Only then will you know you are really alive. There really is no place to go. Feel the love in your heart, the love in your foot, and the love in your armor. Your armor is 'amore'.

Receive Caterpillar Crossing

My attention became captivated by the caterpillar. It was a very wide dirt mountain road for him to be crossing. I stopped to observe his progress and then couldn't leave him alone there, baking in the sunshine. I thought he would be too frightened if I picked him up by hand. So I encouraged him to crawl onto a familiar green leaf and I walked him across to the shade on the opposite bank.

Was I of service there or did I interfere with his plan at his pace? I think about Susan in her dying process and ask the same question. When Susan and I started to talk about her regrets, her relationship with her daughter and possible needs for forgiveness in her life, her physical condition worsened. We never did talk much after that. I did *metta* practice and *tonglen* at her bedside and in my own practice at home.

I told her after sitting with her one day how I appreciated being part of her journey and thanked her. She then became quite clear and even sat up a bit more and said, "You're welcome." Those were her very last words to me. It is a common politeness, yet seems quite profound. She gave me the message, you are and have been welcomed into my life, you are welcomed on this earth and welcomed into relationship with all beings, including caterpillars. You have done well to choose this lifetime and to choose the loving people and beings you encounter.

This life is a very short journey and there are many gifts to be had. Susan was a gift, the caterpillar was a gift, and I too am a gift to others. There is no time except the eternal now moment. I want to really be present for this one precious life of mine as I cross its many unpaved roadways.

Receive A Place to Rest

Find a place to rest in the middle of things. Rest is so important in grieving. Finding the place and taking the time to do that is another matter. I cannot always be grieving, nor writing this book, nor supporting the dying.

Today I went for a hike near Eldora at 8,500'—not too long a hike, just to the waterfall. At my favorite spot were three young men and their two black Labrador retrievers. Observing them was a refreshing break. The dogs explored all the rocky surroundings and then settled in a small pool where the water was not running so swiftly. Their owners encouraged them into the spot. On their own they would have continued to frantically follow scents and the natural excitement of being off leash. I felt myself settle down, cool down with them. It was so pleasurable to be in a place of rest in the midst of the strong currents rushing over the rocks.

Grief has created its own currents for me. It has been the master and the river and it has offered pools of solace. I have learned to recognize over the years the places of rest, sometimes taking advantage of them and sometimes not. What seems most important is to recognize them. My meditation practice has been a source of rest, as have short breaks in my day with a cup of tea or a longer break spent hiking or just stopping in place and taking a breath. It doesn't have to be complex. There is always a place to rest.

Receive the Buddhist Path

I met His Holiness Gayuno Cealo at the First Methodist Church during an evening lecture one of my friends invited me to. While walking down the aisle, many thoughts and emotions, my history with the Christian path, memories and feelings from my childhood in the Protestant tradition rose to the forefront.

Cealo entered, followed by a petite, beautiful woman, his translator. He began with a greeting and then a silent meditation.

Cealo is a Buddhist monk who was enlightened after having a dream about climbing a mountain. In 1990 he was a Japanese businessman who traveled often and one day found himself in the very town where the mountain from his dream was located. He decided to make the ascent and as he hiked up people started to bow at his feet. He asked why they were bowing and he was told that their guru, Sai Baba, had spoken of a holy man who would be coming soon dressed in a suit. Somewhere along the road Cealo woke up—became enlightened. He later took the robes of a simple monk and has been known as the one who heals and blesses with love. He now works as an advocate for the women and children of Burma and Cambodia. He brings much needed support through rice, vegetables, blankets, books, pencils, medical supplies and, most important, education for a self-reliant society.

Many people in the audience had questions for him. Someone asked, "What is the source of your healing?" He pointed up and spoke the only word I have heard him say in English: "God." I was deeply moved and felt I had found a teacher who brought together my beliefs, my trust in God and my deep faith in following the path of study and meditation practice of the Buddhist tradition.

My private interview with him the next day focused on Inga. I told him about her death and my deep sorrow, which seemed immobilizing. I wanted to know where she was and if she was OK. He replied, yes, Inga has died and she is fine. You don't need to worry about her. But you are alive and you need to focus on what you want and how you want to live this present life you have. I felt raw when I left him, as I cried nonstop in his presence. I also felt so much love from him. The veil of darkness was lifted in my time with him. I wanted to spend more time with him, be near him and become his student. This was not possible but it is an important piece in my spiritual questing.

There was also another teacher in the Buddhist tradition with whom I sought to study back in 1990. Dr. Ed Podvall was the founder of the Contemplative Psychotherapy masters program at Naropa University in Boulder, Colorado. He has written extensively, including articles on the Windhorse Project for recovery, which provides individually designed and comprehensive treatment in home environments for those with psychological disturbances. In *The Seduction of Madness* (1990), Dr. Podvoll describes the methods of compassionate care that involve a team of skilled therapists working closely with the client in his or her home. The network of these individual treatment households together with the households of the staff members then form an extended therapeutic community. This community initially began in Boulder in 1981 as Maitri Psychological Services.

I was so impressed with what I read that I enrolled at Naropa and was looking forward to studying with Dr. Podvoll. I arrived on campus in August 1990 and found out that Ed had just left for a 10-year retreat in France. I was disappointed and more than surprised by this.

Twelve years later I heard that Ed had returned to Boulder because he was diagnosed with colon cancer and did not have a good prognosis. I wanted to meet him, yet every opportunity seemed to present an obstacle for me.

I received word one day that Ed had died and that there would be a *sukhaviti* (a Buddhist funeral) held a few days later at the Shambhala Center. I definitely wanted to attend. Since meeting Cealo, I had been spending more time at the Shambhala Center meditating in the ornately decorated Tibetan-style shrine room. There was a long line of mourners waiting in the stairwell. Each person as they entered the shrine room continued to file by the open casket, in order to pay their respects and see death up close. I was in tears as I made my way into his presence. I felt comfortable and open-hearted and I had the thought, "I am a Buddhist." While I never heard Ed speak words directly I have learned great lessons through him and seeing his corpse awakened me to my own mortality and to my living fully with grief. The next year I took my refuge vows to formally become a Buddhist.

My labyrinth walks in the cathedrals and churches have brought me to my heart of hearts, to faith and trust in life again, to Buddhism and seeing clearly the joy in my life along with the reality of death and grief.

Receive Giving to Myself

The center of the labyrinth is the place to receive after releasing thoughts, feelings, people, events, grief and even myself. My relationship with receiving has developed over the course of my lifetime.

When my brother died in July 1969, I started to look at what I wanted to give to myself. At that time, I was in a relationship with Fred and I wanted to get married and have children. He was accepted to medical school in Brussels, Belgium later that summer. We talked about my desire to marry and start a family and he could not make a commitment. Medical school was his focus, not starting a family. I was devastated when I saw him off in late August. I returned home alone feeling lonely. I had lost my best friend and my vision for us. I cried and walked the beach for hours in the upcoming weeks, until one day I realized I had choice.

I could do whatever I wanted. What did I want to give myself? I had money saved and the ability to save even more. I decided to take a one-year sabbatical from my work as a systems engineer with IBM to travel in Europe. This would give me the opportunity to visit Fred in Belgium, go ski the Alps, and visit my father's family in Sweden and Finland, most of whom I had never met. Soon my friend Lynne decided she too wanted to spend the summer traveling in Europe. Therefore, we planned a route together to explore southern France, Spain, Greece and Hungary.

I had turned an important corner with a new beginning after the loss of what my dream had been. I said yes to my passion and everything fell into place easily, which is always a sign that I am on the right track. I tell myself to take note of this lesson, since I often forget it.

To know desire and specific wants is the precursor to receiving. Yes, we can simply receive what is offered in life and I love when that aligns with my values and wants. However, being more specific about my needs and wants does get me on track.

When Inga was diagnosed, I wanted her to be cured and our lives to return to normal. I also wanted her to find healing and wholeness in her life overall. Then there was a reoccurrence. I wanted a miracle. Maybe that is what I always wanted. A miracle. When options for medical treatments ran out, I continued to want that miracle. A miracle is based on faith and hope. In my view, a miracle is usually not based on medicine, but I now think there are also medical miracles. As time went on, my desire for a miracle turned to a desire for mercy. I wanted grace, mercy, and death without suffering. I do not know the exact moment when that shift occurred. It was in the last weeks of her life that I wanted the truth to be unveiled, the elephant in the room to be named. I wanted us all to talk about death. I wanted to talk about Inga's death, which was looming closely on the horizon. I remember saying "this is the beginning of the end."

Once the truth was spoken, I was able to receive. I knew I needed more support from my friends back in Colorado. The flowers, cards, phone calls and endless offers to help started flowing in. The pipeline of support had been stopped up. When I spoke the truth, it cleared the way for the flow of kindness, support and blessings, and I no longer felt so alone.

Receiving can be challenging for me. I have a very old belief about needing to take care of everyone else. To receive makes me feel a bit anxious because I am not so accustomed to being at that end of the cycle. I never modeled receiving with Inga when she was growing up. Or did I?

There was a time when Inga was in high school and she was having difficulty at school. She had little motivation, her grades were dropping to C's, she was bored and she just didn't want to go to school. Both her father and I encouraged her to explore the possibility of going off to a boarding school. She was most thorough in examining what she wanted for her education to blossom. She came up with two possible schools to attend. She and her dad visited the school she favored the most. Upon their return both were most excited to take steps to enroll her there for the next school year.

I started a downward spiral as they continued upward in their enthusiasm. I found all the difficulties with the plan. It was very expensive. It was very far from home, so we would only see her once during her semester away. It would be setting a pattern for her younger sisters that I felt very uncomfortable with.

As Inga became clearer about just what she wanted, I became more convinced that she was too young to leave home. The main reason I didn't want her to go was that I would miss her terribly. She drove me crazy with her demanding nature at times and yet I couldn't bear a separation. I didn't want her to be in the world without her family so soon. I convinced her to go talk with a psychiatrist whom I thought could help her look at other reasons she might be wanting to go away to school. After her session, I was most dismayed with the outcome. It did nothing to help her and made her dislike psychotherapy.

This process went on for several months when at last an acceptance letter came from the school. I was agonizing over what would happen when a week or so after the letter arrived, Inga announced to us her decision to stay at home and make the best of her public school education. She said she appreciated the process of knowing there was a choice and she chose what she thought best for her. Of course, I sighed with relief and there were many lessons. Inga had a choice and so did I.

Now looking back I feel grateful I had her close to me at home for those last two years and also that she had the opportunity to choose. She did not try to appease me and my anxiety, and I gave her the space to come to her own decision. I am proud of us both.

Receive Simplicity

I got it. Yes, indeed. I woke up this morning at daybreak, the shining sun on my face reminding me it was a beautiful day and I could have everything that I wanted. I got up with a smile, even though I did not recall any of my dreams from last night. What I would have liked was in the past. Today I get everything.

I go to the bathroom and the door is ajar. I get what I want. No one is in the bathroom. Now this is a treat, since I share this bathroom with two men I don't know very well and countless visitors at the Shambhala/Buddhist Community House where I currently live. I put my towel on the hook next to the shower and I am sleepy enough not to notice the mildewed grout as I turn on the water. Yep, I get what I want. It is simple. Hot water, soap and my scrubby unused and dry, all mine. Sure is good news.

I stopped hanging my towel in this communal bathroom because others seemed to think it was for their use. Yuck! How could they? So, I thought I would be kind and I put out a guest towel with a little sign "offered" and next to my towel another sign saying "not offered" in capital letters. The next morning I wandered into the bathroom to find my unoffered towel soaking wet. Damn, I didn't solve that problem with kindness. It might have been the guy who couldn't read, besides being color blind. So I decided to keep my towel in my room, like others have done before me. There is a solution, but it is sad when kindness doesn't rule.

I love brushing my teeth. My electric toothbrush provides a gum massage that reaches almost down to my toes. Relaxed am I, as I dress in just what I want, black stretch pants and a dash of color on top. No decisions to be made. I love my uniform of sorts, my Marpa House black and something. Jim, one of the directors here, said I looked like a priestess sitting on my *gomden* (my meditation cushion) this morning in the shrine room. Just what I want: a man noticed me, saw who I really am. Yes, I do get what I want.

Today I stop at the Brewing Market Coffee Shop for my decaf with a shot of real flavored stuff and my Australian Ginger Biscotti for my drive to writing group in Denver. The time is now. I get to write today and I am getting everything I want. Whoopee! Life is a lot more simple than I ever thought.

Receive Trust

While at my office today, I parked in a three-hour zone, so I was prompt walking back to my car to move it. The meter maids of Boulder seem to be very efficient workers and I didn't want yet another parking ticket. There near my car was a parking authority man ticketing someone just ahead of me. I sighed with relief knowing that I had gotten there on time and avoided a ticket. I decided to ask him about the exact rules of this neighborhood permit parking areas. I told him that I would be down at my office another couple of hours and questioned him as to where I could move my car. He asked which car was mine and then told me that this was his district and it was alright with him to just stay put, he would not ticket me. In fact he would not be back on this street today.

I at first thought that I would just move my car anyway. Actually I just didn't trust him. I had a plan and wanted to stick to it. I chatted with him for a few more minutes and then thanked him and walked back to my office.

So I did trust, didn't I? It wasn't about whether I thought he was honest, it was all about me. My hesitation to trust was an act of defiance, of wanting to be in control and stick with my self-imposed limitations—only three hours. I was a bit uncomfortable but managed to stay in that trusting place. I am not shutting down but staying open to possibilities, not staying fixated on the old rules when the new truth presents itself.

Inga's death shattered the world as I believed it could be. In some unconscious way I am continuing to attempt to put the world back the way it was before Inga died. But writing this book goes against my plan. Just like her death went counter to my plan. I can no longer limit myself just so I can feel safe.

To trust what the man said seems like such a simple act, yet it required me to be open to the reality of the world as it was. I enjoyed my brisk walk in the sunshine and talking to the man was pleasurable. I did not shut the world out; I openly welcomed it all. The pleasant surprise was receiving the gift of two hours in my current parking place. Just so simple. The man was a good person offering his generosity.

Receive the Labyrinth Within

The long-awaited pilgrimage to Chartres Cathedral's labyrinth, my 60th birthday celebration, is really happening. My home base for a week is a small, fourth floor studio apartment in a residential district near the Eiffel Tower in Paris. I have no schedule, tours or other people with me to dictate my daily activities. I walk my finger labyrinth each morning, reflecting on what has brought me to this day and asking for guidance. I will visit Chartres at some point but not today—maybe tomorrow. Inga's mantra now is mine also.

On my fourth day in Paris I decide this is the day to fulfill my entire trip's purpose. I negotiate the maze of the central train station, purchase my ticket and find the departing track rather easily. I may even look like a confident local since someone stopped me to ask directions. It has been many years since I have felt the familiar jolts and sounds of travel by rail. When I was a young girl, my mother and I would take the train from Bridgeport, Connecticut into New York City several times a year. The anticipation of the ride and destination send bubbles of excitement up my spine. Then I notice nearby a mother and what seems to be her daughter opposite me. They look so natural, so normal. I want to speak to them. The little girl is reading her book and her eyes look up to her mother with questions or comments. I want to tell them how fortunate they are to be with each other. I feel a twinge of jealousy. Yes, I could be on this train with Jill or Erika, but I could never be here with Inga. I want to cry and I hold back the burning tears. Thoughts of my family travels mingle with the passing scenery. The countryside is lush farmland, so alive, yet tranquil. It seeps into my bones. I do not want to disembark when the conductor awakens me from my reverie with "Chartres, Chartres."

Walking to the cathedral, I hesitate anxious about reaching my destination. As if taking the first bite of a sumptuous dessert, I want to savor this moment.

All I can whisper silently is "Wow!" like a child in awe as I step into the sanctuary. This is magnificent. I feel the grandeur of the divine present here as if I were on a mountain peak with an expansive view of nature. Then I see the labyrinth covered with many small wooden chairs. My heart sinks into my belly. The labyrinth is not accessible. I cannot walk it. Friends forewarned me about this but I did not pay much attention. The labyrinth is not accessible every day for walking since church services and other events require extra seating. I am very disappointed. I walk into a small gift shop to inquire about the labyrinth schedule for walking. They tell me to come back tomorrow, when it will be open. The woman suggests I get a room for the night and invites me to the organ recital here in the cathedral this evening. In fact, she says I am fortunate since it is a special event. So here it is. Things do change. The new plan seems great to me. I have my toothbrush in my handbag and I will just walk over to the hotel a few blocks away and inquire about a room.

The setting sun brings a chill to the air and I wrap my thin red cotton shawl over my arms as I search for a suitable place for dinner. I read a menu posted in a cute little place and then seat myself at a small table next to a large family. I hate eating alone, but I hear English spoken at the table nearby and feel more at ease. Eventually I say hello to them. They are six, two parents and four children ranging in age from seven to sixteen. Their conversation appears animated and lively. No loud bantering or conflict. How nice. They interact respectfully, yet warmly. I wonder though if they have fun together. If they roughhouse or laugh hilariously over silly things too. They are traveling for six weeks in Europe. What an opportunity. I wish our family could have taken an extensive summer vacation together before it was too late. Each of my daughters has gone to Europe with their grandmother, but I felt left out. I wanted to show them myself where I had been, share the adventure together with them as this family was doing. They were not going to the concert later, although they thanked me for letting them know about it.

Bach, the sounds of earth and fire fill this expansive cathedral. I am embraced by the music, lulled into a comfort of just being here. The warmth of the bodies on either side of me balances my feelings of aloneness and desire for togetherness. What a special day this has been, without plans. It could not have been any better. I make my way to my hotel with the stream of other concert attendees under a star-filled sky, walking briskly, chilled by the fresh night air.

I awake excited. Today is it. This is the day I walk the famous Chartres labyrinth. I am here. The labyrinth was built in 1205 AD, but has the original stones, which date to even earlier than that. A fire destroyed the cathedral twice, but it was rebuilt both times. People have been walking this very same pathway for more than 700 years. I am awestruck at the thought of this. I wonder what will happen, what miracle might occur, what the culmination of my pilgrimage will be. There I go, moving ahead of myself. Therefore, I come back to my breath and my moving feet, taking me closer to this sacred site.

I bathe in the colored, sunlit rays coming through one of the many stained glass windows. I meditate and reflect on what has brought me to this day. I ask for healing in my grief. I think about Inga and what she would say if she were with me now. I quiet my mind and thoughts and walk slowly, barefooted, to the labyrinth's entrance.

I clasp my hands in front of me and take my first step in. Thoughts, feelings of excitement arise and I release them. The stones are very cold and smooth. My breathing starts to take on the rhythm of my pace. I feel so grateful to be here. Ahead of me is a group of young women, maybe in their twenties. They walk with a very distinct style. They take two steps forward and one shorter step backward, which creates a very graceful dance. I slow my pace even more and my attention keeps being drawn to one or another of these women as we pass by each other in the many curves of the pathway. As they begin to enter the center, they start a very soft chant in German. It gets louder as more of them enter the center. At first I am annoyed to have the silence broken, but the melodic voices call out to me in what I would imagine is a "remembrance of women," an honoring of the Virgin Mary, of all women—their journeys, their pain and their joys of womanhood. I let all this go and do look forward to joining them in the center where they all are now. Within a few steps, a man in a suit, looking very distraught, walks straight through the labyrinth to tell them to hush. I do not actually hear what he says, but I understand. And the result is silence. Quieting the feminine voice in this holy of holy places. The masculine rules in this centuries-old gothic cathedral.

I am stunned; I try to ignore what happened and I enter the center as the young women begin to leave respectfully, quietly with their rocking determined gaits, which seem to say, "We know the truth, we walk the truth, we dance the truth, and we cannot be silenced."

I am in the rose center of the labyrinth in my own heart of hearts and I know nothing. I hear nothing. There are no radiant lights, no feelings of great love. Just a sense of having done it and a feeling of disappointment. I am alone for a short time when a young man arrives, dressed in a dark suit, white shirt and tie with a knapsack on his back. He is wearing dark, thin-rimmed sunglasses, and looks almost sinister to me. I imagine him to be a spy or something. What am I thinking here in the sacred center of the lab-yrinth of Chartres Cathedral? This is so bizarre. I want to pinch myself to be sure I am not dreaming. Then the man kneels down and meticulously takes off and opens his knapsack. I think maybe he is getting a drink of water. No. He takes out a small piggy bank, one of those highly glazed, dime store varieties with a rubber seal on the bottom so you can take the money out without breaking the bank. He reaches in, places a book and a few other objects down, and sits facing them. He has made an altar of his belongings. What am I receiving here? Shall I stay or leave? I am baffled. I am also annoyed with him. How dare he interrupt my sacred pilgrimage? This is my receiving gift of my labyrinth walk? I am puzzled. So I just choose to return, to leave, to make my walk back out. I cannot shake the disturbing feelings I am having.

What does this mean? What I found was not what I expected. I wanted a mountain top experience. I did not get what I thought I wanted. I believe this visit did have a very profound message. It showed me the power of my feminine voice, which cannot be quieted. There is a need for the outer reminders to help me to remember my inner journey, but I do not need to worship them, make them more important than they really are.

I have a labyrinth within me. When I walk the outer labyrinth, I am anchoring an experience into my body memory to help me to remember where I have traveled, where I have touched the pain of my grief, where I have denied the reality of Inga's death and my own death, where I am compassionate with others, where I trust the journey and where doubts creep in. This distance is not tracked by physical miles, but the spiritual and emotional miles of life. I have an inner support system to help me to negotiate the challenges of everyday life. I have inner guidance to set my course with reflection, releasing, opening to receive what is now available and returning anew to the reality of life. I do have an inner compass. It is the labyrinth within me.

Return

After reflection on Inga's final days and my grieving process, and the release of many memories and emotions, I received healing, many lessons, a sense of renewed trust in myself, forgiveness and peace. Now it is time to turn around and walk the same path to return and reconnect with the world. There is a wide range of experiences on my labyrinth walks. Sometimes, I returned feeling like a very different person. Other times I felt as though nothing had really changed.

The labyrinth walk offered a container for my grief, a time when I did not have to grieve or think about her. It gave me respite before returning to face life without Inga's physical presence.

I remind myself how grief works itself through me as I continue each day and commit to my path. Sometimes I would want to stay in the center, stay in the comfort of feeling Inga's presence and go nowhere. How can I be of some help to others because of what I have gone through? I want to make a difference in this world. I return in order to be of service, to help others. I return in order to live my life fully, not knowing when I too shall die. I return in order to enjoy nature, my family, friends and opportunities that may come to me. I return to prepare for my own death. I return to love more and worry less. I return to study and practice the dharma. I return to dance Argentine tango. I return to enjoy this one precious life.

Join me in returning, walking, dancing, jumping, reconnecting into the world. What gifts do you discover as you return?

Return to Ask for Changes

I have been back working at QuaLife Wellness Community for nearly five months after my sabbatical following Inga's death. The staff, especially the executive director Naomi Sullivan, has been so supportive. I requested copies of all of Inga's medical records because I doubted the adequacy of the pain management provided to her at the hospital. Naomi was a former nurse and hospital administrator. She said she would be happy to review Inga's medical records to give me her impression about what had happened. As a result of her review, I wrote the following letter to the CEO of the hospital where Inga spent her final days.

June 27, 2001
Dear Sir,

I am taking this opportunity to write to you for two purposes. My 30-year-old daughter, Inga Van Nynatten, died on September 2, 2000 at Christopher House Hospice after a long battle with breast cancer. She was admitted to your hospital on August 25, 2000. My first reason is my need in my own grieving process to share information and take some action, which I hope will help others. Second, it is important for me to communicate my thoughts and feelings around the care that my daughter received while hospitalized. I would like to offer insight and education for personnel who were involved in her care. Future families should not have to face the frustration and suffering in the pain management and alleviation of pain of their dying loved ones if there can be learning from Inga's situation. Other mothers, daughters, fathers, sisters, perhaps, will not have to remember, as I do, the needless discomfort she experienced prior to admission to a hospice.

As I have reviewed Inga's chart with medical assistance, it is my understanding and observation that hospital personnel had the order and opportunity to alleviate Inga's pain more completely. It is clear in the chart that from admission, and over the course of her hospitalization, her doses of medication were increased dramatically. What is also apparent is that in the last 10–16 hours of her hospital stay, the order to receive full pain relief care was in her chart, yet it was not adequately administered to relieve pain and agitation. We, her entire family, were begging for more relief for her, with the full understanding that the medication could cease her respirations. We were all informed and gave consent for more medication, including her medical power of attorney. We fully understood what the outcome could be. Yet, there was hesitation on the part of the staff to fully medicate her.

During Inga's other hospitalizations, she received wonderful care. It is my belief that your staff are very effective at managing surgical pain and surgical situations. These patients need to be able to turn, cough, deep breathe, etc. for their well-being. This is not the case in an end-of-life situation. Much emphasis is now being placed on pain management in end-of-life situations, and rightly so. To that end, I would like a commitment from you to make Inga's situation a learning opportunity for your staff. I have reviewed the chart and documentation and would like to assist in furthering staff education in the area of pain management for the end-of-life. In any scenario, I need feedback on what action steps you are taking.

One of the things that Dr. F, her oncologist, committed to us was that her pain would be managed, that she would not suffer. The process fell short for Inga, me and my family. Through some corrective educational steps, it can improve for the next patient.

I will expect to hear of your action plan by August 1, 2001. To discuss this in more detail, feel free to contact me at 303-999-9999.

Thank you in advance for your commitment to improving patient care.

Sincerely,
Carole Lindroos

The president of the hospital wrote me his apologies for the shortcomings in Inga's care and took responsibility to take positive steps for the future. There would be educational events in the months to come. One of the staff members would be attending a national conference on palliative care. He assured me the hospital would be making the necessary changes. I did consult a lawyer to help me decide if I wanted to file a lawsuit, which I chose not to do. I felt as if my speaking out made a difference.

Return to My Professional Work

I have had an intense week. Inga has been with me as I prepared and then presented at the Colorado Hospice Organization's Conference on Friday, followed by being a facilitator at the Healing Life/Healing Death Weekend sponsored by QuaLife.

About forty people attended the annual CHO conference session I facilitated, "River Ride to Renewal," a self-care offering for hospice healthcare professionals. As expected many at the conference chose to leave the conference early instead of coming to my closing session. Leaving early is of course a way to take care of oneself by beating the commuting traffic. I have learned over the years as a healthcare provider the importance of self-care in order to best care for others.

My intention was to provide learning through doing ritual, reflection, releasing, a relaxing river ride visualization, remembrances, re-commitment and take-home rock reminders. Where did all those "R's" come from? The creative juices were flowing for me, as this presentation seemed to unfold magically over the weeks I was preparing. I would get ideas as I drove to work or was taking a walk. I brought flowers and some special things to create a shrine and sacred space to be the central focus in the room. Most importantly, Inga was there with me through it all.

I used a suitcase on wheels to haul all my stuff, from the shrine makings to QuaLife brochures, and then of course there were all those rocks. I took many 7–8" diameter river rocks. These could have been like many that are in the Boulder Creek bed beneath the bench placed in Inga's memory near Eben G. Fine Park in Boulder. The suitcase itself carries a special story.

During one of my many trips over the years of Inga's cancer treatments, the zipper on my suitcase broke. I told her that I wanted to go out and buy a new one. She responded with, "Mom, why buy a new one when that one should have a warranty?" I had used it for more than five years and could not imagine it to be still under any kind of warranty. However, she insisted and preceded to wheel my old suitcase straight into J.C. Penny's. She was determined to get mine replaced with a brand new one. I was too embarrassed to go with her, so I scurried off to shop for something else and left her on her own, expecting her to return with my original suitcase. However, that was not the case. In a short while, with a huge grin on her face, she was wheeling over to me a brand new suitcase. She was a determined young woman.

Later she painted my initials and a big heart on the luggage tag with red nail polish so that I could easily identify my black bag from among the many others on the airport luggage racks. I have since bought a new suitcase, but still use the identification tag she painted. In this way, Inga always travels with me.

Back to the conference. Woven into my presentation were stories of my experiences with death and dying. The rocks, both large and small, remind me of Inga. Throughout Inga's dying process, I held a white rock that my friend Laura had sent me from Findhorn, Scotland. In the midst of so much letting go, I found great comfort in holding on to that rock. There were close to a hundred rocks on the shrine along with flowers, candles, and a photo of Inga. And then there was the chocolate, Inga's favorite food. I found pleasure in welcoming people with, "Those who sit in the front row get chocolate." These brightly red-wrapped dark chocolates have sweet messages written inside, such as, "Life is better with chocolate" and "Sweet dreams." The presentation closed with everyone gathered in a circle around the shrine where we remembered those who had died by saying their names aloud. Then people stepped forward to choose a rock to take home as both a memento of the day and a reminder of their self-care.

Then on Saturday and Sunday, I was the director for the QuaLife Wellness Community's *Healing Life/Healing Death* weekend. There were nineteen people registered to come. I was delighted that we had a full house for a change and that I did not have to be recruiting for participation at the last minute. I love lots of folks attending whatever I am offering. There were a few families and four men attending (a rare occurrence), along with many women of varying ages.

My colleagues and I had developed this weekend in 1996 in response to cancer patients who were coming to support groups at QuaLife. Some of them would come up to me after the group was over to talk about their fears about dying. They did not want to "bring the group down" so were hesitant about speaking up. Therefore, the staff designed a weekend program whose objective was to transform fears of death into living more fully and with more meaning. We even did a pre-, post-test that measures death anxiety, and over the years see the results that demonstrate very much a consistent lowering of death anxiety.

When Inga became ill and my fears of her dying of cancer were so overwhelming, I stopped staffing these weekends. When she died, I never thought that I would even return to work at QuaLife with people with cancer and certainly never imagined that I would work with people who were dying. Yet that is exactly what I did and feel called to do.

My teacher Frank Ostaseski, with whom I did a one-year training program in End-of-Life Counseling at the Zen Hospice of San Francisco, told the following story.

> *There was a man who was training another worker to install those really huge poles that support power lines. He told them ... there is one very important thing I want you all to remember. If the pole starts to get away from you, do NOT run away.* ***Always run towards the pole.***

This is just so profound. Death terrified me. Yet when I moved towards it, then it didn't have the same effect on me. Through Inga's death there was the opportunity to actually heal my greatest fear. We only get to die once, yet most of us don't prepare for it. We are born into this life once and for most of us we die once. I say for most of us, since there are those who have had near-death experiences and those who have been pronounced clinically dead and have come back.

When I was in my twenties, my brother Carl, who was three years older than I, was diagnosed with Hodgkin's disease, a form of cancer. My family didn't communicate about his illness, but I did know that it was very serious and that when he got married shortly after he was diagnosed he didn't have long to live. Two years later, my mother called to tell me that Carl was in the hospital and I should pay him a visit. So I bought a package of strawberries, which my brother loved, and went to the hospital. He looked terrible—pale and thin, and barely smiled at me or the strawberries. The next day he died. I had not been prepared at all.

I felt like I died. I couldn't sleep and would wake up in the middle of the night. I couldn't sit or lie still. There was something unknown that I needed. So I would drive the Connecticut Turnpike and stop where there were people, at truck stops. There I would sit and drink coffee and eat donuts. I was drawn to be near others. There really wasn't anyone I could talk to, but just being near those strangers seemed to help. I did this for three nights and then I was so exhausted I finally fell asleep and had the following dream.

> *I am floating at the ceiling and look down to see myself in a casket. I am at my own funeral. Everyone is crying. I yell down, don't cry. I feel wonderful. I am OK.*

When I woke up, I was really alive again. I knew that my brother was OK and while I was sad and grieving, I knew that things would work out. I had a life to live and had found some hope. My dream life had taken me "towards the pole," into my own death, and I rediscovered life again.

Return to Heart Land

My mind has always wrestled with the deeper questions of life, looked for the logic, wanted to dissect the trivia, categorized thoughts, made lists, compartmentalized and searched for understanding. I believed there must be a reason, a plan, and a way to the truth. I touch into mindfulness on my journey now by remembering, sorting, storytelling, seeing the vast horizon of my past, dancing, dreaming and journaling.

In the landscape of my early mind experiences there were heavy burdens, stuck places, stagnant thoughts, darkness, foreign tongues wagging, dirty dishes, loud sounds and unresolved grief. My grandmother was 70 years old when I was born and she became my main caregiver. My family lived in her house, the home of my mother's childhood and the home where death resided. All four of my mother's siblings died before I was four years old, as did my mother's father. The thick mire of grief lived in that house, unexpressed feelings coating the walls and ceilings, enveloping and chilling me as a child. The antique hope chest where linens and lingerie were to be gathered for the bride became the receptacle for all the unspoken words and tears. "Be strong" was the approved formula for being loved. Silence was the rule of understanding. Staying too busy to feel was treasured.

When I was seven years old, I was made to take piano lessons. My short, little fingers barely spanned the glimmering, white keys as I played endless scales. It sounded terrible to me, though the adults told me I would get better with practice, practice, practice. Practice makes perfect and perfection was what they all wanted. But what did I want? They never asked. I wanted to dance, to move, to wear those pink ballet slippers with satin ribbons tied up around my ankles. I would observe the dancers from a distance on my way to my piano lesson. Someday, I thought. I pleaded with my mother. She said we couldn't afford both piano and dance lessons. And I said, then please just let me dance.

Finally she gave in and I danced. Ah. Ooh. The music was beautiful, the shoes a delight. My awkward, plump body awakened to its first glimpse of something wonderful inside me. What was that feeling?

Barbara Hull was my piano teacher. She also became my dance teacher and was my idol. I loved her mother, who ran the school of the arts, and her husband was the handsomest man I had ever seen up close. Kindness and a quiet beauty emanated from her. The perfect picture did crumble though, slowly at first, and then with a final crash when Barbara died of leukemia, three years later. Our time together too short. What did she really teach me? To love to dance, to love to be in my body at one with the music, to improvise and allow the music to move through my heart and soul. She showed me more of that secret place inside me. Loving was possible with someone who didn't have to love me and who spoke into my secret place. Softness, kindness, creativity, compassion, openness, and opportunities are abundant. My family did not have the tuition for all the creative dance pursuits I longed for. I remember that Barbara invited me to attend a summer dance camp at no charge. How generous she was. Knowing and being cared for by her changed my life. She loved to watch me dance, encouraged my being, not just performing. Was I the daughter she was never able to have?

When I was sixteen years old, I went for advice to my ballet master at the time, Jerry Jacqwith. There were some decisions for me to make. Did I want to be a professional dancer? What were my realistic chances? I am still grateful for his kind and clear words. "Carol, you will always dance. Go get a college education, now is the time to do that. And dance in all your free time." So I went off to college, took a modern dance class and performed with the modern dance club. When I graduated, I tried out for and was accepted in a professional troupe but decided to focus instead on my new job in the "mind industry" of an aircraft manufacturing firm where I was a novice programmer.

Years later, at age 36, with dancing long absent in my life, I was diagnosed with breast cancer. My three daughters were ages eight, five and four. My days were hectic. What were my heart yearnings then and the thoughts that went with them? I don't know. No journals, no dancing. My mind ruled then and a keen, sharp, organized, mind it was to manage the lives of three children in elementary school with gymnastics, swimming, baton twirling, birthday parties and runny noses. I was a walking computer of schedules, three meals a day shopping lists, and two part-time jobs as a systems engineer and an administrative assistant at my husband's office. My mother and in-laws lived close by, which was a help, but also a burden. My body was constantly constricted and tense, with no dance, no play, no freedom, no time for me. No space, no pink ballet slippers, no notice of my heart's longings.

It wasn't until a year after I had breast cancer that I slowed down enough to feel anything at all. It was then that my heart came alive, not only with the sadness of the loss of my breast, but with all the losses of my life and the lives of my family. I had returned home to my heart, the secret place in me.

Heart place exploration. Darkness, lightness. My body knows my heart better than my mind. The arterial railroad to my heart knows many stopping places and obstacles. Friends have come on board. Mentors and many teachers, oftentimes disguised, presented positive detours. Yet I eventually show up in my heart—my big, juicy, sweet, heart of all hearts.

What resides there deep in destination heart land?

Hardened hearts have high risks. Lifestyles based on the mind have a high risk for a heavy heart. When frozen in terror and panic, I did know one thing. To stay still means death. Movement is life, and even the very smallest lifting of my hand to journal the stirrings in my heart is movement. And writing is life giving. No matter how stunned, shocked, or blown over or away I am, I do have choice. A choice to put pen to paper and write something, a choice to lift my hand to wipe away my tears, a choice to stand up and leave the room. Choices are abundant. I can stroll the streets of my neighborhood, taking in the sounds of the night air. I can go into my heart to feel what is there. I can even turn on music and allow it to shape my experience of movement. And I can dance. Dance the sorrow, dance the stuckness, dance the anger, dance the grief in my heart, dance the prayer, dance the smiles. I can dance my heart's vision. I dance, feeling my feet touching the soft carpet, dance the laughter of children, dance the boredom, the jealousy, the panic, the joy and the inspiration.

Discovering movement was possible after years of not moving. My life's journey traces my movement from head to heart and back to mind, armed with a fuller understanding.

Return to the Real Estate

On May 1, 2005 my home of fourteen years was sold. There have been abundant changes and many to come. I did trust the process of letting go of 1667 Mapleton Avenue and here is the story.

I was sitting at my computer looking out over my front yard, which is located at 17th Street and Mapleton Avenue in downtown Boulder, when a man walked by. This is rather unusual since it is a very private area and I had a flash thought that he would buy my house. Naturally, I immediately doubted this. My house wasn't even on the market; I simply was toying with the idea of selling, since a change of lifestyle might offer me freedom to write more and living simply seemed quite appealing. A few months ago, I completed a kitchen remodel that I was pleased with along with stripping the carpets off my oak floors and having them refinished. So I was really pleased with my home, and at the same time, had a very strong inclination to sell and create a change in lifestyle.

I went outside and introduced myself to the man and he told me that he was buying the townhouse on the corner. I quickly responded with, "That's too bad because my house is so much nicer." He asked me what mine was like and I eventually invited him in to take a look. He loved my kitchen and the whole place and asked me my asking price. I told him a figure which was my ideal price and he said that sounded reasonable. He said he did want to buy it if I indeed wanted to sell it. I was stunned and he understood. He said there was no rush and suggested that I sleep on it and call his realtor if I wanted to proceed. I knew even in my daze of disbelief that I would sell the house and felt much excitement at the prospect of moving on.

During the month of May after signing the final papers, I continued to clear out fourteen years of house stuff. When I moved to Boulder in 1990, I had done a similar process of sorting and giving away my furniture, clothing, knickknacks, books and collections. So I was not a novice at this and yet I was amazed at how much I had accumulated since my move to Boulder. I invited friends to help me, which absolutely kept me sane. I had impulses to just put everything in black trash bags and put it out for the Veterans Administration to pick up. And while I did give away many bags, my friends helped me to choose things to keep. I even wanted to rid myself of all my journals and a friend helped me to see that I was not ready to do that yet.

I moved into a Buddhist/Shambhala Community house in Boulder near Chautauqua Park and the university. It was originally a fraternity house and there was a corner room that did seem to call out to me. It was very small, only 8' by 10' but I found a way to furnish it that made it feel a bit more spacious and welcoming. The rent was very reasonable and the community meditation practice was most appealing. So I made a commitment for a retreat in the world for one year. My goal was to write the book, pursue my Buddhist studies and practice daily. Also immediately upon moving in I received an offer to join the staff of a small local hospice founded by Peggy Quinn that provided traditional and complementary services to the dying and their families. Because the hospice was just starting up, my work commitment would not be more than six hours per week.

What seemed unreal became my real "estate;" my body home is with me wherever I go.

Return to Death

In the first weeks of living at Marpa House I had a dream that I titled "Giant Raving Horse Emerges out of the Snow Bank and Threatens Me, But I am not Scared" The following is the dream in its entirety.

I am talking with Mark, who lives here at Marpa House about a black horse in the field. He tells me that he had a special relationship with that one when he first moved here to Marpa House. Now I am attracted to the very same horse. I tell Mark that I am not particularly fond of horses but I did really like that one. Then another, taller horse dives into a snow bank. Out then comes a brown huge horse that is four times larger than the first one with a head like a lion and a snarl that was scaring everyone but me. I was very calm. There was a square two foot high box or feeding trough on the ground between us and I simply held my ground while he snarled at me and made a small attempt to charge me. I was asked what I was thinking at the time when he was threatening me. "I may die right here right now and I have lived a good life."

While this dream has many layers of interpretation, the coming back to my awake life informs me of my relationship with death.

Death is not the enemy. I remember my teacher Frank Ostaseski saying this during my training in early 2003. I traveled to San Francisco nine times that year to participate in an End-of-Life Counselor Training program at the Zen Hospice. I didn't believe Frank when he first said those words. In fact I found those words offensive. My reference point was Inga's death and death was the enemy for her and for me too at that time. There was such a battle and there had to be blame and something that was "bad" in all this. There has been much softening for me around this. I feel the familiar burning of tears that arise. Isn't it really a universal truth? Birth happens and death happens. My daughter died and many daughters die. I have met many mothers who have lost daughters and sons. It is no longer only about my pain, my grief, my loss, my suffering. There are many parents who suffer the death of their children and I am one of them, but not the only one. My heart is more open and available to other people's suffering because of Inga's death. Death is not the enemy. Death simply happens due to the fact that life happens.

Return to Trusting Life

Today is Inga's birthday. Thirty-five years ago I gave birth to her at just this time of day, 10:15 AM. It was a beautiful sunny and bright morning in Brussels, which was very unusual. The weather was hot, just like Inga always liked. The labor room where I had been for about ten hours was where she first saw daylight surrounded by many people. They brought in stirrups so I could "pousser" (push). What an incredible feeling to have my body moving this mass of life through my birth canal. When her head came through the rest was so simple and natural. My legs shook, vibrated with all the excess energy stored that also needed to find a way to move through me. They put her on my chest for too short a time before they whisked her off to get cleaned up and to tend to the placenta delivery.

Thirty-five years pass so quickly, leaving a potpourri of memories. especially through all the photos I sit with now in my room.

I have created a very large shrine, including a photo wall of Inga. I am listening to violin music and then inquire of my Tarot cards for guidance today. Trust, the knight of water was my random selection. Tears just exploded as I read the documentary of it by Osho. "Don't waste your life for that which is going to be taken away. Trust life. If you trust, only then can you put your mind aside. And with trust something immense opens up. Then this life is no longer ordinary life, it becomes full of God, over-flowing. Now is the moment to be a bungee jumper without the cord! And it is this quality of absolute trust, with no reservations or secret safety nets that the knight of water demands from us."

I have a photo of Inga as a toddler, naked, holding her father's finger as they walk into the Delaware River. I call that photo "Trusting." Yes, Inga, today I choose to trust and step courageously into the unknown.

Return to Writing

I enroll in a class with Kirsten Wilson, "Letting the Body Speak," a writing and monologue performance class. There are eight of us in this class and we do movement exercises followed by seven-minute, spontaneous writing exercises and then read them aloud to one another. Sometimes I am over-whelmed and I begin to enjoy letting words flow onto paper with no hesitation. Every week we have homework assignments. Over the next ten weeks, I write a lot, most often with Inga as my focus. Here are some of the short pieces.

- Please ask me. Please do ask me how, why, when, where she died. She did die, you know. No one asks anymore. And I always say it so matter-of-factly. I have three daughters: my youngest, Erika, lives here in Louisville; Jill, my middle child, lives in Atlanta; and Inga, my eldest, died. She was 30 years old and she died of breast cancer. Period. The end. It is usually the end of the conversation. Well, some people say they are very sorry and ask a bit more, but mostly … "Auck, Auck, Auck", a bird screeches in the tree as I write this. Inga used to actually make that sound. What bird is that? Is it her? Where is Inga now? Off the bird flies. And off she flew. But where to? Where is Inga? How can I be alive when she is not? It just isn't the right way. It just isn't right that I should live and she should die. And she did. And I did.

- Writing is my best friend—dependable, honest, direct, humorous. She is my helper. She doesn't know where she is going when she grabs a colorful pen and draws the pictures of her mind and heart on paper. She always knows what she is feeling when I barely know the list of my daily chores. Never without her notebook, I may even get through dinners seated alone.

Writing is my grief ointment, soothing the scars of Inga's death. It carries me through a process I have denied and avoided. Writing is creation in the moment. Instant birthing. Oh, what shall I write next? It is always a surprise and even tantalizing. Even when I judge my written thoughts, it takes only an instant to recoup my dedicated commitment to be mindful and kind to myself and others.

Writing is a path to discovering who I have become day-by-day as the reality of life and my choices mold me. Who is this person holding this pen scrawling aimlessly until yet another flow of ideas spills onto these milk-white pages? Nothing to tidy up. There is always another page and another notebook of beginnings. This writing life is endless. Writing will never die. I just hope some of these notebooks will be bound into a book, so my great-great-great-grandchildren might know me.

My writing began when as a child I had a little diary with a key to safeguard my thoughts and feelings. I could write anything I wanted and no one would know. Then there were the beautiful journals given to me by friends and the one that I started as a summary of my life. It has just a couple of pages per year, my life at a glance.

Writing is my resting place. I can nestle down with my story and let it be. Writing is my best conversation with myself. When I write I feel safe and connected with myself. Writing is my small, still voice buried under my chore lists. Writing calls me out of my complacent self. Writing also shows me my darkest side, my self-judgment, my less than nice traits and jealousies. Writing is my humorous self taking care of all the rest of me.

- What I don't want to talk about is what I really want to talk about. It's Inga who brings tears and that familiar choking feeling in my throat. How can I write with all the tears and needing to blow my nose every minute? There, that has settled down a bit. I have settled down a bit. Perhaps the seven minutes can start now.

Inga asked me to come down to Houston for a consultation visit and a possible treatment at M.D. Anderson Medical Center. She calls a few days before I was to meet her there with a question, or rather a request. "Mom, I know you may not want to do this but I really want you to." She proceeds to tell me that she wants me to run the Race for the Cure with her in Houston the following Saturday. She needs me to get her through that race. I am stunned, since I haven't run in twenty years and I honestly don't know that I can get myself through it, nor get her through it. Inga just laughs. Mom, you are healthy and it won't be any fast pace or anything—after all, I am pretty slowed down with all this radiation. So I just naturally say yes of course I will do it. After I hang up, I reflect on what just happened. She had a need. She needed me, her mother, in a very direct way. She needed to know that she could ask me for support and that I would say yes. She needed to experience my getting her through something. No, not just the race, but the cure. She wanted to be cured and she was asking me to guide her through. I did jog with her to the finish line that Saturday morning, but the cure never happened.

- Death is the cure. Not what I expected, or really could accept. We all want to live forever. We all want to have all our children at our death beds. Inga won't be at my bedside or maybe she really will, just not in the form I thought. Yes, she will potentially guide me to the other side. Nice thought, Carole, but it just doesn't cut it. Put the pieces into some fine order then I will feel better about my life—living it fully and Inga being dead. She is dead—dead, dead, dead. I need to keep saying it, writing it. No flesh and bones, no spirit. I don't feel her presence comfort me. She's simply gone and I am left with this constant ache—this abominable ache in my throat—in my body, in my fingers, in my buttocks, a pain in my own ass, I am. How am I a pain in my own ass? What else do I feel? Flat, numb, shocked, blank, tense—NO, NO, NO—it's not true.

Five years, it's five years and it's not true. How can I not see her for five years? How can I not have her here? Where are you, Inga? Where are you? Where are—where, where, where are you? Where am I? Am I? Who am I now that you have died? No death is not the cure.

- The car is green, a box on wheels with the RAV4 symbol on the rear tire. There are lots of them around driving the streets nearby and far away, all across the country. It's a popular car; a friend wanted to buy one as her next car. Sitting having lunch, enjoying the sunshine on my back, with chili in the bowl in front of me. No place to go, just be with the fresh air, warmth on my back, solid ground beneath my feet. It is all solid; earth supports these buildings and chairs. Like the chair I sit on. The one you sit on. Then the green RAV4 drives by—it doesn't have a purpose or any intention in its path—passes down the street. Maybe it could have driven down 11th Street instead of 12th Street. It is all random, or maybe not. Because in this moment sitting in the sunshine feeling the spaciousness of the world, that green RAV4 drives down the street where I live and the person driving it is not Inga. Where are you, Inga? Where are you, Inga?

I had just talked with Kathy about Inga and my middle granddaughter Emmy, who will be four years old tomorrow. In the Buddhist view, 49 days after death Inga could have reincarnated. Emmy, is that you? Inga, is that you in Emmy's body? Where are you, Inga? Where are you?

- The marathon began one day before New Year's Eve. Inspired by Inga, I accepted the challenge to run that race. Raise money for the Leukemia Society and run again after a hiatus of many years. I never enjoyed running, always said I would rather walk for twice as long to cover the same distance. But Inga insisted; she said, "Mom, you know you can do anything you set your mind to. Mom, it's a great cause. Mom, I can't do it now, please do it for me." So it was the last line that got me moving that first day of January 1999. I ran 5 minutes on day one. By week two I was up to 10 minutes and then by the end of the first month I was running for 20 minutes or more. And that's just how it continued. My body was sluggish until I got up to the one-hour mark, then I started feeling some pleasure with the movement through the wind and the scenery along the way. By the 5-month mark of training, it was time for my one really long run—18 miles before the actual race day. I plotted out my course and had a great time, feeling confident, even blissful at times, until a very strange sensation appeared in my left knee. At first it seemed like just a twitch or a squeak, which became a sensation of heaviness. I just kept going. I was very near my finish line. I was feeling so euphoric, but my left leg couldn't seem to keep up with the rest of me. It was an anchor weighing me down. I felt heat, or was it pain? If I could just cut that leg off, I could get to my finish line. I would be a winner—a bloody, legless winner. Yes, Inga was right: I could do anything I set my mind to.

- Here is the final monologue piece which I performed in November 2005.

My daughter, my 30-year-old daughter, Inga.
She died.

No. Yes. No. Yes. No. It can't be so. No. No. Back and forth. Death. Life. In and out of my feelings I dive. Anger, guilt. Sadness, Remorse. I step out of myself in order to step more fully inside. (step forward)

She died. She really did die.
Where is my dead daughter?

No. Yes. It just can't be true. She had cancer, I had cancer. She's dead and **I am alive.**(space) She was supposed to be at my death bed, not I at hers.

Over and over again for five years I have revisited sobs and cries that leave me feeling skinless. How can I be alive, be in my skin, be in my body when she is not in hers?

Where has she gone? (move hands) I see her not, I touch her not, no mail, no chats over the phone, no email, no juicy news, no advice, no peace, no laughter, no "Guess what, Mumford?"

Mumford, that's what you called me. Call me now, Inga. Where are you? **(gesture up right, look with hands)** I have pleaded with you relentlessly. I have begged, I have asked quietly. No. Nothing. I am an aimless, skinless wanderer, searching, looking for you.

Deep deeper diving into **my** abysmal sadness, diving into the sadness of all those who suffer. The abysmal sadness of all the parents who have children who have died. All of us skinless parents aimlessly wandering looking for our dead children. Sad. So sad.

Oh I remember now you did come in a **dream** to me once. You were lying across my bed and all you said was, "I am OK". I remember feeling a calmness back then. But that faded. I miss you so very much.

Please don't be dead. Dead is not OK. It's not OK for you to be dead. **I am not OK. Where are you? Where am I? Where am I without you?**

MUSIC: "Adios Nonino" by Astor Piazzolla (written by him the day after his father died)

Slow. Slowly. Ever so softly. Ever slower yet. Slowed down am I. Slowed down. To find my breath.

To find his breath..... Breathing into my breath. Relaxing into my body, my skin with his body so close, so powerful and at the same time gentle, barely there, bare. YES. WE are bare—Chest to chest. Heart to heart. **Soul to Soul**. My head lightly resting beneath his chin. His arm surrounding my life breathing ribs. **He leads me to lead him.**

I dance after putting on my high heels and taking off my jacket.

I smile, comforted by his presence, her presence. <u>Yes I see her</u> being held by him, being held by me, and being held by you.

There is an oasis right here right now.

An oasis in the chaos of death and life. His arms, my arms, his breath, my breath, guide me into sweet surrender, as we glide along the floor to music familiar yet unfamiliar.

We are one for this dance. He and I. She and I. I am in my skin, in my body, in his embrace, her embrace. And there's a sacredness, a radiance, that captures, enraptures us in this, our last dance.

Yes, yes yes. I am alive, and Inga, she is alive in me.

After the performance, Erika and some friends took me out for a drink to celebrate. I really did feel Inga's presence in me when I was on stage. I am so grateful for all the support I received and with which I now really return to the world. My teacher Kirsten Wilson was an incredible inspiration and source of encouragement. All my fellow classmates were amazing. I didn't get to see all of their performances because I was backstage preparing, but we were in this together and that really made a difference. I feel less alone in my grief. Writing and performing has helped me immensely.

Return to Talking with Inga

Dear Inga,
Today I am thinking of you as I look at your high school graduation picture and try to remember what your life was like for you then. I remember your white beaded cashmere—like sweater. How you wanted to look grownup and sophisticated. How very many dreams you had back then. You wanted to be a veterinarian; you had gotten over wanting to be a professional model. You told me many years later how depressed you were then

in high school and how I was never really there for you as I was so absorbed in my own struggles and inner demons. I wish I could have talked with you about what you were feeling. I was in training to help other people with their depression, yet there you were suffering right in my house. I know you had such a mixed up relationship with your father as well as me. How he would ignore you, forget about you. Not remember your birthday or even what you told him the day before. How painful that was to me as I know it was for you. I would get so angry with him and I then again was angry about a lot of things back then. I loved that short time when we were all at the beach together, you and both of your sisters and your dad. We would take long walks on the beach talking things out, but then it never did work out at all. Everything fell apart. How did that happen? What do you remember? I wish we could talk about it. Then you left for college and I was happy that you were so excited about your new life, the adventure of being away from home and creating your own place. You told me over and over again that I needed to move on and forget about your father. I wonder what you think of my life now.
Love, Mumford

January 15, 2006
Dear Inga,

Today I sit here at my very small desk in this very small room at Marpa House wondering what you would think about this life I have chosen for myself. I have changed since you died. I am calmer, less reactive, less angry and more authentic. I continue to find death challenging, yet I find being with my patients in the hospice I work for and also their family members offers a mirror to me that helps me to heal. I just have to be real with them and there is no way to protect my vulnerable places. I would really like for you to be with me more—be with me when I visit my patients, be with me when I write. I sure do miss you and I feel my nostrils start to burn with tears that are welling up in me. I always feel better and closer to you when I write. That is reason enough to continue writing. The next step is to edit a bit and get input from others. Erika has agreed to reread what I have writ-

ten and I think it is time to invite others to read this also. I need input and
support.
Love you lots,
Mumford

January 26, 2006
Dear Inga,
    The days, weeks, months and now years are moving past since you died. I
write the words and I feel an emptiness and deep sadness that you aren't
here.
    You would have enjoyed swimming with Erika, Anna and me yesterday.
Anna is really a delight with all her squealing laughter and you should have
seen her gaze set on the lifeguard. We thought she was already taking after
you by checking out the cute guys. I sat in the splash pool with her while
Erika swam laps. Anna jumped into my arms off the side of the pool to the
count of three. Seems that she really loves the water just as you and your sis-
ters all did at that age. I really enjoy watching her grow.
    Thank you for being with me.
Love, Mom

Return to Life as a Grief Journey

Inga lost her health, which she cherished, with her diagnosis. Her body
failed to fight off the cancer cells. Her body no longer did the job that it
was supposed to do. Inga encountered many losses.

Her first physician, whom she consulted when she discovered a lump in
her armpit, said she had mononucleosis and treated her with antibiotics.
He misdiagnosed her failing her miserably. The body is not a perfect system and the medical system is not either. Inga's life changed dramatically
as she entered a new world of doctor appointments, tests, blood draws,
insurance forms, endless questions, research and consultations in order to
help her to make the best treatment decisions. At the end of her life she
asked, "Did I make the right decisions? Was there something else I could
have done?"

Disbelief and denial were my constant friends as I fought with deep sadness, anger and guilt that my daughter had cancer. I was a cancer survivor; my mother was a cancer survivor. Was I the cause of her disease? How could I deal with her illness and with my guilt? I had lost the illusion that I could protect my children from harm, from suffering and pain.

My entire life has been a journey with grief. I imagine at my birth having been handed an antique trunk loaded with the unresolved grief of my family. The first half of my life I traveled dragging that trunk along unconsciously and in the second half of my life, I am becoming more and more aware of grief directly—facing it, feeling it, releasing it and helping others to do the same. The trunk has grown lighter over time.

I had been working with cancer patients for a decade and questioned now whether I could be helpful to Inga and also to all the patients I was serving in my professional life. How would I balance caring for myself, Inga, the rest of my family and my professional clients? I was grieving and questioned whether I could continue to support others in their grief. I would continue to hold that question as I proceeded along, one step, one day and one week at a time.

In the present, I continue to question and have learned to embrace the questions, uncertainty and ambiguity and relax into what is here right now. There is no fixed course for the grief journey, no 30-day program that guarantees a peaceful acceptance as the outcome. There are many resources in the community where I live, but each that I choose may not be ones that the reader would find useful. It takes trust to find your way through grief. Yet death itself dissolves trust. The truth does set us free, yet the truth of death is not palpable. Some say they don't fear death, but ask them about the death of their loved ones.

I believe it is very important to have at least one person with whom you can be completely honest and share your journey, someone who will also give you direct feedback too. They need to mirror your behavior and show you why your denial and resistance many not be helping you, as well as to celebrate turning points with you. They can reflect your discoveries and gifts along the way. They can celebrate your great joy and be present with you in your deep pain.

Some of the biggest lessons that I have learned concern being present for others with all that I am feeling. I have learned to trust myself and even when I doubt, I do not get stuck in that feeling. The world is full of suffering and I have opened more to all of it.

I really love life and appreciate the mystery of it and the serendipity that happens every day. My heart was broken open by Inga's death and there is more room now in it for living fully. I no longer fear death. I am more relaxed overall. I have been blessed with gifts and recognize life is a grief journey.

At my work at QuaLife, the staff art therapist built a labyrinth in the garden and we often had workshops revolving around it. A participant who attended a "Grief in the Labyrinth" workshop that I co-led made an impression on me about trusting her inner wisdom. The format for the program started with choosing a rose and walking into the labyrinth remembering our loved one who died and plucking rose petals that symbolized memories that we were ready to let go of. Then as we walked we dropped petals on the path. This was a very powerful ritual and embodied the letting go process. However, one woman did not pluck any petals and placed the rose intact in the center. Later she told the group that she wasn't ready to let go of any memories and wished to take the rose home with her and put it to dry out in a special place. She followed her own instincts to make the ritual work for her. She said she felt empowered by doing what felt right for her even though it was different from what everyone else chose.

Return to Dance

My new dance class is salsa. I laughed and smiled the entire time. Inga would have loved it. I remember the one class we did take together in Austin many years ago. I remember her smile as she danced, which was my smile tonight. The energy of salsa evokes a playful sensuality, which she always seemed to be very comfortable with. I think about how beautiful she was in her little sparkling black dress and heels dancing that night in Austin.

However, Argentine Tango is really my dance. It has been an important part of my life since 1994 when I first saw it danced by Al Pacino, who played a blind man in "Scent of a Woman." When I saw him dance with a partner on a beautiful shining wood floor with much feeling I knew that I wanted to be there too. Just a month later I was in Seattle visiting Erika and when I spent a day with my friend Jane, she asked me if I had my "scent." I had no clue what she was speaking of. She then took me to a perfumery. The owner greeted us at the door, looked me up and down, and said, "Tango? Yes?" And I said, not yet. I chose two scents that day which she recommended. One of them was Byzance, which I wear every time I go to an Argentine dance party, called a *milonga*. When I returned from Seattle I found an article in the paper about an Argentine Tango Class that would be starting the very next weekend. So I signed up and have been dancing every since. Today I go to teach a tango class in Peachtree City where Jill lives.

Tango has been a healing balm. It has given me a venue for my sensual nature. It has been space away from grief, a safe haven where I don't need to talk, explain or delve into emotions. When I traveled to Austin to be with Inga during her illness, I had a tango friend with whom I would check in. I often went to a milonga there and she helped me to just dance a little with the best dancers and then I would leave. Nothing had to happen. It was just a rest from everything going on with Inga.

To dance tango feels as vital as breathing and eating. I am present in my body, synchronized in body, mind and heart with the music, and completely at one with my partner. The music touches my soul. I feel a happiness in every cell of my body. Tango is a universal language, with its basic walking steps and improvisational nature. I have danced nationally and internationally with men whose names I have never known, yet the dance we shared is still with me. There is a unique intimacy in tango. To dance tango, I am called out of my ordinary life, out of my grief, to embrace a culture and a way of being steeped in tragedy, passion, love, sensuality, fantasy, aliveness and drama. We dance and then it is over. Then we dance another dance. And we let that one go too.

Return to Seduction

Seduction to madness. Seduction to peacefulness. Seduction to grief and pain, so long my best friends. What is this pull, this tug in me to stay in the known familiar place? My place. Yes I know my place, where my mother and her mother stood bravely, stoically, strict, being strong. My mother would say, "You must be strong for your family."

But tonight, seduction. It starts in the afternoon as I lie down with one of the many books stacked on my nightstand. My headphones are on and a violin concerto fills my head. The music lulls me into a daytime dream. Soft waves of unconsciousness meet my tense frame tenderly, lovingly and sleep takes me over with my glasses still balanced on the edge of my nose. The seduction to sleep is so comforting, so enticing. Friday afternoons are special. Having an hour nap refuels me for my late Friday night dancing at the Mercury Café in Denver. Eight PM brings the sounds of rushing water seducing me into my very hot bath, scented with aromatic sandalwood, orange and ylang ylang. Melting into the waters' invitation I do relax and then dream again. Bathing is my lifetime ritual of seduction.

Wearing black on black. That's my usual, yet I add a unique pair of earrings that sparkle like a mirror of my inner, flirtatious self. Carefully applied eyeliner, a hint of color to my cheekbones shape my ageless, best features. Seduction. Oh, seduction. Walking up the stairs of the Mercury Café, the music like a fine aroma seduces me. I feel overcome for maybe the hundredth time by my passionate heart and the aliveness in the air. The tango rhythms call me to dance, to move, to fall in love, to be seduced, to be a flowing, sensuous woman and *not* be strong. I hear the music and taste its sweetness, soothing the wounds of my broken, grieving heart.

Return to Mirthful Frolic

If I were listening I would sing, sing into the wee hours of the night. I would wake up dancing naked in the sunrise. I would write words that were gibberish and love the sounds of them in my mouth. I would do the body painting I always wanted to do, feeling all the sensations of squishing colorful paint as it sloshed on the paper, between my toes, along my arm. I would paint highways that led to enchanting places everyone knows exist. If only I would take off the irritations that burden me, confine myself to a path that isn't mine. I would trail blaze new, colorful avenues where I am completely engaged with all my senses, dancing a novel into a musical sunset of gleeful bliss. Oh, what a day that would be. Oh, what a mirthful, merry, captivating, fantastic, frolicking good time. Timeless temptation to touch the tantalizing truth.

Return to the Mother Lineage

What is the mother lineage? I gave birth. I gave birth to a beautiful baby girl. What is the mother lineage? I became a mother. I didn't know what to do. Motherhood wasn't a class I took in college. In fact I never held a baby until my firstborn. What is the mother lineage? She was born out of my body. That makes her my daughter. One day I had hoped that she too would give birth. What is the mother lineage? There is my mother. I was born out of her body. She was born out of her mother's body. But what about birthing into death? Dying is a birth too. What is the mother lineage? I gave birth to my firstborn and I witnessed her death. My mother gave birth and she witnessed the death of her firstborn. My grandmother gave birth many times and she witnessed four of her children's deaths. What is this mother lineage? The line that ages knows pain. Birth is pain. Death is pain. Birth is joyful. Death has pain and even joy. Death comes when it chooses. Mothers do not know when it will.

What is the mother lineage?
To mother is to nurture. To mother is to love.
To mother is to bear the burdens of life.
To mother is to open to the divine nature of life.
Mother lines know no end. Mothering myself to be at my death bed.
To die each day to what I believe is the truth is to find nothing.
Nothing is reality. Loving deeply is living deeply.
Dying is living deeply with love.
What is the mother lineage?

Knowing love lives everywhere.

Knowing death brings an end to the obstacles of love.

Love lives in death.

Deny not what death offers.

She is our friend, not our enemy.

What is the mother lineage?

Ageless, timeless, openness that carries the soul's journey of all my
     mothers.

You are my mother. He is my mother. She is my mother.

All those hellish troublemakers out there, they too are my mother.

Yours too. So smile.

Inga as a child speaks here through me.

*Freckles. I sure have got freckles. I love the sun and the sun grows freckles.
That is what you see, those brownish red spots of all sizes and shapes on me.
That is what you see, don't you? Can you find your favorite freckle—the one
that surprises you with its beauty? Now follow that freckle on a stream of
light energy inside of me. Come play in the wonder of my inner life. This is
no four-lane highway. It is a cycling path that veers off, leaving you on a
walking path, a path that few have chosen to venture on. Don't be scared
off; don't go timid on me now.*

*Our journey has only begun. Come along now, no shuffling those weary
feet of yours. The day is young. I am only eight years on this planet myself.
Let me show you the way. This fork in the road is not a choice. Turn right,
see the wing of that airplane, and hop on in with my dad and me. We are
on our way to my summer camp. My dad, he's not a real pilot, but he flies
small planes for fun. (Kind of like not being a real writer, just writing for
fun.) My mom asked him to drive me to camp because she had so much else
on her schedule with my two sisters. She is always in the car chauffeuring us
someplace. So he said, "Sure, it will be a great opportunity to practice flying." That is what he said. Now what kind of a mad man practices flying a
plane with his eldest child aboard? That last line was really my mom speaking. She couldn't believe he really meant it, that he was actually going to fly*

me to camp. I think she prayed for rain that day because she knew he wouldn't fly in the rain. He needed to see the ground in order to navigate. And even that was a challenge. Well, it didn't rain and I was very excited to be the only kid that got to camp via plane.

We both could see the ground, but we still got lost. Dad is asking me, "Where are the railroad tracks?" What on earth was he talking about? I was going to camp via plane, not train. Oh, am I ever going to have a great story to tell around the campfire tonight. They will all be impressed.

Right now, I am hoping though that we will actually get there. Wasn't the sun starting to set?. Dad had said we'd be there in time for lunch and I am mighty hungry. Oh! Why is Dad scratching his head in that funny way? He sure looks stumped. What a puzzle this is. We did arrive at camp, but not in time for registration. I was angry about missing the opening event, but Dad was proud that we made it. Me too.

Traveling the foot path of my life. Right there, coming up on the left. Can you see it? There's the beach. Those ocean waves sure are inviting. Dad loves the beach and so does Mom. That's where most of my freckles grew to maturity.

Return to the Magical One

Inga, you weren't always magical, but you made magic happen. When you were ten years old, you got your first magician's kit. Let me back up though; first, you met Ron Knopf who was your Sunday school teacher. There was a time I had to drag you to church, but not after you met Ron. He was magical and his magic rubbed off on you. He was a full-blown magician, black cape, rabbit and all. He inspired and molded you. I knew why you wanted a magician's kit. You practiced your tricks for hours on end entertaining your sisters. You even entertained their friends when there was a birthday party. They loved your magic, they loved you and they thought you were magical.

There was the little tree house in the back ditch of our property at Trail in the Pines. You would keep your sisters hopping with collecting special red berries to create brews for transforming leaves into magic potions. It would be almost dark and I would be yelling for you all to come for dinner. You would call back, "Just five more minutes, we have important stuff to do." Now I was afraid of the snakes in the ditches, but you, you loved the snakes, which carries me ahead of myself many years.

That first year after you died, I visited your bench by Boulder Creek to think about you and something quite mysterious happened. A snake came crawling right in front of me, just three feet away, straight as an arrow. I am scared and I am not scared. This is Inga up to her old tricks with me. She is teasing me to see if I will just jump up and run away. A smile crept over my face, no an ear-to-ear grin, an Inga kind of grin. I breathe and watch that four-foot long snake traverse the sacred soil that surrounds your bench.

Inga, you are magical. You made magic happen when you were ten and you are still magical. I just want to hug your boney body one more time. I miss you so very much. I am carrying a book inside of me and it's slowly making its way out of its hiding place. Now that too is magic. I too am a magician.

Return to Family Memories

Eating pizza. Pizza crust. Let's start with the basics, the crust. Flour and lots of counter space. My kids loved it when we all were in the kitchen and cooked together. Even Dad was home that Saturday afternoon. Music played on the old radio and we donned aprons.

Ready. Set. Go. Let's skip over the mixing the dough. There are soft balls and elbows knocking, not enough space and some shuffling. The tone of this scene was friendly at first, just jockeying for the ideal place to roll out the crust. There were high kitchen stools and the littlest one would sit on her knees up there with the most enthusiasm. The eldest teased her that she was not big enough to really roll out a good enough crust. Yes, no, sure am! Stupid, don't yell at me. Can if I want to. Let's turn up the music and drown out the bickering.

When I was in high school my friends and I would go out for pizza at the very best place in town. I am salivating right now as I think of that pizza. My best friend Barb would want pepperoni and I green peppers. After we reached drinking age, we had beer with our pizza. I never liked beer but with pizza, it was a great solvent for all that cheese. Can't remember the name of that place, but my taste buds get stirred up thinking of it.

Back to the kitchen at our family home at 105 Trail in the Pines. There are some crusts ready for topping and we are now down to two kids in the kitchen. Dad is off reading his magazine. Yes, Erika, you can spread the tomato sauce. Now I prefer a basil pesto topping, Nick 'n Willie's style. But back then it was the straight-up tomato version. Who hid the pepperoni slices? Fred are you kidding me, you ate it for lunch? But I told you we were making pizza today. Oh well, there is always more cheese. Didn't worry about cholesterol back then, or being lactose intolerant.

Yes, let's get the oven preheated. It's getting late and all this cooking sure does make me hungry. Where are you all going? There are dishes to be washed, bowls to wipe and flour to be mopped up. Who's screaming now?

I sure did a great job back then. Didn't always seem like it, but when I see all five of us sitting down with that fragrant brown-crusted, stringy-cheesed, piping hot pizza on our cheerful white plates, we have a moment to remember. A single slice to savor, seeing the family all together.

Let's end with returning to the basics. Family. The family is what is really the best ingredient. I never thought back then that we five wouldn't be able to all sit around a table again after my hair turned grey and my little ones had kitchens of their own.

Return to Being Kind to Myself

Just be. Be still. Be with the first thought; whatever arises is fresh. How lucky am I. Be quiet and know whatever comes through is basically good, and kindness is abundant.

I loved her. I loved Inga and I continue to. My meditation practice, Shambhala vision has helped me be kind to myself. Grief is so demanding. There were the days early in my grieving when I beat myself up non-stop. Then I was at least in control in the midst of my unrelenting pain. I would blame the world and people around me and then turn the same aggression on myself. Remembering this is a good thing. It shows me how far I have come. Back to my breath, gently, sweetly; what a good practice.

The teacher taught today about the different ways in which doubt arises and the importance of befriending doubt. The little doubts for me are like annoying gnats and I swish them away. Early in my grief, I wondered if I would ever be cheerful again. There were moments, distractions that would make me smile, but I doubted life would ever be really joyful with a relaxed sense of peace.

The really big doubts can trap us and immobilize us. I doubted when I first started writing that I could write anything at all. I doubted calling myself a writer, a person writing a book. Now I have little doubts occasionally, but they don't overwhelm or trap me.

Stopping long enough to notice the thought in meditation and going with the out breath provides a great deal of space for me. Grief and all its emotions can be claustrophobic, consuming and stifling. Meditation taught me to practice touching my emotional states and not fixating on them. There is enormous relief in being with sadness just as it is. To simply be with a tear or a river of tears that flow down my cheek and to notice all the sensations of this very natural body response to sadness is life-giving. I really know and feel my aliveness when I pay exquisite attention in this way. There is nowhere to go, nothing to do but simply be with the river of tears. Often in our society we apologize for crying. Why? Crying is as natural as breathing. Crying is a way of being compassionate. What a lesson it is to grieve with gentleness and kindness!

Return to a Place to Rest

Finding a place to rest in the midst of grief can be difficult. If we haven't experienced this before in our regular lives, how do we suddenly find it amidst the emotional turmoil of grief? Walking the finger labyrinth today as I was sitting on Inga's memorial bench in the sunshine reminded me that I have learned a lot about resting, sitting in peace for a moment, or for extended periods of time as I did today. Nature was Inga's place of solace and it is for me too. To discover what really works for each of us is the important part. You might want to try out my favorite resting places, but what works for me will not necessarily work for you.

One of my hospice patients named the sound "ker-plunk" of the ocean as a resting place. Even when away from the ocean, imagining it in one's mind eye can bring a sense of peace and relaxation. My elderly patient wasn't able to articulate this but I trust that is what she was getting at. She was drawn to the sound of the ocean and she offered that to me.

Many different sounds can be places to rest. It might be classical music, the sound of the creek rushing over rocks, a cat purring, or maybe the sound of silence. To enter into the sounds, fully resting with them, creates an oasis from the outer world of chaos, confusion, grasping and aggression.

When space is created to relax, it draws most people in. Walk into a gothic cathedral in Europe and one feels a sense of peace. At my meditation retreat this weekend, we were having tea, laughing and enjoying each other's company. Then the gong rang to call us back into the shrine room. As I entered into that space I could feel my body slow down and adjust to the space. It was a place of rest.

During my first year of grief, I was not able to step into a meditation room. I think the contrast was too great for me. My first meditative experience was at a full labyrinth in the First Methodist Church. When I returned to doing a sitting practice of meditation, it was for very short periods of time and then grew over time.

Resting is critical to support oneself and it is also how we recuperate to face the journey's ups and downs. When I walk the labyrinth and enter the center, I am reminded that everything and nothing happens while waiting there. I follow my breath, and today I am thankful for all the resting places I have had on my grief journey.

I remember to rest. I can't grieve twenty-four hours a day, seven days a week, even when it feels that way. It's OK to rest. I am OK as I return to the world having rested.

Return to Blueberry Smiles

I try not to think about Inga's death every day, every hour, every minute. Today I haven't yet, until now when up death popped. I see her smiling face and I smile into the tight place. The pit of my stomach aches and I wonder what has happened to her. Has she come back yet? Will she ever? I do believe in reincarnation.

My second granddaughter Emmy was born thirteen months after Inga died. Emmy reminds me often of Inga. When Emmy was three years old and was sitting on the sofa with a big bowl of blueberries as she watched a kids' TV program, she very abruptly looked over at me and exclaimed wholeheartedly, "I love blueberries." Oh, I love Emmy. I love Inga or I loved Inga. Is it from the past or is it in the present? It just still seems strange to me to say it in the present tense, yet in the past tense it is so painful.

Inga loved blueberries too. She and her sisters, her dad too, we all loved to go to the blueberry fields and pick those ripe, huge, sweet, juicy berries ourselves. The kids' faces, hands and clothes were all blue when we were finished and smiles were broad. The field attendant once said, "Maybe I should have weighed those kids of yours in before they went into the fields."

I smile still for the pounds you collected. I smile. Still am smiling, thinking about Inga today. So it's a good day. Her smile that makes me smile. Oh no, I didn't want to think about that smile, the last smile. The smile on her face after she died. How can she be dead and smiling? I am not dead. I cannot smile thinking of that death smile. Not today. I just won't think about that smile. Not today. I'll return to the blueberry smiles.

Return to Heart Talk

My heart says, "Da-dum, da-dum, da-dum. Tra la, tra la." "Da-dum". I'm still beating about sixty beats per minute, like clockwork. I am working, doing what I do best. What more do you want from me?

Yes, I have a layer of annoyance around me. You are expecting some-thing right here, right now. Doesn't work well for me that way. Give me a break. I have already opened up today. Isn't the once-a-day plan good enough for you? Want me to unlock more heart-filled, wet tiers of sad sto-ries. Is that what is in your plan for me today?

No, not today, right now. This moment. What's happening? "Da-dum da-dum." Still beating. At least I am not beating on myself today. Used to do that when I was a young mother. That has gotten much better.

How did I handle all the roles? Working outside the home as well as inside the home with my husband gone twelve hours or more a day. I am shocked. I got angry with myself, I got angry with all of them. I was rigid with anger. I kept everyone at bay.

I liked vacuuming. I used to vacuum to have some peace and quiet. Even the dog ran and hid when I plugged in the old Kirby upright. I could only hear the white noise roar of that cleaning machine in motion. It had a light, like a railroad train pointing the way to solitude. No one dared disturb me when I vacuumed. What a genius I was! Proud of my cleaning alone times, designed to rid the house of dust and rejuvenate my spirit. Then I was ready for the next round of whatever came my way.

How sweet. I feel a soft spot there in my heart thinking of those roaring times. How hard it was on me. I worked more than 20 hours a week in the professional world and more than 70 hours per week at home. Not much time for living in the heart world.

Sweet isolated moments, picking green beans for dinner in our garden, being served breakfast in bed for Mother's Day, six-arm hugs all at once, chocolate mousse binges, all five of us in our king-size bed watching silly movies, doors slamming, kitchen floor scrubbing, picking gardenias, walking the beach and wading in tidal pools. Heartfelt. Heart full. "Da-dum da-dum."

Return Remembering

I remember your face. Your smiling vibrant face. Your smile that broke through any cloudy doubt. I remember your hands. Your nails were chewed down. You were so proud of yourself as a teenager when your grandmother Bonma challenged you to let your nails grow by giving you a $20 reward. The money incentive worked and you were so happy with your new nail life.

You always loved shopping for clothes. I recall the shopping day that you bought nothing and it was I who made many purchases. It was a first.

It was during your cancer treatment when you were feeling pretty well. Did you ever really feel well with all that chemotherapy in you? It was all relative. I loved to go shopping with you. It was always so helpful for me. You had an eye for what colors and shapes would work well on me. I remember that day in the mall in North Carolina when I bought several outfits that all worked well together. The blue jumper with white shirt and a necklace that I still have. The beads are red and blue, very brilliant. I hardly ever wear it anymore but it reminds me of that day with you. I also bought pants with a beige jacket that was very comfy. Everything I got that day was interchangeable and I wore every item. Today my closet is filled with black clothes and spots of color—burgundy, various shades of blue and much red. It all works but I sure would love another shopping spree with you.

We were always trading clothes too. There would be something in my closet that you wanted to borrow. It usually started with a "just wear it today" and would lead to a borrow for the week. I would worry that you would get a spot on it. You were such a messy eater. And then again I am a messy eater. Just this past Saturday night, I dripped olive oil from my bread onto my sweater. My friend pointed it out to me, which I appreciated. Now it's at the cleaners. Inga, I miss you when I recall all this. I do have you inside me too. My nails are very short, but I don't chew them. My wardrobe does all go together. My smile is broad and bright, especially when I dance.

What else do I remember about you this minute, this second, right now? A plaid, pleated skirt. Did I sew that for you? I don't think so. You wore argyle knee-highs with it. Makes me shudder and smile thinking of your outrageous taste in clothing. And I love you.

Return Not Remembering

I don't remember a lot about those early years of being a mother. I don't remember when Inga started to eat solid foods or said "mama" for the first time. I don't remember the feel of her skin. Did I take time to just be with her? I don't remember when I had those headaches while living in Belgium. Her dad and I decided to put her in a little French preschool a few days a week. The headaches went away, but I don't remember what it was like taking her to school; she was only two. I don't remember her first day at kindergarten. I don't remember her riding a two-wheeler for the first time. I don't remember her first date or when she started menstruating. I am so sad not remembering the details of so many important times.

I just can't remember anything. It is all blank in me. All those precious days and years I got to be with her and I can't remember them. I want to go back to what I do remember, what I want to remember, what I can recall.

But that's not the point. I missed out on so much. All that I don't remember, I will put in a box. A brown box with a hammered brass latch and a lock. Piece by piece, I will let each unremembered event go into the lost memory box. How sad. I don't remember her struggles with homework or writing assignments. I don't remember her being sad yet I know she was. I don't remember how much she wanted to play the violin and how adamant I was for her to practice out in the utility shed because I didn't want to listen to those screeches. I don't remember if she even played anything that she liked. Her grandmother also played the violin, but I never heard her. I don't remember if I talked about that with her. How sad. In the midst of all the chatter, did we even talk about anything meaningful? What did Inga remember? What silent sadness did she die with? What didn't she remember to tell me? I can't remember anything. Sometimes I want to open the box of lost memories and sometimes not.

Return to an Unforeseen Occurrence

A ship comes into the port where I am waiting aimlessly one fine summer day. The sun is warm, and my skirt is gently waving from the cool sea breezes. I wait and I watch. Wait and listen. Wait and savor this scrumptious day. How could it be better than it is?

The ship is docking with a flurry of activity by the deck hands with their large coils of rope. It is a timeless day when no concerns hammer at my head; only the sensations, the smells, and the contentment inside hold my attention.

I am waiting—not something I excel at, if one would even desire such a skill. Then the ramp is lowered and I wait, breathless, as I anticipate the crowd. There must be many people and someone must be smiling for me. So let's just wait as I consider all the possibilities. My rational mind overtakes my contentment on this sweet summer day.

Then it happens at the bow: she appears no more than a teenager. Long and lithe with a very broad, beaming smile that seems to whisper, here I am. She waits, as I waited, the energy of light years between us like an eternity that knows no distance, only love. Yes, love crossed over. Love came forward before she even took a step. Still holding my breath, I want to call out to her with my voiceless yearning. I know you. So beautiful you are. So innocent and fresh, like a budding rose of purple lilacs—confused but blooming.

The air does not stir. The stillness surrounds us. The birds swirl above, calling down to us to be still and know this moment fully. To be here now, and here I am, there she is. Once more. Again and forever she sees me and I her.

No words are needed. We have everything we need. Friends forever, saints we are not, but mothers and daughters know what it is when there is no separation yet space exists. I am your mother. I am your daughter. I am your friend and sister. I am your aunt and grandmother. I am a woman and all who came before me leave again, come back again. We are still friends; we are safe, surrounded by empathic listeners, no words spoken. No time lost. Endless eternity of oneness.

Return to Another Auto Accident

Compression. Pushed, crushed, condensed, wiped inwards, crunched, smacked into myself. Today's car crash molds my future. My auto accident in June 2000 also informed me of my future. This one is my ending "bookend." I need to write. I need to finish the book. No more running. I will not be leaving for Buenos Aires on May 1. Be the teacher. Write it out. Find the truth within and put it into words.

I am spaced out this morning at 9AM. Driving to the Health Fair in Longmont for a checkup, I encounter a traffic jam ahead due to construction. So I take a quick turn onto Baseline Road. Sipping water, then carefully closing the lid, the next thing I know is my car is crammed under a red jeep Cherokee in front of me. I never saw this car. My chest really hurts and I question if I cracked a rib. Grey smoke circles up in front of me and I hear my Spanish lesson tape talking to me. Bizarre. It is all so strange and surreal. What happened? Stopped in my tracks, I have no place to go.

I have really done this. It is my fault. Mindlessness, carelessness. I hope the driver I hit is not injured. And my chest really burns. A woman comes over and says she will call an ambulance. I refuse. She will call 911 to report the accident. I sit motionless. Someone tells me to shut off my engine.

I guess I am not badly hurt. I can stand up outside of the car. I am stunned, shocked, embarrassed. How did I just ram right into that car? I apologize to the young, dark-haired man with tears close to the surface. He tells me accidents happen and to not worry about it.

What does all this mean? Just two weeks ago, my back was crunched on the ice and now my front too is crunched up. I had just been to my acupuncturist and my back was really feeling better. I was thinking I would go dancing tonight and maybe I could go to Argentina. Now I cannot go backward and I cannot go forward.

I want meaning and I know I must write. I must finish the book. Not just for me, for Inga, for all my daughters, but I think for all those mothers crying in solitude. I also must meditate each day before I write. No more distractions. No more metaphors needed. Wise woman self, come on out and take the lead here and I will follow. You have my full attention.

Return to Serve

Today, I feel accepting of where I am, the plans I have for the future and my sense that everything is just fine. Today Inga is with me, inside me. Her spirit resides deep in a cavern of my soul. The loud winds of the outer world don't stir the soil of calm, only clear the decks. Outside my room is a patio with a large table and umbrella. The wind blew the umbrella over and it landed on the glass tabletop, shattering it into fragments. I heard the crash and then saw this very beautiful pile of glass glimmering in the sunshine. When I had the auto accident that shattered my windshield and later Inga died, I saw nothing beautiful, I saw nothing but loss. Now I do understand as well as feel that in tragedy, there are wondrous gifts. It is a horrible thing that happened. And my life has been put together in a very new way and is still changing. But in the midst of that "crash" I was frozen in time and space. For months I lived in a daze, barely relating to life. All I could do was to feed myself and sleep (and not very well at that) most of the time. I continue searching for meaning within those shards of glass.

I miss Inga. I love her and she died. Her pain and my pain in grief no longer make me feel broken inside. I want to talk about her, but I don't have to. My life feels integrated with her death. I feel whole and complete. My outer world no longer needs to affirm and support me in my grief. There is an end to a phase of my grief. I will always miss her yet I feel I can move beyond my grief. And I am doing so. I know I will hold her close, but not too close. I know I will love her always and have learned much about love through her. I know the emptiness of losing her and I know the form of the grief process that has supported me. I do trust life. I do trust death also. Through my dying daughter, the death of many others and the death of my life day by day, I have been blessed with much joy and the appreciation for life.

Now I want to serve others who are looking for their way through the labyrinth of grief. Service in the world is bringing my whole self into any situation with an open heart and mind. The structure of my entire life guides me. The more I release the past and feel the earth beneath my feet in this magnificent present, the more I can serve others.

Rachel Naomi Remen says, "Serving is different from helping. Helping is based on inequality; it is not a relationship between equals … Service, on the other hand, is an experience of mystery, surrender and awe. Our service serves us as well as others. That which uses us strengthens us. Over time, fixing and helping are draining, depleting. Over time we burn out. Service is renewing. When we serve, our work itself will sustain us."

Appreciation and gratitude are a way of life. Even in the midst of the darkest nights, appreciation can be a loyal friend. I have opened my heart, been kind to myself, and no matter what happens, I can choose to extend kindness to others. And when I don't, I can choose to forgive myself. This is service.

Return to "Shake and Bake" Grief

It was an assertive and confident part of me that was determined to have my baby. I was happy to be pregnant even when we hadn't planned it. When the doctor told me I was pregnant, I cried. She asked me, what does the father think and I said he wants me to not have this baby. I cried when she started talking about my options. I ask myself if I cried with Fred about this. I did very much want my baby and I also questioned myself about it. My tool kit of courage was well equipped with denial. How skillful I was. How fortunate I was. I didn't talk with anyone else about my decision, only the doctor and Fred, the father to be. There was a "grab the answer and run" mentality that I followed to a "T." Kind of like "Shake and Bake chicken." My mother used to make that dish. Drop the chicken in a bag with some seasoning crumbs. Yes, shake it up and then bake it. Don't question, don't grapple with the dilemma, don't talk to people, don't make lists of the plus and minus points. Just throw it all in the bag, coat it with something palatable. Those are the ways my mother knew how to deal with grief. Slather it over with sappy sweet messages that said, "It's for the best."

My mother cooked our family chicken and she handled her grief in that fashion. She never really said how sorry she was about Inga dying. She coped as best she could with "shake and bake" grief. Mother baked her grief about Inga inside with all the rest of her grief. She didn't know what to say so she said nothing. She told me many times, "No matter what I say it's never the right thing." That was true for many years. But when Inga died, I was beyond needing anything from her. It was I who was taking care of her. Her body was failing, her mind was failing and emotionally she was unable to be present for me. She did the very best she could.

Inga always seemed so sure of herself. I am so uncertain about many things, but about this I am painfully clear. I must work my way through my grief and get it out. I must paint with words the lackluster color of my life without her on this blank page. I must find the words that fit the circumstance of having a dead daughter and give them shape on this page. I must discover and remodel the shake and bake grief model of my mother's ways.

Return Softly

Grief has returned me to a soft place, like the lamb's ear plant growing in the gardens all over Boulder. I feel the pleasure of my softness. Grief has opened my heart to feel the suffering of the world and my shield of anger has melted into tears. When I place a dollar bill in a homeless person's hand, I feel his pain in my heart and tears flow easily.

I was driving home very late after dancing in Denver last Saturday night. The mountain roads are still unfamiliar to me and I passed only one car over the many miles of twisting turns. My fear started to build as I thought I heard a strange noise in my car and wondered if my car was responding safely when I braked. I feared I might get a flat tire and tried to think out a logical plan of action if something went wrong. I did arrive home safely, but the next morning I saw my rear tire looked quite low. I drove thirty minutes to Boulder and went to my tire dealership to have it checked.

Indeed, I had a slow leak due to a small screw imbedded in the tire. After repairing the tire, the salesman also informed me the level of my threads was low and recommended I purchase a new set of tires.

A simple lesson, handled easily. When fear arises, it is important not to feed it and also to check out the reality and take action if need be. Tires do wear out and the small screw seems like my feeling of not being good enough. This needs attention; I ask myself how I might be of better service to others. I thank the screw and all the opportunities I receive to learn and grow. I can be soft and take care of myself.

Return to Surrender

My basic nature has always led me to dive deep emotionally and explore my psyche. I am introverted, intuitive, a thinker and a visionary. The rawness of grief was not unfamiliar territory for me. However, the breadth and

intensity of it was. I surrendered and felt often that I succumbed to it
Where was my lifeline? I had no faith that I would survive Inga's death.
felt I was dying. Over and over again I was pulled under into the ocean o
grief's undertow. I had no control, I could only surrender.

I recently heard a story about a man who went rafting, fell into th
churning rapids and got caught in a deep eddy. He tried with all hi
strength to swim out of it. He could not. His will gave out and he literally
threw his hands up in the air and surrendered to the swirling waters. H
was sucked to the bottom and then spit out further downstream
unharmed.

For me this is like the power of grief's natural flow, which churn
around me and then it too drops me at a new place along my life journey.

I love my children and grandchildren immensely. I love them more
than life itself. Inga died and I died too. When I saw the beginning of th
end, I knew she was dying and nothing could stop the natural force o
nature.

I surrendered when I returned home and knew I could not return to my
life as I knew it. I stopped working. I went to bed, got up and ate and
walked and then went back to bed.

With a sense of confidence I did return to the world. No matter what hap
pens, everything is workable. The word confidence seems to be derived from
con (with) and *fidence* (faith). I face the world with faith, trusting its natura
flow. Sharon Salzberg wrote a book, *Faith Trusting your own Deepest Experi
ence*. She says, "The first step on the journey of faith is to recognize tha
everything is moving onward to something else, inside us and outside. See
ing this truth is the foundation of faith. Life is transition, movement and
growth. No matter what is happening, whenever we see the inevitability o
change, the ordinary, or even oppressive, facts of our lives can become alive
with prospect. We see that a self-image we've been holding doesn't need to
define us forever, the next step is not the last step, what life was is not what i
is now, and certainly not what it might yet be." This book has helped me to
name my experience. I can relax to a greater extent. I feel more at peace with
the world as I step forward into my unknown future.

I am in my body with all my senses. My finger glides along the return path of the labyrinth as I glide over silky threads.

When I met Cealo, the Japanese Buddhist monk, I immediately felt love from and around him. In a private interview, I told him of my agony over Inga's death and asked his advice. He told me Inga was fine. He said I should let go of Inga and focus on what I wanted in my life here on earth. So I made a list, as is my way.

I want to love more and struggle less.

I want to surrender to the natural flow of life.

I want to be of service to those dying, their family and to others who care for the dying.

I want to assist people in their grieving and living with dying.

I want to dance more with abandon, surrendering to my partner, the music and the moment.

I want to travel to Argentina, Mexican beaches, Italy and Greece.

I want to live in a contemplative co-housing community.

I want to flow like a river with my writing.

I want a life partner.

I want to dance, sing and giggle with my grandchildren.

I want to know my daughters better and for them to know me.

I want to play more and fret less.

I want to see beauty where my eyes have been closed.

I want to love myself more and judge less.

I want to live fully into my dying.

I want to leave a legacy.

Return to Be Seen

Sawdust riddles the dark earth surface and hillside reaching down to the creek. The trees were trimmed; no, someone has decimated this place. They felled a towering tree two feet in diameter, which once shaded and protected this place. Now there is more sunshine here on Inga's bench. I try to see the brighter side to this loss. This is my sanctuary for being with Inga and it has been remodeled. I feel tears burning their way to the surface. I am distressed the tree couldn't be saved, upset with the mess from the surgery, which clutters the ground, distressed to have not visited here earlier, to have not had the chance to be in the this place as it used to be. I am simply sad not to have Inga here with me right now. Another entry way into my grief.

I am pulled into the ache in my heart and gut once more. It all happened and I could not stop it. I could not save my daughter and I could not save the tree. This bench no longer is secluded and hidden from the Boulder Creek path of cyclists and runners. The tree used to shelter me from on-lookers. Now my tears and piles of wet Kleenex are visible. I am visible.

Will new trees spring up? I want to plant something here. I want to go back to how it was. I want to sit with Inga just one more moment. The trees shed their leaves, sprout again, die and are often cut to the ground. Like Inga, another loss. Thank you, tree, for your beauty and protection. Thank you for being part of the legacy of this sacred earth world.

I touch into the jagged edges of my grief. I am actually happy to revisit my tender-heartedness once again. The creek sings its endless chorus, soothing my tremors of pain. Another journey through my labyrinth, another loss, another moment to rest in peaceful abiding, this time being seen.

Return Walking My Talk

My heart's tears flow easily like the aspen leaves responding to the wind. I miss Inga so very much today and feel her arms around my shoulders, comforting and reminding me to go out into the world and love everyone in my life. A woman called me yesterday whose sister died in a tragic accident just six weeks ago. She said she doesn't know what she is doing most of the time. She can't focus. She can't believe her sister is dead. I will visit with her tomorrow. I know I can offer my presence and be of some service to her. What I have been through with Inga has shaped me in a new loving way. I do have much to offer by my presence.

Walking the labyrinth helps me focus and connects me to my sensate journey of circuitous yet forward movement. I feel transparent and often times confused. The labyrinth grounds me and helps me to find my body's truth, especially what is in my heart.

I walk the labyrinth again and know my head is struggling with my heart. This is not an unfamiliar feeling. My heart says to be patient with my life. My heart says to be nurturing of myself and my struggles. I am reminded to give others what I have given to myself. Walk your talk, Carole. My head says I have all this time and spaciousness and need to finish this book. Make goals, set a plan, create an outline and just do it. I feel this tug of war is between my masculine and feminine aspects. I want to respect both, for each is very valuable. So I join a writer's coaching group for support and goal setting.

The trees respond to the wind's energy. When the weather turns cold they will change colors and drop their leaves for the long winter ahead. I am in the summer of my life, reaping the harvest of all my efforts and the seeds of many teachers and mentors. I have pulled out the weeds that have strangled my sense of the basic goodness in me and others. I am well. My head knows my heart's desires. My heart appreciates my head's thoughts, plans and ideas.

Return Within Me

Within me there lies the past, memories vivid with people I have loved and still love. Within me there lie dreams and fantasies, luring me to live in other worlds, special places inhabited by me alone and some incredible friends. Within me there lies spirit, a mysterious world where I am safe and embraced.

I have walked the labyrinth so very many times, seeking solitude and peace. This outer tool for spiritual connection has served people of all faiths and beliefs over hundreds of years. I have felt God's presence within me as miraculously landed in the center place, my inner sanctuary. But what exactly is God's presence? Is it surrounding me, is it emptiness, is it peace and love? Is it the voice that says, "You are not alone" and "You are loved"?

Recently I watched the movie version of the well known book by Neal Walsch, *Conversations with God*. He heard voices loud and clear only after he had given up all hope. Does my will, my ego mind act as a blockade? What does lie within me? There are times Inga speaks to me as if she were alive. Her death cut through my desires for what I wanted. My prayers were not answered. I wandered the dark night of the soul for days, months, years. I walked the labyrinth asking for help and I often received help. I found how much I am loved. Inga told me over and over and over again. She says to write this down, so I'll remember.

Listen to me, I am with you. There are many tools, many ways for you to seek and find help. Those are all good. And within you, you have everything you need. You have a labyrinth within you. You have God and Buddha within you. You are pure love. You are and you continue to be my mother, the very best mother ever. So travel to wonderful beaches, exotic places, but always remember the truest sacred place is within you, where the invisible world meets the shore of this physical land, evergreens and roses. You are supported throughout eternity. Listen to the timeless whispers. Tune in, stay tuned. I am here. I am endlessly yours.

Return to the Anniversary of the Death

Today is Saturday, September 2, 2006 and it is the sixth anniversary of Inga's death. I am in Portland, Oregon officiating at the wedding of Daniela Nikolic and Alex Krebs.

I met Alex first. He is a very fine Argentine tango teacher, musician and dancer. He traveled to teach in Denver, so I knew him before I met Daniela in Buenos Aires two years ago. She was 36 years old at the time. Her six-foot stature was goddess-like. My traveling companion Dvora and I were both drawn to Daniela and the three of us became shopping fanatics as well as best friends.

One day we had a marathon shopping adventure, starting at 11 AM at Abasto Shopping Mall where we browsed, tried on lots of clothes, had lunch, shopped some more, shared our life stories, laughed, cried and, hungry again, had dinner, which sustained us to close the place down at 10 PM. Daniela became like a daughter, though I'd known her only two weeks.

So when she announced her engagement to Alex, I was just thrilled. I love them both. A few months before the wedding, she said their plans were falling into place. They had the location, a photographer, a caterer and a wedding gown, but they didn't have anyone to marry them. My spontaneous "I can and would love to marry you" was well received. Her smile was beautiful, just like Inga's.

The date for the wedding was set for September 2 and I had no second thoughts about doing this on the anniversary of Inga's death. I was turning another corner of my grief journey to be celebrating life, relationship and marriage. I was honoring Inga as I stepped into this new place.

It is a bright sunny day and the log cabin setting near a small river is shaded by enormous pines with years of shed needles creating a cushioned groundcover. Sitting in a chair beside the rushing water before the guests arrive, I contemplate the ceremony. I remember Inga's wedding more than a decade ago on the beach in Wilmington, North Carolina. I think of Inga's memorial bench positioned on the slope of the creek bed with the water coming to my right, and here today the water flow is coming on my left. It is as though I have crossed over the creek/river. I am churned up with emotion and a sense of peacefulness. This is a beautiful place; this is a beautiful life. I miss Inga and I love life.

The guests gather near the band and a dance floor laid on a flat section behind the hill leading down to the river's shore. Watching Alex's face as he awaits Daniela in her processional along the wooded path from the cabin to his side is mystical. He is in love and it shows. They each have written their own vows and Daniela is the first to speak. Alex says a few words, then takes his saxophone to play his vows. It is very moving and very beautiful. Following the exchange of rings, I pronounce them married and offer the blessing I wrote:

> *We are gathered here to celebrate the love that has brought you Alex and you Daniela both to this day. Blessings from his holiness the Dalai Lama. (Rice thrown blessed by the Dalai Lama)*
>
> *May you be blessed in body, mind and spirit.*
>
> *May your marriage and vows be blessed.*
>
> *May you know life's meaning and its mystery-how you become truly one in sharing yourselves with one another, and yet, remain truly two in your own uniqueness.*
>
> *May your house be a place of happiness for all who enter it, a place where the old and the young are renewed in each other's company, a place for growing, a place for music, dance and laughter.*
>
> *May your lives together flow like this stream beside us with clarity, sweetness and calm abiding.*
>
> *May you be blessed with abundance, vitality and silly surprises.*
>
> *May you be blessed with all your hearts' desires.*
>
> *May you find comfort in each other's presence and when you don't, welcome the opportunity to grow beyond your differences.*
>
> *May your larger family be the family of all humankind. May those who are nearest to you and dearest to you constantly be enriched by the beauty and the energy of your love for each other.*
>
> *May we all be blessed.*

Afterword

I return over and over again to the labyrinth with my grief. I have struggled, healed and grown. I know I will continue to revisit the grief of Inga's death. Life's basic paradox is that where there is birth, there is death. Thus grief is always present. There is a beginning, a middle and an ending to every day, all relationships, adventures, pain, and delight. Losses are a part of our everyday scenery.

Now I am faced with another loss, the completion of this book. I could not imagine when I started writing five years ago that there would be an end to it. It is time to face my grief over this ending. I have been identifying myself as the writer of this book. Who am I with its completion? What will happen next? Will anyone want to read it and find it worthwhile? I take time to step into my grief using my own labyrinth grief roadmap.

I go to Inga's bench beside the Boulder Creek in the early morning, wanting to wrap my arms around myself, this book, my grief and my future readers and just be still. I have had the luxury of space, time, resources, and support to write this book. With my finger labyrinth on my lap and my writing journal beside me I rest, reflect and review my process with this book.

In 2002 during a two-month sabbatical in the mountains, I started transcribing journals and only wrote 45 pages when I had hoped to complete an entire book. I remember all the people who came into my life, encouraging me to write more and take all the time I needed to finish. A year ago, I had my first rough draft and proclaimed myself a writer. This year with the help of my editor, I have written missing pieces and delved into background grief needing to be revisited from earlier times of my life. I feel like I am a very pregnant mother long overdue and I want to deliver this book baby immediately.

I enter the labyrinth, hesitating as if this were my first trip. I make my way slowly through the many curves. I let go of judgments about what I think about my writing style and my worry about what others will think of this book. Will anyone like my baby? I take a deep breath and feel the silk path with my finger and smile.

Reaching the center with a sigh of relief then a burst of excitement. Yes I have completed my book. Hallelujah! Then these words come to me "grief mixed with joy is a rare commodity." I contemplate this phrase and feel the power of the ingrained nature of the labyrinth within me. Yes, have experienced the treasure of joy embedded in my grief. I feel immeasurable gratitude.

My return walk is with confidence and I release this book to its next phase. I will continue to walk the labyrinth, write, do workshops and presentations. My grief is not finished but is now the bedrock of my existence and supports me to step into my unknown future with courage.

While I hope this book, my grief map and my journey will be helpful to others, I don't presuppose it is for everyone. In sharing my story with you I wish that you may better find your unique healing path with grief.

May you, my readers, find trust in your lives.
May confidence spur you to walk courageously with all your grief.
May labyrinths be a source of support.
May you ask for help even when you don't think you need it.
May you remember your loved ones.
May you release your painful attachment to them.
May you be happy.
May you find something you are passionate about.
May you be filled with loving-kindness.
May you find solace and peace.
May your journeys unfold smoothly.

APPENDIX

RESOURCES

Some books I found helpful were:

Artress, Lauren. *Walking a Sacred Path: Rediscovering the Labyrinth as a Spiritual Tool.* New York: Penguin Putnam Inc., 1995.

Blank, Jeanne Webster. *Death of an Adult Child: A Book for and About Bereaved Parents.* Amityville, New York: Baywood Publishing Company, Inc, 1998.

Chodron, Pema. *When Things Fall Apart.* Boston: Shambhala Publications, 1997.

Dass, Ram. *Still Here: Embracing Aging, Changing and Dying.* New York: Penguin Putnam Inc., 2000.

Kubler-Ross, Elisabeth. *The Wheel of Life: A Memoir of Living and Dying.* New York: Touchstone, 1998.

Lattanzi-Licht, Marcia; Miller, Galen W.; Mahoney John J. *The Hospice Choice: In Pursuit of a Peaceful Death.* New York: Touchstone, 1998.

Levine, Stephen. *Unattended Sorrow: Recovering From Loss and Reviving the Heart.* USA: Holtzbrinck Publishers, 2005.

Levine, Stephen. *Who Dies? An Exploration of Conscious Living and Conscious Dying.* New York: Anchor Books Editions, 1982.

Lewis, C.S. *A Grief Observed.* San Francisco: HarperCollins Publishers, 2001.

Orloff, Judith. *Second Sight.* New York: Warner Books, 1996.

Rosof, Barbara D. *The Worst Loss: How Families Heal After the Death of a Child.* New York: H. Holt, 1994.

Sarnoff Schiff, Harriet. *The Bereaved Parent.* London: Penguin Books, 1977.

Taylor, Jeremy. *Where People Fly and Water Runs Uphill: Using Dreams to Tap the Wisdom of the Unconscious.* New York: Warner Books, 1992.

Wilbur, Ken. *Grace and Grit: Spirituality and Healing in the Life and Death of Treya Killam Wilbur.* Boston: Shambhala, 2001.

Zimmerman, Susan. *Writing to Heal the Soul: Transforming Grief and Loss though Writing.* New York: Random House, 2002.

Websites:

www.compassionatefriends.org The mission of The Compassionate Friends is to assist families toward the positive resolution of grief following the death of a child of any age and to provide information to help others be supportive.

www.growthhouse.org A non-profit organization working with grief, bereavement, hospice, and end-of-life issues.

www.hospicefoundation.org/griefandloss Hospice Foundation of America provides leadership in the development and application of hospice and its philosophy of care with the goal of enhancing the American health care system and the role of hospice within it.

www.labyrinthsociety.com International resource on labyrinths with a link to a world-wide labyrinth locator.

www.mettainstitute.org established to provide education on spirituality in dying. Inspired by the Buddhist tradition, it encourages the integration of the spiritual dimensions of living, dying and transformation through professional training, educational programs and materials.

www.naturaltransitions.org Help with creating your own home funeral. Their mission is to reclaim after-death care for families and communities, educating and empowering them to make choices that are more meaningful, affordable, and environmentally conscious.

www.shambhala.org It is the Shambhala view that every human being has a fundamental nature of goodness, warmth and intelligence. This nature can be cultivated through meditation, following ancient principles, and it can be further developed in daily life, so that it radiates out to family, friends, community and society. There are Shambhala centers all over the world.

Author's Note

I will be facilitating workshops and presentations based on the grief labyrinth and also the Healing Life-Healing Death Workshop. Visit my website at www.clindroos.com for more information.

FORGIVENESS MEDITATION

In this moment give yourself time for deep reflection. You have the opportunity right now to explore forgiveness, to open yourself, and your heart to experiencing forgiveness. This is about you, not about others; it is for you and about your caring for yourself.

Prepare yourself for meditation by making yourself comfortable in a chair (or bed). Use cushions and a blanket if you need one so your body can get relaxed. You might want to put a scarf or Kleenex over your eyes to block out the light and help you to turn inward. Having Kleenex in your hand may also support your emotional process.

If at any time during this guided exercise, you cannot hear me, just gently raise your hand and I will speak louder. Also as you listen to me, allow my words to guide you. If my words don't seem to fit for you, then change them so that the words really do work for you. Trust your own knowing about what is right for you here today. And breathe easily, without effort or trying to make anything happen.

Allow your eyes to close now if they aren't already, and focus on your own breath—the bridge between your body and consciousness. Feel your breath flowing in and out of your body. (repeat) Visualize each inhalation filling you, expanding your body. Visualize each exhalation emptying you, relaxing your body, releasing all tension and fatigue as you breathe it out with your breath … Go ahead breathe it all out.

Know that you are safe, surrounded by this caring environment. And remember that at any time if you feel overwhelmed, you can open your eyes to come back into this room.

As you **give yourself permission to go deeper into relaxation**, you go deeper and deeper into yourself … until you find the very center of your being, that place of unity between body, mind, and spirit. Adjust your body at any time to give yourself more comfort and relaxation.

Staying centered and with your breath, allow yourself to reflect for a moment on the word "forgiveness" ... forgiveness ... What is forgiveness? ... How might it be to know forgiveness in your life right now?

Be curious and explore forgiveness. Open to the possibility of experiencing forgiveness for yourself. How might it be to bring forgiveness into your life for yourself? If it feels all right for you right now, gently and with great tenderness, acknowledge how painful it is to hold yourself not forgiven, out of your own heart about something that may have happened a very long time ago or in a recent time ... and breathe.

Where have you been angry with yourself? ... Where have you been resentful with yourself? ... Now just touch it and then let it go. Let go of the pain. And breathe. Call out to yourself, using your own name, and say, "I forgive myself." I forgive myself for whatever has been holding pain. Gently open to making room in your heart for yourself. Open to that self-forgiveness. And say it to yourself over and ... over slowly. Say it as many times that is needed to really feel a shift occur. (pause)

Let yourself have some space ... let anything that has kept you from forgiving yourself fall away. Let all the regrets fall away ... let the hardness, the judgments about yourself ... fall away. And breathe ... breathe gently, not trying to make anything happen here. Let yourself be touched by forgiveness. **Allow yourself back into your very own sacred heart**. Allow yourself to be forgiven.

Let that forgiveness fill your entire body. Feel the warmth and care that wishes you well. And breathe ... Let yourself be loved. Know that in this moment you are wholly and completely forgiven ... It is just up to you to allow it in. Let yourself be loved, and now too let yourself love. And breathe ...

And as you allow yourself to love … I invite you now to open to the possibility of forgiving someone else. For this moment, it doesn't have to be something big, maybe it is a small thing. Checking in with yourself, seeing if it feels all right at this time, without forcing yourself in any way to forgive someone.... just breathe.

Begin by slowly **bringing into your mind and heart the image of someone for whom you feel or sense some anger or resentment, someone who has hurt you.** Gently allow a picture, a feeling, a sense of them to gather here with you. Notice whatever fear or anger may arise to deny them entering. Be with that, and if you choose, allow yourself to soften all around it. Feel for a moment the spaciousness of relating to that person with the possibility of forgiveness … and breathe.

Now allow those walls of resentment, to melt so that your heart may open. So **YOUR** life may be lighter. Let the distance between you to dissolve in compassion. Open to a sense of his or her presence … And if it feels right to you, say to him or her now. "**I forgive you.**" Say it out loud if that seems right. "**I forgive you 'So-and-so'** for the pain you have caused me in the past, intentionally … or unintentionally. **I forgive you '_____.'**"

Letting go with the breath, allow that being to go on their way, touched by your blessing and the possibility of your forgiveness. Gently bid this person farewell and let them be on their way, having shared the one great heart of forgiveness even for a millisecond. **Thank yourself and that person for allowing forgiveness to be experienced.**

Now begin to share this blessing of forgiveness and awareness. **Breathing in forgiveness, and breathing out forgiveness,** let it extend out to those around you right in this moment. Let all who are here be touched by the power of forgiveness. All who also have known such pain. Touch them with your forgiveness, with your loving—kindness, that they too may be

healed as you are ... Feel the heart we all share filled with forgiveness s
that we might all be whole and free.

Gently now, breathing in forgiveness and breathing out forgivenes
know that this meditation is coming to an end. **Begin to bring you
senses back into your body as much as you choose at this time.** Fee
your body making contact with the chair (or bed) and the floor. Becom
aware of your breath and bring the experience of your heart of forgivenes
with you. Feel your embodied self, your feet, your fingers starting to mov
slightly and feel your urge to stretch. Maybe you yawn and wiggle you
toes.

Slowly open your eyes. Stretch and come back as much as you ar
ready at this time. Notice how you are feeling now in your heart, min
and body. Thank yourself for your willingness to step into forgiveness fo
yourself and for everyone around you.

DO AND DON'T LIST

Some Guidelines for Grief Counselors
And Friends
Supporting Grieving Mothers

- **Do** listen to me with your heart (which may mean you cry with me)
- **Do** ask me questions about my daughter or son
- **Do** ask me how I feel and know that may change moment to moment
- **Do** say that you are sorry
- **Do** help me express what I am feeling
- **Do** reflect back to me that I am hurting, that my daughter (son) died, that you don't know what to say
- **Do** help me find structure and ground to rest on
- **Do** guide me with rituals
- **Do** ask me about my spiritual life
- **Do** your own emotional work about being with me
- **Do** know anger intimately
- **Do** know how to work with guilt
- **Do** help me to trust myself and my inner knowing
- _____

- **Don't** hand me Kleenex the minute I start to cry
- **Don't** tell me that I will feel better in time
- **Don't** tell me you know how I feel (even if you too are a grieving parent)
- **Don't** say that my grief is still "fresh"

- **Don't** ask if breast cancer runs in my family
- **Don't** keep asking me what I need when I don't know
- **Don't** listen with only your head
- **Don't** think that you know what to say to me
- **Don't** try to fix me or rescue me
- **Don't** think you know what I need
- **Don't** say I should go to Compassionate Friends when I say I am not ready
- _____

GRIEVING SELF-CARE

- Be kind to yourself.

- Drink plenty of water and herbal teas: avoid caffeinated drinks.

- Take time-outs and breathe deeply and fully two or three times.

- Walk a labyrinth; meditate; pray; take a contemplative walk in nature.

- Listen to soothing music (or music that helps you to express all the emotions of grief including anger).

- Exercise a little if that is all that feels right or go for a rigorous hike

- Walk barefoot inside or out to bring you back to feeling the ground beneath your feet; especially helpful if you feel "spacey."

- Reach out to people. If there is no one you feel you want to call on then find someone, join a group or consider doing some grief counseling.... Ask people to call you or check in on you.

- Physical contact and comfort is important. Ask for hugs, get a massage, take a hot bubble bath, adopt a kitten.

- Ask for help and accept offers of help. When people offer assistance, tell them if you don't know what you need and ask them to suggest something concrete.

- Be aware of the negative effects of alcohol, drugs and caffeine on your well-being. Choose wisely.

- Keep a journal; write what you feel and think, and your dreams.

Compassionate Communication

Whether you are in a workshop, in the workplace or in a private conver-
tion, these guidelines can support you to be a good listener and speak
Both as a listener and when you are speaking it is helpful to start w
being present with yourself, taking a breath and noticing what you need
be comfortable and not distracted. This does not need to take a lot of tir
Let us choose to listen and speak from our hearts, respecting ourselves a
others.

As a Listener

- Listen without giving advice
- Concentrate and focus on what the person is saying to you
- Appreciate silence
- Don't think about what you are going to say or do next
- Seek clarification if you do not understand something said
- Verify nonverbal "messages" that you receive, by stating "you see
  (sad, angry, scared, etc.); is that true?"
- Take time to breathe
- Remember confidentiality
- You can disagree with the message, while affirming the pers
  speaking
- Be mindful not to interrupt the person speaking

As a Speaker

- Use "I" statements to share what is true for yourself
- Appreciate silence
- If needed, remind the person(s) who are listening to you to ke
  what you are saying confidential
- Share as much or as little as you choose

- Separate the importance and value of speaking your "truth" from the response you receive
- Honor time commitments and ask the listener(s) for their response to what you are saying

INTRODUCTION TO THE FINGER LABYRINTH

The labyrinth on the next page is from the Cretan design which is intended to be traced with your finger. In a meditative process, you may choose to decorate your labyrinth using the colorful cording and beads to suit your taste and make it your own. Any multi-purpose glue that dries clear is suitable.

USE OF THE LABYRINTH

There is no "right" way to use the labyrinth, but below are some suggestions on how to approach and be with the labyrinth experience.

- Sit comfortably with the labyrinth in your lap or on a table before you. REFLECT and REVIEW your life.

- It may be helpful to set an intention for this time (e.g. a time of healing, quiet, prayer, life review, being with your fears of the unknown, asking for an answer to a question)

- With your non-dominant hand (for most people this is the left), begin to follow the path from the entrance at the outer edge of the labyrinth and moving along.

- As you move towards the center of the labyrinth, reflect on RELEASING, emptying and quieting your mind, and body. Focus on your breathing, feel the sensation of your finger on the path. Close your eyes if this is helpful and notice any changes in your body or in your breathing. Take as long as you would like and are comfortable with in this process.

- When you reach the center of the labyrinth, pause for a period of reflection and RECEIVING. Pray, meditate, or just take time to further quiet your mind and to deepen your relaxation.

- When you feel ready, follow the path from the center back out of the labyrinth from where you began. As you do this, reflect on your reunion and RECONNECTION with the world, taking this experience with you as you exit the labyrinth. Reflect on any insights you may have had and what you want to bring into your life as you RETURN from your labyrinth walk.

- After the labyrinth experience, you may want to continue your time in quiet, prayer or reflection. Some people find it helpful to write or journal their labyrinth experience, or to share it with another person.

- Remember, the finger labyrinth is a tool for quiet reflection and can be very helpful during times of grief.

A FINGER LABYRINTH

978-0-595-47712-8
0-595-47712-7